Contents

About the Author

John Smart was born at Farnborough, Kent in 1960 and was educated at Alleyn's in south London and Nottingham University, his main academic interests being historical geography and history of architecture.

In addition, his forebears included E.G. Blythe and E.H. Niemann, 19th century artists, and Colin Blythe (1879-1917) a renowned bowler for Kent and England, leading to a further interest in matters historical. As a result he undertook genealogical work at home and abroad over many years.

Meanwhile, his family supported Millwall from the 1920s and he followed them from 1970. Indeed, it was this football experience that provided the initial inspiration for his writing career.

After visiting numerous football grounds he researched soccer history and produced *The Wow Factor - How Soccer Evolved* with two editions in 2003-05, followed by a fiction book *The Wizards of Wight*, and a seminal work on the first F.A. president entitled *Arthur Pember's Great Adventures* in 2007.

The current book is a detailed story of the founders of soccer, exploring their lives in Victorian times and beyond, combined with a history of the game's development and of the grounds.

The Founders of Soccer

With a History of the Game

John Blythe Smart

Published by Blythe Smart Publications in 2008

A CIP catalogue record for this book is available from the British Library.

ISBN: 978 - 0 - 9545017 - 4 - 7

Cover, Type: Blythe Smart Publications
Printers: Imprint Digital

Note 1 - The facts are correct at the time of printing, but this does not preclude later adjustment in the light of further research.

Note 2 - There are a number of Civil Registration records where the quarter date has been used so, for example, June 1865 covers the period April to June 1865.

Blythe Smart Publications
Freshwater - Isle of Wight - England

Introduction

What could be more fascinating than delving deep into the history of our national pastime? Having watched football on a cold Saturday afternoon one might consider its roots, and ponder how money now dominates the modern game.

The founders of soccer pursued high ideals and envisioned an amateur sport, however the professionals soon arrived as did entrepreneurs with their greedy cheque books. Yet, it was only recently that the game was changed beyond all recognition.

To investigate this revolution required both a passion for soccer and a fascination with history. This was perhaps an unusual combination but the author had such attributes and spent many years watching games, visiting historic grounds, and studying archival records.

When others concentrated on pre-match refreshment and nourishing pies, he surveyed the exterior of once famous venues and stands then in a state of terminal decay. In fact, the fabric of soccer history provided a buzz comparable to any excitement on the pitch.

In the late 1980s there was a football legacy little changed from the early days, and many grounds were a fixture in the soccer calendar. Indeed, the terraces inspired a degree of awe and were as permanent as any primeval monolith, but this was not in fact the case.

There were many famous grounds whose names evoked great matches, iconic players, and heaving swaying crowds of wildly exuberant fans, with examples like Anfield, Goodison, Old Trafford, Highbury, and Stamford Bridge to name but a few.

However there were many speculative ventures that stood the test of time, which were impressive in the extreme and stunning in their scale, although they were perhaps somewhat less familiar.

Imagine travelling to the four corners of the country and walking on these vast and disappearing terraces, with their inherent atmosphere and ghostly reminders of crowds long departed.

One could marvel at the sweeping vista of St. Andrew's, the stunning scale of the Long Side at Turf Moor, the roar of Roker Park, the idiosyncrasies of Molineux and its South Bank for 30,000 making one last stand, the curving mounds and red brick of the Hawthorns, the unusual tunnels and wooden stands of Deepdale, and the vast amphitheatres of Leeds Road or the Valley where 75,000 once stood.

However, the forces of change were soon to take a hand and alter the game forever. In the first instance there was new action against hooliganism and the arrival of well-heeled sponsors in the game, but it was the disasters at Bradford and Sheffield which saw the end of a soccer' phenomena and probably a whole way of life.

Indeed, the experience of going to football matches was completely altered with the arrival of modern all-seater stadiums. These saw the demise of the extensive terraces with their capacious crowds, and for some a degree of passion and nostalgia was removed from the game.

Clearly safety was paramount, but such regimentation was possibly allied to other elements of governmental social control. Whatever the case, this signalled the death-knell for old grounds, their rambling terraces, and also the associated football experience. In fact, many were gone in the blink of an eye, whereas others succumbed during the last decade.

A whole generation now enjoys football in state-of-the-art stadiums, and not one large terrace remains, although some clubs in the lower leagues still provide reminders from those earlier times. The power of the dollar was all pervading however it was once very different in the extreme....

CHAPTER 1

Codes and Rules

The origins of soccer are open to conjecture and there are several theories available, however there is evidence that the Chinese and Japanese enjoyed games where a ball was kicked back in the dynastic times.

Clearly there was a correlation between leisure activities and economic prosperity, thus both Greeks and Romans indulged in a number of games involving a ball. One of the first mentions of cricket was in Guildford, but perhaps an old tablet may contain the truth about soccer.

Some exhausted centurions were enjoying a break in the spa at Buxton, but became tired from too much bathing, and gazed wistfully at their helmets lying by the bathtub (with their tunics stuffed loosely inside).

One day Soccerundus climbed from the hot tub and accidentally stubbed his toe on a protruding column. He was hopping mad, thus he kicked his helmet with all his might and it flew through the air past some Britons who were defending the baths. The projectile shortly lodged in a fishing net hanging between two adjacent columns.

At this, his fellow centurions leapt from the hot tub with their arms raised in the air and shouted themselves hoarse, some hugged one another, others climbed pillars, and all of them gesticulated and jeered at the Britons.

Crikey, this was more fun than invading another country and a fledgling sport was born, therefore they arranged a game against opponents from Londinium, who promptly travelled up Watling Street. Meanwhile, their supporters caused a large degree of mayhem along the way.

During the game the Romans enjoyed much possession of the helmet, and won when Soccerundus deflected the item past a line of Britons using his shield. Soon afterwards it sailed through the door of a nearby villa.

The game was a great success lasting for three days with only twenty-three casualties, whilst the Roman supporters invaded the pitch and the Britons felt cheated and dubbed the goal "The Shield of Athena." In fact, they were still griping about it when the Romans left the country several years later. However, this was just one possible version of soccer's emergence!

It is a more certain fact that a rough game was played throughout the country - the most notable example being at Ashbourne, Derbyshire, where such a tradition is claimed from as early as 217 A.D. In general, however, the game's origins are traced to Shrovetide football which traditionally took place in English villages on Shrove Tuesday.

The contests involved an unmarked pitch with streams, ponds, roads, or cottages, whilst a primitive ball was carried or kicked between two goals. There were no rules and no restriction on the number of participants, thus the game was a rough, rowdy affair over several days with many injuries. A yearly re-enactment takes place at Alnwick, Northumberland where the ball is kicked-off from the castle walls, whereas other traditions still remain at Atherstone, Chester, Corfe, and Sedgefield.

Within this rural idyll of farmers and crop growing there were limited prospects for the game's development, thus the early history was ultimately centred on the sporting activities at England's public schools.

Many of them played football in the 19th century viz. Charterhouse, Eton, Harrow, Shrewsbury, Westminster, and Winchester, although each had different rules and this led to some serious controversies.

OLD SCHOOL TIES

Disparities within the rules made it difficult to have inter-school contests, whilst many played on rough common-land beyond the college precincts, making the chance of injury to the boys' ankles and legs very great.

Westminster School engaged in soccer as early as 1710 however a decree from the Church authorities tried to stop such games, since boys would waste valuable time kicking a ball about in the cloisters. There were many idiosyncrasies at first and games might continue for two to three days (as with cricket); whereas the numbers were unrestricted hence the 'Dowling Game' at Shrewsbury, familiar to Darwin, involved fifty-a-side.

Eton College, meanwhile, indulged in two forms of early football. The most famous 'primitive' form was the Eton Wall Game, which was played against a boundary wall built near to the school in 1717. The first such games took place as early as 1766 and were traditionally played between the *Collegers* and *Oppidans* on St. Andrew's Day (30th November) from 1844, whereas the rules were formalised in 1849.

The game was contested on a pitch 120 yards long, but only six yards wide, next to a wall bordering the college playing fields and was like a long drawn-out rugby scrum. No hands could be used however a 'shy' was scored when the ball was touched against the wall at each end.

A team scored 1 point for a success and then had a throw at goal (a door and a tree) the conversion adding 9 points, although the last 'goal' was in fact scored in 1909. Indeed, such a tradition is continued up until today.

Variations within the rules were an issue in the mid-19th century, and the two most controversial areas centred upon attitudes towards handling the ball and rough practices such as hacking, shinning, mauling, and tagging. In fact, with regard to this there was a famous incident. William Webb Ellis astounded his team mates by picking up the ball at Rugby in 1823, whilst the game of that name was first played at the school in 1841, and the rules were formalised in 1845. As a result many of their old boys preferred this version of the football code.

Schools such as Eton, however, with their Field and Wall games forbade the use of the hand, whilst Charterhouse and Westminster developed the skill of 'dribbling' to gain possession of the ball (rather than a scrum).

There were many anomalies and Charles Alcock noted "a peculiar species of football" at Harrow, which prevailed up to the end of the 19th century. The goal was referred to as a base and there was the extraordinary "Three Yard Rule," where a player could catch the ball, shout out "Three Yards," and jump through the goal posts to score in three strides.

The emphasis in all the public schools was on the physical aspect, and many believed kicking the opponent's legs to obtain the ball was an integral part of the game. It was a test of courage and resilience similar to other character building ideas at these public schools.

CAMBRIDGE RULES

The most significant events, however, took place at Cambridge University where players attempted to unify the football code as early as 1846. Indeed, in this respect, two of their students led the way.

John Charles Thring (1824-1909) was the son of Rev. John Gale Dalton Thring of Alford, Somerset and grandson of John Thring a banker of "Alford House," Warminster. He matriculated at St. John's, Cambridge in 1843 gaining a B.A. in 1848 and was a curate in 1848-55, but spent the next decade as a schoolmaster at Uppingham. Meanwhile, in later years he was a curate at Alford and Bradford on Avon in Somerset.

His peer Henry De Winton (1822-95) was born at Hay-on-Wye and the son of Walter a clerk of Hay Castle and vicar of Llanigen, Breconshire. He matriculated at Trinity in 1842 gaining a B.A. in 1846 and was a deacon in 1848, then was the rector of Boughrood, Radnorshire in 1849-81 and the Archdeacon of Brecon from 1875.

These ministerial pioneers arranged a meeting at Trinity College and thus compiled the Cambridge Rules in October 1848, which were tried out on Parker's Piece. This swath of open ground is just east of the town among Georgian and Victorian housing, and today is of considerable importance in terms of the game's evolution.

The eleven rules were for all players with a number of precepts including a goal scored 'under' the tape, throw-ins from the side, and an offside rule (with three players), but included a free catch and kick towards goal.

Further developments took place in the schools, although the rules still differed greatly and this was only the first step, thus there was a movement to establish the game on a firmer footing during the 1860s.

Edward Thring (1822), elder brother of John, gained a B.A. in 1845 and was a curate and private tutor, whilst he was headmaster at Uppingham in 1853-87 and raised it to a foremost position among the public schools with 11 boarding houses, 30 masters, and 320 boys.

His brother John was an assistant master there in 1859-69 and continued his interest in soccer, thus he developed the Uppingham Rules in 1862 which were based on his days at Cambridge University.

No tripping was allowed whereas Rule III stated, "Kicks must be aimed only at the ball." However, there was still a free catch and a player was 'out of play' when positioned in front of the ball.

Another issue was goal size and Harrow stipulated 12 feet but increased this to 24 feet during a replay, whilst Cambridge established a distance of just 15 feet. The F.A. set the present width of 24 feet in the 1860s, whilst the goals had two uprights with a tape at a height of 8 feet.

The only development outside the schools was in the unlikely northern enclave of Sheffield, where a half-day Wednesday (holiday) encouraged the playing of local sports. Indeed, a number of sports-venues were developed as a result and the area was a pioneer of the game.

The Bramall Lane ground was initially laid out for cricket in 1854, whilst Nathaniel Creswick and William Prest, who were both former Harrovians, formed Sheffield F.C. on 24 October 1857. As a consequence the eleven Sheffield Rules were developed later that year. [1]

However, these differed from those in London and the schools since they allowed charging at the kicker, a push with the hands, and also a knock on, although carrying the ball was still strictly forbidden.

The reputed first club football match between Sheffield and Hallam F.C. (1860) took place at Bramall Lane on 29 December 1862, whilst Sandygate home of Hallam became the oldest ground in the world, and John C. Clegg played for Sheffield, the Wednesday, and England (and eventually became the F.A. president).

---

[1] Sheffield F.C. are now the oldest club in the world, Cray Wanderers (1860) are the second, and Notts County (1862) are the oldest in the League.

CLUB FOOTBALL

Charles W. Alcock, an early pioneer, then provided a useful commentary, "There was little progress in the sport before 1859 however there were some developments in Sheffield whilst the Crusaders played games against Charterhouse and Westminster Schools in London."

In addition, he noted important centres where the game evolved: Barnes, Richmond Green, Thames Valley, and Mincing Lane in the City, while the main progress was in London and Ebenezer C. Morley led the way.

The latter initially played games with his some friends on Barnes Green, whereas he formed Barnes F.C. at Limes Field, Mortlake, Surrey, near the historic railway bridge (1846-49), during 1862.

By a strange coincidence this was next to White Hart Lane and today the truncated Limes Field Road bears witness to this historical venue. The side then played Richmond at Barn Elms Park in November that year, making this the first ever 'unofficial' club football match.

Blackheath was an important centre and Rev. Selwyn, headmaster of the proprietary school, encouraged football on the common, whilst other early pioneers such as Edward E. Bowen attended the institution. [2]

Meanwhile, Charles Alcock and his brother John helped form the Forest F.C. at Snaresbrook in Essex - they later became the Wanderers and won a total of five F.A. Cup Finals from 1872-78.

The Barnes Club played Forest F.C. in March 1863 and *Bell's Life* noted that, "Mr. Morley was a pretty and most effective dribbler.... We cannot abstain from saying that the play of Mr. Morley of Barnes and Mr. C. Alcock of the Forest Club elicited great applause from the spectators of whom there were a large number present."

Westminster School was another of the trendsetters especially with regard to their games against the Crusaders. Indeed, Arthur Pember, the first F.A. president, had links to the school through his brother George and with the Stewards viz. Francis a stockbroker and Herbert of the Crusaders.

As a result Pember was founder of the No Names Club of Kilburn, on fields opposite to his home, in the early 1860s. The name may have been a quip regarding Lloyd's Insurers and the side probably had members from the Stock Exchange, as the Civil Service and War Office also had teams.

---

[2] Rev. Edward John Selwyn a relative of Bishop Selwyn N.Z. was headmaster in 1847-64, and curate of Lee in 1859-64. Indeed, his son Edward Carus Selwyn was headmaster of Uppingham from 1887-1907 - after Edward Thring.

Other teams of significance during these early days were successful school sides from Charterhouse and Clapham, and amateur clubs such as Clapham Rovers, Crystal Palace, and the Royal Engineers.

F.A. PIONEERS

Ebenezer Cobb Morley has been described as the father of football, whilst Charles W. Alcock with his ubiquitous connections to the Oval has been accredited as the father of modern sport; however Pember's role in this process has generally been ignored.

The first meeting of the Football Association was cordially arranged at the Freemasons Tavern, Great Queen Street on 26 October 1863 (now the New Connaught Assembly Rooms). Indeed, the gentlemen present wanted to produce a code to replace the existing local rules and arrangements, thereby gaining control of the whole sport.

Arriving by carriage they congregated with some noisy anticipation in the tavern's upstairs rooms, and once called to order the first action was to appoint a chairman. It was proposed by Mr. Morley and seconded by Mr. Mackenzie (and carried), "That Mr. Pember do take the Chair."

The latter represented the No Names Club at this first meeting and his appointment was not an anomaly, but a clear indication of his leadership qualities and the esteem in which he was held by his football peers. Even more so, since unlike Morley, Alcock, Marindin, and Kinnaird he was not recorded as a sportsman of note.

Some other significant appointments were then made i.e. Arthur Pember president (proposed by Herbert T. Steward), Ebenezer Morley of Barnes secretary (proposed by A.W. Mackenzie of Forest), and F.W. Campbell of Blackheath treasurer (proposed by Arthur Pember). Indeed, Arthur Pember was to head the list of only thirteen presidents of the F.A., with many of them being esteemed Royal patrons.

Other committee members were then likewise appointed i.e. John Alcock of Forest (later the Wanderers), G. Wawn of the War Office, J. Turner of the Crystal Palace (unconnected to the present club who formed in 1905), and Herbert Steward of the Crusaders.

After the committee had been established and some initial matters were concluded, eleven clubs joined the fledgling Football Association, and their names are recorded as follows: Barnes, Blackheath, Blackheath Proprietary, Crusaders, Crystal Palace, Forest of Leytonstone, Kensington School, No Names Club of Kilburn, Percival House (Blackheath), Surbiton, and the War Office Club.

Of those present only Charterhouse School did not take up membership at this stage. G.F. Hartshorne their captain believed the public schools should be prominent, but he first wanted to ascertain the attitude of the other top schools since few were present, and only then would they commit to the new Association.

Ebenezer Morley concluded the first meeting and his last instruction was to contact all the schools regarding this issue, whereas they placed an advert in *Bell's Life*, *The Field*, and *Sporting Life*.

The second meeting took place on 10 November 1863, and the main matter of debate was regarding the schools - Charterhouse, Harrow, and Westminster replied to the Association with little enthusiasm, whilst Eton, Rugby, and Winchester did not reply at all.

The committee, however, remained positive and Pember who had read the laws of Charterhouse made an observation. He noted that their laws were simple to understand, and he believed that if two schools joined then the others would surely follow their lead.

Ebenezer Morley had formulated the first set of rules at his home 26 The Terrace, Barnes and these were duly approved. At the third meeting on 14 November 1863 letters were received from Uppingham and Lincoln F.C. although the latter soon created some problems.

Meanwhile, Charles Pritchard, an astronomer and headmaster of Clapham Grammar (1834-62), promoted soccer on the common, and their player Charles C. Dacre hastened some decisions regarding the rules. He was an excellent 'dribbler,' a skill much admired at the time, and played for the school and Clapham Rovers, however a serious injury he received on the common intensified the debates about hacking. [3]

The fourth meeting was on 17 November 1863 and the Cambridge Rules were incorporated into the existing code, but this action was taken without the approval of all members - leading to some considerable trouble.

Indeed, the fifth meeting on 1 December 1863 was a stormy-encounter with much heated debate about these unendorsed changes, in particular the issues of handling the ball and the practice of hacking.

Mr. Pember of the No Names Club spoke with passion, stating, "Perhaps you will allow me to say that I took down 'fifteen' the other day to play a match, and I was the only one who had not been at a public school and we were all dead against hacking."

---

[3] Alcock recorded that Dacre of Clapham Rovers took the game to New Zealand. He was born in Sydney in 1848 and went to Auckland in 1859, but was educated in Clapham. He returned in 1870 and started a soccer team plus an inter-provincial contest between Auckland, Wellington, Canterbury, and Otago.

F.W. Campbell of Blackheath then took up the exigent argument, and suggested strongly that the Cambridge Rules should not have been added without all of the members' agreement!

In reply, Pember contested the statement most vigorously, announcing, "Hacking is a dangerous and painful practice, very brutal when deliberate and likely to prevent a man who had due regard for his wife and family from following the game!"

Indeed, it was a heart-felt and poignant warning, whereas he also took offence at such insinuations, adding, "I do not submit to the suggestion of un-gentlemanly conduct!" Consequently he put forward a motion to remove both running with the ball and hacking, a motion which was duly carried and then embodied in the rules as follows:

Rule IV - A goal is scored by kicking the ball over the space between the goal-posts (at whatever height)

Rule VIII - If a player makes a fair catch he shall be entitled to a free kick providing he claims it by making a mark with his heel at once

Rule IX - No player shall run with the ball
Rule X - Neither tripping nor hacking shall be allowed
Rule XI - A player shall not throw or pass the ball with his hands
Rule XII - No player shall take the ball from the ground with his hands

Despite some difficulties in reaching consensus there was no ambiguity in these Laws and this was a game of the boot, not the hand, thus the sports of soccer and rugby separated. In fact, these were the basis of today's game and Pember, with his significant role, might be designated as the father of soccer (as oppose to the game of rugby).

The sixth and final meeting then took place on 8 December 1863, and a letter and postal order was received from Rev. J.C. Thring, this being the subscription for Uppingham School.

A second letter also arrived from Lieutenant H.C. Moore, the secretary of the Royal Engineers, Chatham, containing their subscription and comments strongly deprecating running with the ball and hacking.

However, F.W. Campbell stated that although his club approved of the objects of the Association, the rules as they stood took away all interest in the game therefore he and Blackheath departed to play rugby.

SOME TEST MATCHES

The members decided to play a test game at Battersea on 2 January 1864, but some became impatient thus the first experimental game was Barnes against Richmond at Limes Field, Mortlake on 19 December 1863.

This was fifteen a side but the rules were quite easy to understand and no disputes arose; Barnes had six "tries at goal" but failed to score and the game was drawn after 1½ hours - not the best of test matches.

Richmond F.C. played a few soccer games but preferred rugby as several of their members were old boys. In fact, they played the first such game against Blackheath on 2 January 1864, and their founder Edwin Ash was instrumental in the formation of the Rugby Union in January 1871.

Meanwhile, the first exhibition soccer game was at Battersea on Saturday, 9 January 1864 with two representative teams chosen by A. Pember and E.C. Morley. However, there were few other developments until the annual meeting at the Freemasons Tavern in 1866.

A member of the No Names Club complained it was hard to play under the existing rules, as they were only being followed by Barnes and Crystal Palace. In fact, the Lincoln side announced they were also unhappy, and promptly cancelled their membership.

Pember was greatly disturbed by their actions and stated, "Lincoln are strongly opposed to anything but hacking, throttling, and other harsh practices." This ill-advised comment caused outrage and led to a strong denial by the Lincoln captain in *Bell's Life*, with twelve paces at dawn!

In fact, the F.A. wanted their rules to extend to the whole country and sent a letter to Sheffield, who had recently joined. W.J. Chesterman, their secretary, replied and suggested a contest against southern opponents, thus the club captains met at Morley's chambers, No. 3 King's Bench Walk, Temple to discuss the matter.

R.W. Willis the F.A. secretary arranged a match between a representative London side and Sheffield at Battersea on 31 March 1866. This was to be played under the F.A. Laws, whilst the following rules were to apply:

1. The teams to be eleven a side
2. The ground to be 120 yards long by 80 wide
3. London dress white jersey (or flannel shirt) and trousers
4. The ball to be Lillywhite's No.5
5. The play to commence 3 p.m. and terminate at 4.30
6. Notice to be sent to *The Field, Bell's Life, Sporting Life,* and *The Sportsman*

The London side included Morley and Willis of Barnes, C. Alcock and Kinnaird of the Wanderers, Pember (captain), C.M. Tebbut, and A. Baker of the No Names Club, whilst W.J. Chesterman was captain of Sheffield. Both sides delivered some hard knocks and Morley was credited with the first ever goal in representative soccer and Alcock the first offside.

The game took place under the F.A. Rules and London won by 2 goals and 4 touchdowns to nil. Such a description seems unusual since the rules stated a goal 'must' be kicked, and it was possibly a romantic version, as soccer and rugby were well defined. The occasion was rounded off with a splendid dinner for the contestants at the Albion Hotel.

Indeed, there was a return match under the Sheffield Rules later that year and this became a 'fixture' throughout the 19th century, leading to a union with the northern game in 1877.

The original Cambridge Rules stipulated a ball passed to a player could not be touched unless three of the opposition were in front, but Association Rules stated **any** player forward of the ball was offside. This was rather restrictive and the F.A. tried to gain greater appeal for the game in 1867, thus they amended the offside rule to coincide with that already being used at Charterhouse and Westminster.

Once the new rule was introduced the tactics of play were changed and the skill of "middling" became important, although in many schools old rules persisted, and it took some time for their players to adjust.

The F.A. then announced in the press, "The rules shall be tested in a county match, Middlesex v Kent & Surrey, and the game will be played on Saturday November 2nd, 1867, at Beaufort House" - the headquarters and rifle ground of the South Middlesex Volunteers. The venue had a path or track around a pitch, as well as a rifle range, and backed on to Lillie Bridge Cricket Ground (the venue of the 1873 Cup Final).

A large crowd assembled however Lord Ranelagh and the secretary of the Amateur Athletic Club had a disagreement, thus the players and spectators had to seek refuge in the 'wilds' of Battersea Park.

Middlesex included Charles Alcock and the dribbler Charles E.B. Nepean of Charterhouse, whilst Kent-Surrey had R.G. Graham and R.W. Willis of Barnes and Charles Dacre of Clapham Grammar.

Bell's Life stated the game was a goalless draw and success, although, "The ground was in a most objectionable state and totally unfit for football purposes and the grass, which was several inches long and extremely thick, effectually prevented all attempts at dribbling or any exhibition of play which we might have expected from the reputation of many of the players engaged in this contest."

There was a second match Kent v Surrey at the West London Running Grounds, Brompton (i.e. Lillie Bridge) on 25 January 1868. The Kent side included A. Kinnaird (captain) of Trinity, Cambridge and E. Lubbock of West Kent F.C., whereas Surrey had Morley, Willis, and Graham (captain) of Barnes and A. Thompson of the Wanderers.

This secondary game was twelve a side and ended in a goalless draw, but was a considerable success hence the press stated, "The Rules now meet with universal approval." Not long afterwards the "fair catch" was also abolished and a goal was scored solely "under the tape."

Pember did not play in these two games and immigrated to America later that year, with some significant consequences in terms of soccer's history. Meanwhile, E.C. Morley replaced him as the F.A. president, and with his colleagues soon took the game forward.

CHAPTER 2

Barnes Association

The pioneers of soccer generally emanated from the higher echelons of society, although their personalities and family backgrounds were found to be very different in the extreme.

Indeed, the official histories often furnish a somewhat limited perspective of these gentlemen, concentrating on pompous stereotyped Victorians and pithy rule-changes within the game. These accounts are possibly aimed at those who have a passing interest, and not those of a more enquiring mind who require a new and contemporary viewpoint.

The following accounts come well within the latter category and include extensive genealogical and historical research. In fact, they give a detailed and rounded account of the founders of soccer, thereby illuminating every idiosyncrasy of their lives in a manner previously unavailable.

In the first instance the discussion takes on a parochial aspect with three portraits that are reminiscent of a Dickens' sketch, namely the solicitor, the merchant, and the broker's man!

RELIGIOUS ZEAL

All soccer histories begin with Ebenezer Morley due to his great longevity within the game, and regarding the formulation of the first set of rules. However, less is known of his background, which is of some significance being rooted in the religious revivals of the later 18th century.

The Victorians themselves maintained strong values and drives although they often possessed an ambiguous morality, whereas missionaries took their 'versions of the faith' to the four corners of the globe.

Meanwhile, at home there was a paternalistic vision for the lower classes termed muscular Christianity, which promoted sport as a panacea for all kinds of social ills. The idea was initially associated with writers Charles Kingsley and Thomas Hughes (regarding the moral and spiritual aspect), whereas modern research has confirmed the benefits to mind, body, and soul, showing sport to be a galvanising force within society.

Indeed, Morley came from such a background and brought high ideals to the game, whilst he contradicted those of a more cynical nature who said, "Rugby is a game of hooligans played by gentlemen, but soccer is a game of gentlemen played by hooligans."

John Morley was born in central London in 1770 and his parents intended him for a business career, however at seventeen he experienced salvation and described his conversion in the most eloquent of terms:

"The thunder rolled tremendously loud and the lightning's flashed vividly; there was an earthquake in my conscience and I feared the earth would open and swallow me up."

He found himself in a dark place, but added, "My mind was set at happy liberty under a sermon preached in the Tabernacle by the Rev. Edward Parsons of Leeds from Acts 13th, 38 and 39 verses.... The reading of the text melted me into tears and every sentence in the sermon came with holy unction to my spirit."

Having received such grace he put himself forward for baptism and this was carried out by Andrew Kinsman (a coadjutor of Whitefield) in the Tabernacle House near Finsbury Square. The whole direction of his life was then altered and he later became a Congregational minister.

Initially, he had a connection with the fellowship of Spa Field's Chapel, situated at the junction of Spa Field Street and Exmouth Street (Market) in the northern enclave of Clerkenwell.

The chapel was a devotee of the Countess of Huntingdon's Connexion and followed the same Calvinistic Methodism as Whitefield. Indeed, the children of George and Jane Morley were baptized at Spa Fields in 1786-89 and it seems likely they were his relatives. [1]

Morley received his early training there but soon afterwards entered into public ministry. He was ordained as a pastor at the Independent Church, Alford, Lincoln (part of the Countess of Huntingdon's Connexion), in 1793-1800, but was then invited to preach at Thorngumbald, since Sir S. Handidge of the Hull Corporation erected a small chapel there.

John Morley married his wife Mary Elizabeth at this time and a son Ebenezer was born in 1801, but soon afterwards he adopted Congregational precepts and became the minister of the Providence Chapel, Hope Street, Hull - an association which lasted some fifty years. The chapel was erected off Paragon Street in 1797 and replaced the former Ebenezer Chapel, whilst a daughter was born nearby in 1802.

---

[1] George Whitefield (1714-70) opposed the Arminian Methodism of Charles and John Wesley who received their conversions in 1738. The Tabernacle was built in the 1740s and Whitefield carried out the first baptisms, whereas Andrew Kinsman officiated from 1776-86 - although Morley was not recorded.

The Tabernacle became part of the Central Foundation School, Leonard Street; whereas Wesley's Chapel was built on City Road and Tabernacle Street (some forty years later) and remains there today.

However, his first wife died and Rev. Morley married Hannah Atkinson at Sculcoates in 1804. Her family attended Fish Street Calvinistic Chapel and the union resulted in two children, Salome (1805) and Josephus (1806), whilst they lived at Anlaby Road in 1821. Indeed, the town was a hotbed of nonconformity close to the Humber, Junction, and Old Docks.

John Morley finally retired as the minister of Hope Street in 1850, and preached his last sermon at the Sailor's Institute, Hull on 11 October 1857 aged 87. Salome then nursed him through the last years of his life and he died in 1863, whilst he left his worldly goods to the widows and children of Protestant ministers and to his kindly daughter.

His two sons took completely different paths. Josephus attended chapel, but was listed as a brewer at 20 Waterhouse Lane in 1835 and also a coal merchant at Trundle Street in 1842. In later years he worked as a grocer, and his son William was an ale and porter merchant in Hull.

Ebenezer Morley, however, followed his father into the Congregational faith and discussed life after his mother died, stating: "He was left under the care and guidance of his pious father and enjoyed the advantages of a religious education and training."

He became a collector for the London Missionary Society and was also a devoted Sunday school teacher, becoming a member of the Providence Chapel in 1817. At first he was an itinerant preacher and went to Cheshunt College, Cambridge in 1819 - then joined the Zion Independent Chapel, Bridlington his ordination in 1823. He was most prolific with three services on a Sunday and preached at nearby villages in the week!

Matters took a new direction when he married Hannah Cobb, daughter of a wealthy ship-owner and merchant, at St. Mary's, Hull in 1826 (in fact only Anglican ministers could perform marriages from 1754-1837).

Ebenezer continued to preach at the Zion Chapel but was laid low with illness and exhaustion in 1830, and took a short break to recover. During this period his father-in-law built a new chapel at Holborn Street, Sutton, just to the east of Hull, where he recommenced his ministry. Indeed, a son Ebenezer Cobb Morley was born at that address on 16 August 1831, and baptized at the chapel on 11 September.

There was to be a long association at Holborn Street and the family lived at 2 Holborn Place in 1851, whereas the son Ebenezer was aged nineteen and was employed as a solicitor's articled clerk.

However, there was then a complete change of direction and Rev. Morley moved to "that desolate sanctuary" Albany Chapel, Brentford, on 13 July 1853. He also became the secretary to the *Bible Association*, and was much engaged in open air preaching for a period of five years.

Despite this there were still some connections up north and in his will he stated: "I give, devise, and bequeath all that my chapel situate in Holborn Street in the parish of Sutton, Hull and the dwelling-house, yard, and other outbuildings and appurtenances thereunto belonging, unto and to the use of my said wife Hannah Morley and my son Ebenezer Cobb Morley... my money to be equally divided between all of my children."

A temporary chapel was then erected at West Brompton in 1858 and Rev. Morley despite his age worked there with untiring zeal, stating: "He had never enjoyed his ministry more than in that place."

He resided with his wife and three daughters at 12 Victoria (Netherton) Grove off Fulham Road, Chelsea in 1861, but died the following year and was buried at Abney Park Cemetery, Stoke Newington. He was spiritually rich but his probate showed his effects were under £200, whereas his son entered a profession of considerable pecuniary benefit.

EBENEZER COBB MORLEY

Having spent his formative years in a religious home this founder of soccer inherited important qualities, beneficial qualities which no doubt helped him during his future organisational roles.

Initially he trained in Hull and may have worked for his father's solicitors Messrs. Phillips & Copeman in 1851, but came to Brentford in 1853 and was admitted to the Law Society as a London solicitor in 1854.

There was a proliferation of legal families just across the river in Barnes and Charles Ireland Shirreff a solicitor lived at 27 The Terrace. In fact, his son William Moore was also a solicitor and notably the first honorary secretary of the Barnes & Mortlake Regatta in 1858.

Morley was likewise a founder of the latter consequently he resided at the White Hart Inn, at the west end of Barnes Terrace, in 1861. The tavern was a meeting place for leading oarsmen of the time, and a good location for aspiring coxes, therefore he purchased 26 The Terrace, Barnes soon afterwards and remained for some sixty years. [2]

He also entered into partnership with Richard Alfred Goodman (1804-65), a solicitor and nonconformist from Market Harborough, in the firm of Goodman & Morley. Indeed, the partners were based at 3 King's Bench Walk, Inner Temple, which had some considerable significance, while the latter was a counsel for indictments on the Oxford Circuit.

---

[2] The present White Hart Inn was rebuilt on the site in 1899, and is adjacent to the finishing-line of the University Boat Race.

His father died in 1862, but he had a sound domestic and professional base, thus he turned his attention and energies to the fledgling sport of soccer. After playing some games with friends on Barnes Green he formed Barnes F.C. at Limes Field, Mortlake later that year. This was just a short walk from his home and to the west of White Hart Lane.

The club played some important games and although just formed were said to be, "A live proposition boasting a big membership." In particular, they had contests against their neighbours Richmond and the two met at Barn Elms Park, Putney beside the Thames in November 1862.

A large number of spectators gathered to watch the struggle, many being of the fairer sex - whilst the winning team was the first to score two goals. Barnes managed this in just twenty minutes and left as victors, while this game predates Sheffield v Hallam on 29 December, thus Barn Elms Park was the venue for the first (unofficial) 'club' football match.

A return game took place at Richmond Green a month later, but due to heavy rain the pitch became extremely muddy, and the 400-500 spectators were greatly amused as the players failed to keep their feet. Mr. Gregory won the game for Barnes with a single goal, but this was neither soccer nor rugby since the goal was described thus:

"He made a neat catch about 15 yards exactly in front of the Richmond base and after making his mark scored with a drop kick." Meanwhile, the gentlemen of the two clubs dined afterwards at the Talbot Hotel.

During that year Morley succeeded William M. Shirreff as secretary of the Barnes & Mortlake Regatta, whereas he was a member of the London Rowing Club and became its honorary solicitor. [3]

He then continued to play football, although a lack of established rules meant teams played using their own format and this led to some disputes. Consequently, as the Barnes captain he sent a letter to *Bell's* Life, stating that the rules should be established on similar lines to the M.C.C.

As a result the F.A. was formed during six meetings in late 1863 (already discussed), whilst Richmond had an important role - although not properly constituted, and played against Forest F.C. in November 1863. [4]

---

[3] The Boat Race was started at Henley in 1829 and moved to Putney in 1845. In fact, the owner of Barn Elms Estate entertained the crews after the contest.

[4] Richmond Green was impractical, and the *Sportsman* noted in December 1871 that the pitch narrowed at one end due to a number of paths. The club remained until 1873 and moved to Richmond Athletic Ground, shown as Richmond Town Cricket Ground on later 19th century maps. They remain today and should not be confused with non-League Hampton & Richmond (Hampton F.C.).

Indeed, the club attended the later meetings and told Morley they would join the F.A. if the rules were ready for winter. However, despite playing in the test match at Limes Field on 19 December 1863, they departed to play rugby soon afterwards.

Morley was first secretary of the F.A. in 1863-66 and helped establish the early game. In fact, there were stringent offside rules making dribbling an essential talent - a player would progress down the pitch backed up by other forwards, while two strong-kicking backs defended behind.

Meanwhile, outside of soccer he stroked for the London Rowing Club eight in the *Grand Challenge Cup* at Henley in 1864, whilst he arranged an athletics meeting at Limes Field on the day of the Boat Race that year. The latter continued for many years and attracted top athletes of the day.

His partner Mr. Goodman died in 1865 and he then practiced alone at 3 King's Bench Walk, Temple until at least 1868. These red brick chambers were erected shortly after the 'Great Fire of London' and were reached across an erratic, paved and cobbled walkway.

There were some further developments with the contests against Sheffield in 1866, whilst Morley became president of the F.A. from 1867-74. In fact, he remained very active, and with 'Bob' Willis built and equipped a small gymnasium opposite to the White Hart Inn, Barnes in 1867.

The work was carried out by members of the soccer team and the rowing fraternity; however it was only used as such for five or six years and later became the Bardowie Skittle Club.

Morley was involved in the test games in 1867-68 when the offside rules were changed, and this saw the introduction of "middling" as an essential skill (bend it like Beckham). Meanwhile, he married Frances Bidgood the daughter of a woollen merchant at Christchurch near to St. Pancras on 14 October 1869, however they had no children.

The F.A. committee appointed a secretary, president, treasurer, and four other members in 1863, but this was increased to ten members in 1869 and they were then poised to make their most important decision.

A meeting took place at the Sportsman Office, Ludgate Hill, on 20 July 1871, and it was under Morley that the F.A. Cup was introduced, although the competition was the brainchild of Charles Alcock (see later).

An informal international was played at the Oval in 1870 and a full game in Glasgow on 30 November 1872, while the corner kick arrived in 1873; however, Morley retired from his senior role at the F.A. the next year, and the daily business then passed over into new hands.

So what about his professional life? He practiced as a commissioner for oaths in Chancery and was the senior partner in Morley & Shirreff by 1871.

The other partner was his neighbour and rowing associate W.M. Shirreff and their chambers were at 59 Mark Lane, London. In addition, he helped to conserve Barnes Common, and was a keen rider with a pack of beagles, who hunted with the Surrey Union Foxhounds (from the 1870s).

He continued to live at 26 The Terrace with his wife, his sister, and two servants in 1881, whereas his offices were situated at 53 Old Broad Street not far from Liverpool Street Station.

Morley remained the secretary of Barnes & Mortlake Regatta until 1880 and the event continued until 1888, whereas Barnes F.C. played in their last Cup tournament at Limes Field in 1886-87, and First and Second Avenues had covered the site by 1895.

His relatives the Bidgoods were in the wool trade and his brother-in-law Frederick was a woollen merchant, whilst the latter's sister, Emily married William James who was a woollen merchant and hotel proprietor. Their son Dudley W.H. James inherited the aptly named *Morley's Hotel* (1831-1935) at 25 Cockspur Street, on the east side of Trafalgar Square - which was later replaced by South Africa House.

Meanwhile, Morley tried to revive the Regatta on a number of occasions from 1908 but eventually had to concede defeat, whilst he was a president of the Barnes Artizan's Club, a local J.P., and represented Barnes on the Surrey County Council from 1903-19.

He was a member of Devon and Somerset Staghounds from 1902 and his wife Frances died at the Imperial Hotel, Taw Vale Parade, Barnstaple, on 15 August 1911. The F.A. then recognized his major contribution, despite the many changes within the game, during their jubilee of 1913.

26 The Terrace was in a quiet suburb beside the Thames and had a plain front with a conservatory on the east side (and still survives today). Indeed, in a time untainted by motor traffic he could ride past his house. [5]

Ebenezer Cobb Morley of 53 Gresham House, Old Broad Street and Barnes made his last will on 29 October 1918. It was a lengthy document and he left his estate in trust to several relatives, while numerous bequests and legacies went to local charities and his employees.

He was a remarkable man of great energy and died at 26 The Terrace on 20 November 1924 aged 93. His funeral took place at Barnes Church and he was buried in a corner of the Old Cemetery (1854) on the common, not far from where he had first played football.

---

[5] Gustav Holst composer lived at 10 The Terrace (1908-13) and Archibald Leitch ground designer at Lonsdale Road (1915-22); whilst the Ranelagh Club, Barn Elms was a fashionable centre for sport from 1884-1939.

Those at the service included his relatives, partners from Morley, Shirreff, members of Barnes Council, and the Artizan's Club, whilst details of his life appeared in two local papers and his estate was valued at £48,994.

Meanwhile, Barnes Old Cemetery was closed in the mid-1950s and plans for a lawn cemetery failed thus it became a nature reserve. It is completely overgrown, although Morley's grave survives and can be found by virtue of being the last one in the southeast corner.

A blue plaque to "Major Walter Clopton Wingfield (1833-1912), father of lawn tennis," is situated at 33 St. George's Square, Pimlico yet there is none to commemorate Ebenezer Cobb Morley at 26 The Terrace. It is a theme regarding soccer history that remains quite ubiquitous.

ROBERT WATSON WILLIS

The early development of the game had a parochial aspect hence the next two F.A. secretaries came from the ranks of Barnes F.C. In fact, the club enjoyed a monopoly at the organisation which was purely provincial.

Initially, the story entertained a tartan twist, since Robert Willis of Leith just north of Edinburgh married Agnes Hay in 1795 and had four children. Meanwhile, a degree of Highland dew entered into the mix, since the father was a spirit dealer at *The Pipes* in 1801.

His son Robert Willis was born at Leith on 13 February 1799 and qualified as an M.D., being a fellow of both the Royal College of Surgeons and of Physicians in Edinburgh (F.R.C.S.E.). However, he was soon to perceive some new opportunities south of the border.

Meanwhile, David Watson married Ann Mary Underwood a minor of St. Luke's at St. Margaret's, Westminster on 22 July 1793. He then worked as an upholsterer at 14 Bridge Street, Westminster until 1810 and also traded with his brother Henry at 51 Parliament Street.

Four children were baptized at St. Margaret's Church next to Westminster Abbey, whilst local rate books showed the father lived in Parliament Street, the property having an annual poor rate value of £150 with a charge of £9 7s 6d. There was also a smaller charge for the 'watch rate.'

David Watson of Whitehall made his last will in 1810 and left 3/10 of the business to his wife, and smaller sums to Henry Watson and John Watson Esq. of Torryburn in Fife. After his death his wife moved a short distance to Princes Court, Westminster, which was a small street of twelve houses at the end of Great George Street beside Storey's Gate and St. James's Park. Indeed, she was listed in the rate books from 1812-30, with an annual rate value ranging from £30 to £40.

Henry Watson ran the upholstery business at 14 Bridge Street from 1811-26 and was a gentleman of 31 Parliament Street otherwise Whitehall. In his will he left properties to Mary Maria wife of Baron de Berenger de Beautain, and also John Hunter of Torryburn, Edinburgh, whilst he was buried at St. Margaret's on 17 March 1830 aged 69.

Robert Willis M.D. married Eleanor Watson (daughter of David) at St. Margaret's, Westminster on 31 March 1831, and moved to Princes Court then had three children viz. Eleanor (1832), Anne Mary (1833) and Agnes Aders (1836). Indeed, the father was a successful physician and they moved to an affluent property 25 Dover Street, Piccadilly, in 1837. [6]

Two more daughters were baptized at St. George's Hanover Square soon after: Frances La Touche (1839) and Mary Watson (1841), whilst they lived at Dover Street in 1841 and the household included a relative Robert Mason (20) an engineer from Scotland, two students in medicine, and five servants. The property itself was a four-storey Georgian town-house with a plain but narrow façade, and is still present today.

A son Robert Watson Willis was born at 25 Dover Street on 26 January 1843 and baptized at St. George's Hanover Square later that year, whereas the practice had removed to Barnes in leafy Surrey by 1846.

The family then enjoyed a comfortable country lifestyle and lived at Rose Cottage, Church Road, on the edge of Barnes Common (opposite Nassau and Grange Roads). This had a colonial appearance with a pretty veranda, good-sized garden with picket fence, and common land just behind.

There were then some significant unions and Agnes Aders married Henry Edward Vernet a banker with origins in Geneva in 1859; whilst Frances La Touche married Mark Dewsnap who was a widower and barrister in 1865, the witnesses Robert Willis, Eleanor Willis, and R.G. Graham.

Indeed, 'Bob' Willis was a prominent member of Barnes and an associate of Morley and Graham, thus he became F.A. secretary in 1866 aged 23, and played for London in the test match against Sheffield later that year.

Such football activities also provided social connections and he married Helen Eliza Graham at Barnes on 28 August 1867, the witnesses Robert Willis, Robert George Graham, and Emily Sophia Graham (sister).

He also appeared for Kent & Surrey in 1867 and then Surrey in 1868, with both Morley and Graham, which were important in terms of the game's development. However, he then stepped down as secretary of the F.A. and stood on the committee from 1869-71.

---

[6] Princes Court was later demolished during road widening, and the Institution of Mechanical Engineers, 1 Birdcage Walk is now on the site.

Initially, he lived with his wife at 5 Beverley Villas, Barnes, which was one of six semi-detached houses on the edge of the common - next to Clyde Road. It was an elegant three-storey property with white stucco and grey brickwork above, and was re-numbered as 114 Beverley Road.

The couple had a number of children there, however left Barnes in 1872 and the football connection was then ended. Meanwhile, their new home was at "Hinxton House," Upper Richmond Road, East Sheen - a name of some considerable interest regarding the following discourse.

Robert W. Willis operated as a Spanish or wine merchant at 25 Crutched Friars in the City, although he did not trade under his own name; whereas his father died at Rose Cottage in 1878 and was buried in Barnes Old Cemetery, his property being valued at almost £5,000. [7]

The family had some significant connections by marriage and notable neighbours in the vicinity. In fact, the Willis's lived at Hinxton House near Richmond Park during the 1880s, and the adjacent properties were "The Grange" home of Henry and Agnes Vernet, and "Fernbank" the residence of Herbert Williams and Elizabeth Reeves. [8]

Willis was a merchant at Hinxton House in 1891 and lived with his wife Helen E., children Mabel, Harry F.A. (merchant's clerk), Norman (a clerk to the Crown Agent's Office), Enid, Vere, and five servants. However, the family situation was soon to be significantly transformed.

Sir Joseph Napier (1804-82) held senior posts and was M.P. for Dublin University from 1848-58, whilst his son spent some time in Canada, thus a grandson William Lennox Napier was born in Montreal in 1867. The latter was a pupil at Park House School, Tilehurst near to Reading and studied under the headmaster Arthur C. Bartholomew (see later).

He completed his education at Uppingham and Jesus College, Cambridge then established links with both Graham and Forster at nearby Hinxton, and married Mabel Edith Geraldine Forster there in 1890.

As a result William L. Napier a student at law lived at 1 Temple Sheen, Mortlake in 1891, with his wife Mabel, brothers-in-law Arthur E.T. Forster, (stockbroker's clerk), Leopold H.V. Forster (16), and two servants who

---

[7] The 'Misses' Willis or Eleanor and Mary lived at Rose Cottage in 1879, but left soon after, and the former (late of Barnes) died at Florence, Italy in 1881. The property then had several residents including Rev. Walter H. Rammell curate of Barnes in 1884, C. Tonge in 1887-88, and Richard W. Nunn from 1895-1911. It was demolished for road widening on 3 October 1911.

[8] Herbert Williams Reeves was related to Arthur Pember, whilst his wife had local connections and was a relative of R.G. Graham (see below).

came from Hinxton. The property was a large house looking north down Derby Road, situated at the junction with Temple Sheen Road.

The Napiers then moved to Kensington and the father was a barrister at Temple, whilst the Willis's took their old house, however Robert Watson Willis died there after a long illness on 16 January 1892 aged 48.

A local paper noted that he was greatly respected in the parish and a large number of parishioners waited at Mortlake Cemetery to pay their tributes, whereas many carriages of the local gentry followed the coffin. His effects came to £12,357 whilst a large cross memorial was erected on a three step base, although today this is up-turned. Clearly few who pass by realize that he was once a pioneer of soccer.

His widow Helen (née Graham) lived with her children and three servants at 1 Temple Sheen in 1901, whereas Richard W. Cory a barrister lived at No. 2 (see below) and Henry and Agnes Vernet at Nos. 3-4.

Mrs. R.W. Willis resided at "Sheen House," Portsmouth Road, Esher near Sandown Park Racecourse from 1910-30, whereas Anne M. Willis married William Marshall M.D. and resided at "Torrieburn," Church Road, Barnes near Nassau Gardens in the late 19th century.

ROBERT GEORGE GRAHAM

The stories of Willis and Graham were greatly inter-twined and William Graham married Mary Robinson at Wetheral, Cumberland, near to Corby Castle, in 1789, whilst a son John Graham was born on 8 July 1792.

The family had some beneficial connections, and the latter attended St. John's, Cambridge in 1811 then gained his B.A. in 1815. Initially, he was the curate of Wardley, Rutland, and of Swaffham Bulbeck, Cambridge, but gained a B.D. in 1825 and was a fellow of Jesus College by 1828.

Remaining in the district he became vicar of Comberton in 1830-33 and then vicar of Hinxton on the River Cam, ten miles south of Cambridge, in 1833 - he also held a notable sinecure as vicar of Swavesey, a substantial church located to the northwest of the city.

Hinxton had several coach services after 1832, although the railway did not arrive there until 1845; while the church and vicarage were in a central location and several houses exhibited the local art of pargeting.

However, there was much hardship and more than a hundred agricultural labourers gathered in the High Street to protest about exploitation by local landowners in 1833. They received only a small sum for their labours, and eventually there was a fight and an assault, thus the protagonists were sentenced to a month's hard labour.

Meanwhile, John Graham married Frances Maria Gillson at Claybrook, Leicester on 28 May 1834, who came from Greetham, Rutland near Exton Hall home of the Noels. The couple then lived in Hinxton and had seven children including Robert George (1845) and Helen Eliza (1846).

A country vicar had an important role and Rev. Graham soon appeared in the local records. Indeed, he was involved in a heated dispute. Some repair work was done on a few nearby cottages at the request of the church, but there was a serious argument over who should pay.

Northfield Reynolds wanted 42 guineas for his labour but was left out of pocket, thus he could not pay his uncle William Reynolds. The latter took Rev. Graham to court to try and recover the outstanding money from the third party in 1846, and indeed eventually won the case.

On another occasion a young couple arrived at the church to be married. They failed to produce a licence, thus the vicar sent them away and they were forced to marry several miles away at Saffron Walden. Further to this there was a report about Rev. Graham's sick cow in 1854, whilst two years later the *Cambridge Independent Press* noted, "the getting in of some forward oats - the property of Rev. J. Graham."

The latter resided at the Vicarage in 1861 with his wife Frances Maria, children William (student of the Inner Temple), Mary Frances, Helen Eliza, and Emily Sophia, however he died there on 8 July 1862 and a flat stone memorial was placed just left of the church porch.

He had been the incumbent at Hinxton for twenty-nine years, and was followed by two other long-term vicars, namely Rev. Charles Thornton Forster (1865-91) and Rev. Richard Twells (1892-1926).

Indeed, Henry Thornton a banker resided at Battersea Rise and was a member of the Clapham Sect who fought slavery, whilst his daughter Laura was born in 1808. She married Charles Forster a Welsh clergyman at Holy Trinity, Clapham in 1833 and they had two notable sons:

(1) Charles Thornton Forster (1836) was born at Ash, Kent and became the vicar of Hinxton after the Rev. Graham, whereas his daughter Mabel was married to William Lennox Napier.

(2) Edward Morgan Llewellyn Forster (1848) trained as an architect and married Alice Clara Whichelo at Wandsworth in 1877. Their son Edward Morgan Forster was born in the Marylebone district on 1 January 1879 and was destined to become a famous writer. [9]

---

[9] Forster wrote *A Room with a View* (1908), *Howard's End* (1910), and *A Passage to India* (1924), and gave the Clark Lectures at Trinity, Cambridge on his book *Aspects of the Novel* (1927). He referred to *The Craft of Fiction* (1921) by Percy Lubbock and it is thought they were acquainted (see later).

The latter was brought up by his mother 'Lily' and great aunt Marianne Thornton who was also an evangelist, reformer, and writer. Indeed, she left E.M. Forster £8,000 in trust when she died in 1887.

Meanwhile, Robert George Graham was born at Hinxton on 2 January 1845 and spent his childhood living in the village, but was educated at Cheltenham College in 1861-62. His erudition, however, came to an end at his father's decease and he then entered into business.

The family moved to Barnes although the reason for this is uncertain, and Mrs. Graham lived at 2 Lonsdale Villas, Lonsdale Road near Hammersmith Bridge in 1865-67 - the Wedgwoods resided at 4 Park Villas (see later). In fact, her son joined Barnes F.C. soon after its formation and was on the F.A. committee in 1867-68, thus he played for Kent-Surrey and for Surrey (as captain) with his brother-in-law at this time.

He was secretary of the F.A. from 1868-70 and treasurer in 1869-70, whilst he was a stockbroker and married Alice Hackblock at Christchurch, East Sheen on 15 September 1869. Her father John Hackblock was a gentleman and had previously lived at Camberwell where she was born.

The couple then moved to "Lyndhurst," Upper Richmond Road, Barnes near to the "Manor House" (see Merriman), and his mother Frances resided with daughter Emily Sophia at 23-24 The Terrace close to Morley.

There were some good connections and Sir Francis Molyneux Ommanney M.P. of East Sheen married Georgiana Hawkes and had children Elizabeth Acworth (1804) and Octavius (1817); while John and Sophia Prinsep had two sons: Henry Thoby (1792) who married Sarah Pattle and Augustus (1803) who married Elizabeth A. Ommanney in 1828. [10]

Indeed, the Ommanneys had several links in East Sheen while Augustus Prinsep a merchant died at sea soon after and his widow married Samuel Beachcroft. Their daughter Elizabeth (1844) then married Herbert Williams Reeves, a fact that is relevant during the later story.

Octavius Ommanney was born at Mortlake in 1817 and married in 1841, whilst his son Frederick Glean married Emily Sophia Graham at Barnes in 1871, and then lived at "Sheen House," Upper Walmer, Kent (in fact, their daughter was married to Herbert E. Kenyon who was a relative of William S. Kenyon-Slaney).

---

[10] The Pattle family had connections to Edward G. Wakefield a founder of New Zealand, while Sarah was sister of Julia Margaret Cameron a pioneer photographer of Freshwater and Maria the wife of Dr. John Jackson. The Prinseps resided at Little Holland House and their son was a Pre-Raphaelite, whereas Leslie Stephen a publisher married Harriet M. Thackeray and Julia P. Jackson (mother of Vanessa Bell and Virginia Woolf).

Her mother Frances Maria Graham had left Barnes by 1878 and was a funded proprietor at "Wetheral," Keswick Road, Putney in 1881 but died there in 1889. She was buried in Mortlake Cemetery beside Robert Watson Willis and his son Robert Graham Willis. [11]

Of her children, William Graham (1838) was educated at Sedbergh and Cambridge and became a barrister in 1862. He lived at Upper Richmond Road and spoke on the matter of Parnell and was counsel for the *Times*. Charles J. Graham (1839) was educated at Uppingham by E. Thring and at Bury, but became a farmer and member of the Queensland Government, whereas John Graham (1841) was a minister like his father.

Robert and Alice Graham had only two daughters from their marriage, Alice Evelyn Manners (1871) born at "Lyndhurst," and Matilda Winifred Muriel (1873) born at 12 Bolton Gardens, South Kensington. [12]

R.G. Graham worked as a stockbroker for Glyn & Co. from 1876-78 and then moved to "St. Alban's," Hampton on the banks of the River Thames. This red-brick house was of an unusual design being long and narrow, due to the constraints of the site, and backed right onto the road. However, there was a pretty lawn leading down to the river, with a boathouse and horse chestnut to one side, whilst the gardens continued to the east past a series of stepped terraces. [13]

Indeed, this was an attractive location near to Bushy Park with buildings connected to David Garrick the actor, most notably a temple designed by Capability Brown in 1756. The church of St. Mary's was a short distance further on and this was to be the scene of much creativity.

Robert G. Graham of the Stock Exchange resided there in 1881 with his wife Alice, his two daughters (both scholars), a governess, three servants, a coachman, and a horse trainer. Indeed, this was the principal property on Thames Street and the Graham family remained for eighty years.

A serious fire occurred at Rose Villa in Station Road in November 1867, and the attending engine could not find sufficient water, while the hose was proven to be too short! There were similar problems in 1870; however a volunteer fire brigade was established at Hampton Hill in 1876.

---

[11] Nearby there is a memorial to Charles C.B. Dickens (1837-96), who was eldest son of the famous writer.

[12] The property was near to Barkston Gardens (see Leitch) and The Boltons (see Bonsor), whilst Beatrix Potter lived in Old Brompton Road from 1866-1913.

[13] John Wilson Croker (1780-1857) the famous author and statesman from Ireland lived at St. Alban's, Hampton and also died there.

Meanwhile, there were no facilities in the village itself hence there was a vestry meeting in 1885, and the parish asked for an initiative. Several men came forward to form a volunteer fire brigade and Mr. Graham consented to act as their captain. He was a considerable influence on the brigade and was associated with it for the rest of his life.

R.G. Graham was a company director and employer in 1891 and lived at St. Alban's with his wife and daughters, whilst Alice married John Hubert Grogan in 1895 - although her sister enjoyed the more notable life. Indeed, literary talent pervaded the corridors of St. Alban's and Winifred Graham became a writer of some distinction.

A serious fire destroyed the Bell Hotel thus a new fire station opened opposite to the Water Works in 1898, whereas Graham had retired from business by 1901. His sister Helen E. Willis was living at Temple Sheen and her neighbour was Richard W. Cory (a barrister), resulting in a new liaison. The Corys owned a colliery near to Cardiff however their son Theodore John, also a barrister, married Winifred at Kensington in 1906.

The family no doubt spent many pleasant days sojourning by the river, but the father died at St. Alban's on 6 April 1922 aged 77 and his wife in 1938. A notable alabaster tablet was then erected by his two daughters, above the vestry door in the south aisle of St. Mary's, Hampton:

"To the glory of God and the dear memory of Robert George Graham Esq. of St Albans Hampton chairman of the National Fire Brigade widows and orphans fund, for 26 years the beloved chief of the Hampton Volunteer Fire Brigade...." [14]

Winifred Graham (1873) moved to St. Alban's with her husband and it was there that she wrote most of her eighty-eight books. Indeed, she may have known E.M. Forster a friend of the family from the Hinxton days, and thereby received some significant inspiration.

Her education was at home, and she began to write popular novels both dramatic and sentimental at an early age. These were of an easy, flowing, critical style, although not very exacting, and she carried off situations that a more sophisticated reader might have found unbelievable.

---

[14] Nearby is a memorial: "Mrs Susannah Thomas sole daughter and heiress of Sir Dalby Thomas knight governor of all the African companies settlements and of Dame Dorothy daughter of John Chettle of St. Mary Blandford 4 April 1731 descended from an antient family in Wales." This monumental design with Ionic columns appears in Jerome's "Three Men in a Boat" in 1889 - "Harris wanted to get out at Hampton Church to go and see Mrs. Thomas's tomb. 'Who is Mrs Thomas?' I asked. 'How should I know?' replied Harris. 'She's a lady that's got a funny tomb and I want to see it.'"

Amongst her works were short stories for the Strand and Red Magazine and a series "The Idylls of Suburbia" in 1898-1912. She campaigned against the Mormon religion in her work, produced lessons for Sunday school education, and had a great fascination with psychic phenomena.

In particular she published, "My letters from heaven being messages from the unseen world given in automatic writing to Winifred Graham from her father R.G. Graham" (1940). She also wrote a trilogy and autobiography including her association with Aleister Crowley a literary friend.

She died in 1950 and her husband inherited the house, whilst after his death he left St. Alban's to Twickenham Council as a museum. The house was to be a memorial to his wife and her writing, whilst a stained glass window was installed at St. Mary's, with a book to signify her work and a background of the church, St. Alban's, and Garrick's Temple.

However, the plans for a museum came to nothing and St. Alban's passed to Richmond Council in 1965, and the house was demolished in 1972. The grounds then became a public space with a plaque to Winifred Graham, and there is also a memorial in the form of a book at St. Mary's.

Football itself was soon to be played on a wider stage, and the reins were transferred to Messrs. Alcock and Marindin.

CHAPTER 3

American Links

Arthur Pember the first F.A. president was one of the most extraordinary characters in the game, but his contribution was largely ignored. So one might ask, "If he was so important, how did this come about?"

In the first instance he departed from the F.A. soon after the rules were established and went abroad. In the second instance the history of the F.A. was written much later by those whose tenure was more long-lasting. In fact, Charles Alcock, who wrote one of the earliest histories, may have had personal reasons for such a noteworthy omission.

Pember's contribution to the game was largely covered in the first chapter; therefore this section concentrates on the man behind the boots and his family connections. Indeed, his story is quite exceptional, providing a large degree of contrast in terms of his contemporaries at the F.A.

Initially, he was somewhat elusive and enquiries suggested that little was known of him, except that he was a London solicitor who concentrated on the administration side. Yet, further research showed he had an illustrious background with a fascinating history to boot.

THE PEMBER FAMILY

In general the family believed they were descended from the Pembers of Newport House, an estate northwest of Hereford, however this was not in fact the case. Five generations held the property from the 17th century but it was sold in 1712, and there was then an indication that they moved to Ledbury, although this assumption was erroneous and flawed.

Based on such antecedents they were entitled to a coat of arms after a *Herald's Visitation* of 1683. This consisted of a shield of three pheasants, azure and argent, with a single pheasant feeding on a stalk of wheat, whilst their motto of "Cave Calcem" held a warning. Indeed cave means beware, whilst calcem comes from calx viz. lime or chalk, a goal marked by a chalk line, an end as oppose to a start, a heel, or perhaps a kick.

The Biblical explanation Acts IX verse 5 states, "It is hard for you to kick against the pricks," and in this context the word pricks refers to a goad for oxen, whilst the literal translation is "Beware the Kick," "Watch out for the Boot." The soccer connotations are clear and this archaic motto was to be most prophetic in terms of the rules.

Meanwhile, regarding the early history some crucial facts were ignored. John Pember a yeoman was born at Kenchester by the River Wye in 1670 and married Katherine Hodges of Credenhill at Lugwardine in 1692. They had several children including Elizabeth who married her relative Thomas Pember a local glover, and also a son Thomas who moved to Ledbury and established himself as a tailor.

Thomas Pember married Esther Chamberlain at Ledbury, which was once a large minster with a notable raised market hall, in 1721, and had three children there viz. Ann (1725), John (1727), and Thomas (1730).

The common belief was that the Pembers of Newport House removed to the town after selling their grand estate; however two title deeds and a will conclusively showed that this assumption was wrong. The most significant document was a deed of 1756 which settled any argument: "John Pember of Ledbury tailor son of Thomas Pember of the same tailor (deceased) and the grandson of John Pember of Credenhill yeoman…."

There was little likelihood that a gentleman would turn tradesman, and in fact the son John Pember married Mary Parker at Ledbury in 1758 and had five children including Mary, Edward, and St. John (1769); whilst his sons were tailors at Crescent Place, Blackfriars, from the 1800s.

St. John Pember of Clapham married Mary Carless of St. Anne, Blackfriars by licence at Holy Trinity, Clapham on 29 January 1801. The church was on the north side of the common, and had a classical façade with a white colonnade and clock tower, adjacent to a brown brick nave. [1]

The couple lived at Vauxhall Terrace, Lambeth and had ten children but most died in childhood, whilst the father was a tailor at Crescent Place until his decease in 1835. The most significant offspring was their first son John Edward Ross born 1801, since he raised the family in the social scale.

Indeed, he made a fortune at the Stock Exchange and initially resided in Stockwell, marrying Elizabeth Devey at St. Matthew's, Brixton just after it was first consecrated on 9 August 1825. She was heiress to a property in Walsall and died soon after thus it passed to the Pember family.

However, he then made a new match and married Fanny Robson, a minor, with consent of her father at St. Pancras, Euston Road on 9 August 1831. His bride came from a large family of fifteen children, and was the daughter of John Robson a long-term member of the Stock Exchange who lived at Hamilton Place, New Road.

---

[1] William Wilberforce and the Clapham Sect worshipped at Holy Trinity in the 18th/19th centuries - the Macaulays and Henry and John Venn, curate and rector were also involved. They placed pressure on Parliament thus the slave trade was abolished in 1807, and freedom was secured in 1833.

At first the couple lived at Stockwell but soon moved to a large property 4 New Park Road near to the junction with Brixton Hill. This was at the top of an incline in a semi-village environment with a school, several shops, and a prison nearby, and some fields and market gardens just behind.

The father continued to do well and had a large family whilst his children were educated at home by governesses (Kate and Jane Robson), privately in Brixton, and at public school. Indeed, their childhood years were spent at their Brixton Hill home and they remained there until 1848.

Meanwhile, Thomas Cubitt who designed Belgravia and Pimlico purchased some land nearby and laid out Clapham Park with its large stucco houses, extensive gardens, and wide avenues for the upper classes.

Thackeray was taken with the area, and stated, "Of all the pretty suburbs that still adorn our metropolis there are few that exceed in charm Clapham Common;" whilst his book *The Newcomes* was based on a local family.

The Pembers then moved to a mansion "Langlands," Kings Road on the estate, which was situated in half an acre of land with orchards to the rear, whilst their near neighbours included Sir James Youl.

The father sat on the 'Committee for General Purposes' at the Stock Exchange from 1852 and moved to another fine house at Leigham Avenue, Streatham in 1863, then represented Jones Loyd & Co (1858-65), Bank of London (1866-67), and the Bank of England (1868-78).

However, his wife Fanny died in 1873 and he lived at Woodfield Cottage in Mount Ephraim Road, Streatham until his own death in 1881. Much of his fortune was lost by this time although the family have a large memorial at West Norwood Cemetery. His children, meanwhile, took two distinct paths with some immigrating to a new future without façade.

His eldest son Edward Henry Pember (1832) wrote poetry and was "the best talker in London," using his literary skills as a barrister of Lincoln's Inn from 1858. He became a noted parliamentary speaker and was a favourite of both Houses, representing the interests of the Manchester Ship Canal and was counsel for Cecil Rhodes regarding the Jameson Raid.

He lived at Vicars Hill House near Lymington in the New Forest; whilst his son Francis a barrister wrote a family history, and his granddaughter Katharine was married to Charles Galton Darwin.

George Herbert Pember (1845) the youngest son attended Westminster School in 1856-63, and possibly introduced his brother Arthur to football. In fact, he joined his father at the Stock Exchange in 1869, and also formed the long-running broking firm of Pember & Boyle. [2]

---

[2] Cecil Boyle was descended from the Earls of Cork & Orrery, the Spencers, and the Dukes of Devonshire, while Hallam Tennyson was his brother-in-law.

Initially, he resided at Norbiton, Surrey but was a country gentleman at Tangier Park near Basingstoke from 1885-1903. During that time he was master of the Vine Hunt however he moved south to Fair Oak Park near Eastleigh and played a full role in the community, being a benefactor of considerable importance - he died there in 1921.

However, this was just one side of the story, and other family members were not held by such long-standing and ingrained traditions.

THE EMIGRANTS

The eldest daughter Ellen (1833) married William Reeves of Kennington at Holy Trinity, Clapham when aged just twenty. He was also a member of the Stock Exchange but after a business failure decided to emigrate.

The couple arrived with one daughter at Lyttelton, New Zealand in 1857, just seven years after the Canterbury Colony was formed. In fact, Reeves was soon acquainted with the leading pioneers and managed a sheep run, then became a politician in the New Zealand Parliament.

He built a fine settlers homestead "Risingholme," Opawa just outside of Christchurch, and was proprietor of a Liberal organ the *Lyttelton Times*, but despite such successes was bankrupt when he died in 1891.

His son William Pember Reeves worked at the paper and like his father was a politician, being aligned with the Fabians as a radical Liberal. He was the first Minister of Labour in the Empire in 1892 and passed important legislation, whilst his wife Maud helped secure votes for women in 1893, but his radical views meant he was Agent General in London by 1896.

The family were then associated with the Webbs and Bernard Shaw, all Fabians, whilst Reeves published *The Long White Cloud* a detailed history of New Zealand which was the standard view until the 1950s.

He was High-Commissioner in 1905, however there was a scandal after his daughter Amber had an affair with H.G. Wells and became pregnant. The couple briefly eloped to Le Touquet, France, but for propriety's sake she married her mother's lawyer George Rivers Blanco-White in 1909.

Maud did research in Lambeth in 1909-13 and published *Round about a pound a week* however son Fabian a lieutenant in the Royal Naval Air Service died in France in 1917. The father never recovered and died in Kensington in 1932, whilst Amber (also a writer) later received the O.B.E.

Frederick Pember (1837) also emigrated but his motives were different in the extreme. He attended Christchurch College and was influenced by the Oxford Movement, whilst he was ordained by Bishop Wilberforce in 1861 and spent the first few years as a curate in England.

However, he was recruited by Bishop Harper of Christchurch and sailed for the colony in 1868, then became incumbent at Burnham, which was a parish covering a large area up to the mountains. Indeed, Rev. Pember rode on horseback to the outlying regions, and held services that were famous locally for their 'hearty fellowship.'

Due to certain problems he moved back to town and was in charge of Holy Trinity, Lyttelton in 1872-75, but returned to England to recuperate. After working as a missionary in Maine in 1877-86, he moved to Boston and founded Christchurch, Needham in 1894. Of his sons, John was a local reporter and Walter was an architect at Albany in New York.

ARTHUR PEMBER

This pioneer of soccer was born at New Park Road on 15 January 1835 and received his education at a private school in Brixton, with tutors at home, and then in France. He did not attend public school but was well-educated being familiar with both the classics and contemporary literature.

He travelled to France, Italy, and Switzerland and his greatest achievement was the ascent of Mont Blanc, with a friend and two guides, in the early 1860s. He later wrote and lectured upon the subject, providing a vivid and moving description of this dangerous climb.

Pember was married by 1862 and lived at Kilburn, whilst he worked with his father at the Stock Exchange. He also rode a horse and was the stroke of an eight-oared boat for two seasons, and probably met Morley in Barnes at this time. Meanwhile, his brothers were at major public schools thus he started the No Names Club, and was instrumental in the formation of the Football Association.

He was a stockbroker for the Consolidated Bank in 1864 and lived at 26 Carlton Road, Kilburn (Carlton Vale), whilst the bank was briefly closed in 1866, due to a disastrous takeover of the Bank of London. This may have caused financial problems and he resigned from the F.A., and immigrated with his family to New York in 1868.

This was a bold move, the country being under reconstruction after the Civil War. Consequently he had several concerns, and his daughter Lillian was adopted by her uncle Edward in the New Forest.

After arriving in New York he did not enter Wall Street but sought a new profession as a journalist. Initially, he tried his luck in Boston, but soon returned to New York and lived at 1233 Third Avenue in the 1870s. He worked for the leading editors of the day, and in the first instance wrote two articles for *Atlantic Monthly* and *Lippincott's Magazine*.

These provided a deep insight into his character and the first was about "Ritualism in England by an English Ritualist." He discussed the movement in some detail and in particular church riots that took place in 1867.

Many believed the movement was Catholic however this was disputed, whilst he talked of his association with Father Mackonochie of St. Alban's, Holborn, "One of the most advanced Ritualists of the day."

His second article was even more extreme being entitled, "The Coming Revolution in England." In this he talked of a liberalising drive that would soon witness the demise of the House of Lords. The Anglican Church was disestablished in Ireland in 1869 and he believed the same would happen in England (although this never actually took place).

Indeed, "Intelligent observers of the signs of the times can scarcely have failed to arrive at the conclusion that a great social and moral revolution is impending over Great Britain. That the rapid growth of liberal opinion and the gradual accumulation of liberal legislation are undermining the authoritative position, the long claimed right to govern, and the long accorded superiority over the masses, of the British aristocracy."

"The Church is a great and important element in the great aristocratic fabric, and cannot fail in its fall to give a severe shaking to the already tottering remainder." The Lords, meanwhile, was just a remnant of the feudal system and would no doubt soon be abolished (not the case).

Arthur Pember the F.A. president had come a long way from Kilburn to the Upper East Side and lived there among many other immigrants. Indeed, with two articles under his belt he found further work with new journals, initially for John Russell Young editor of the *Standard* a short-lived paper in 1870-72. He also penned satirical rhyming for *Punchinello* with hits against noted men, Sorosis women, and other would-be reformers. [3]

Meanwhile, the papers in Newspaper Row near to City Hall engaged in a number of exposés in the 1870s, the most notable regarding "Boss" Tweed and the Tammany. In fact, Pember did similar work for Whitelaw Reid at the *Tribune* and spent time at Ludlow Street Jail as a poor prisoner.

He also investigated the purlieus of Water Street, the panel-houses and keno joints, and bogus diplomas for doctors. Such investigative journalism was a new art and Pember was very good at this work, however he then joined Louis J. Jennings at the *Times* and did an important series "Our State Institutions." There were 33 articles covering almost every city, which were well-informed with allusions to literature and characters of the time.

---

[3] Sorosis, the first women's society in America, was established at Delmonico's Restaurant in Fifth Avenue in 1868. This took place after female reporters were denied access to see Charles Dickens during his visit.

Indeed, during his travels he met leading industrialists and saw pioneering processes such as Bessemer, whilst visiting prisons such as Sing Sing with their hard regimes. He also detailed asylums with great compassion.

His most important work, however, came in 1872-74 when he explored "people's modes of existence," or "how the other half lives," in New York and its environs. In the first instance he dressed as an amateur beggar and was host at a beggar's banquet in the notorious Water Street. [4]

Later on he ventured forth as a tramp from Jersey City to Philadelphia and worked his passage on the Erie Canal, then explored various "occupations" such as curbstone singer, costermonger, peepshow proprietor, diver, and circus entertainer. In fact, he then spent time in an underground lodging house and met Kit Burns who ran the notorious "Rat Pit."

In addition, he travelled to Pennsylvania and went down a coalmine at Mauch Chunk (Jim Thorpe), explored with some bravery a zinc mine near to Bethlehem, experienced the notorious Tombs Prison and the Five Points locality, and acted as a fraudulent spirit medium.

His twenty adventures, humorous and grave, had a strong social motive and appeared in book form in 1874 viz. "The Mysteries and Miseries of the Great Metropolis, with some adventures in the country: being the disguises and surprises of a New York journalist," by the Amateur Vagabond.

D. Appleton & Co. published this pioneering book which contained 462 pages and 11 plates from photographs by Gurney, whilst a few copies are still held at the New York State Library in Albany.

The reporter was not content with the comfortable life and made strong comments regarding the privileged, whilst his work contained ideas suitable for both the reformer and philanthropist. The *N.Y. Times* then reviewed this significant work and attempted to correct any misconceptions.

There were several similar publications of an inferior nature, however, "It has no place with those other volumes, but will rank far above them, whether we regard it merely on its literary merits, or, more justly, as an able practical exemplification of certain phases of everyday life, as obtained through the courage and ingenuity of a clever journalist."

Indeed the reporter was described as, "A man whose literary attainments and social position are such as to insure the handling of his subject in a manner far beyond the level of merely sensational writers."

"The *Amateur Vagabond* has succeeded in the production of a work which, amongst recent publications, must be awarded a very high place for originality and intrinsic worth. It is a book which will afford a vast fund

---

[4] Arthur Conan Doyle almost certainly used the idea of The Amateur Beggar in his story The Man with the Twisted Lip published in 1891.

of amusement, and provoke many a hearty laugh; but it is also a book which, if rightly read, will be found to have a high social purpose, while in every page it can hardly fail to excite in the mind of the reader admiration for the personal merits of the *Amateur Vagabond* himself."

Pember continued to work as a journalist in the 1870s and remained at Third Avenue but his most important work was already done. He appeared before a Senate Committee in the matter of the panel-houses in 1875, and did articles on Saratoga and the Centennial Exposition, the latter being an international exhibition larger than the Crystal Palace.

However, there were dramatic changes when his wife Alice died in 1881 and he was left with five sons aged from two to sixteen. By then he lived at 1240 Third Avenue but had given up his newspaper career, and classified fauna and flora at the Natural History Museum. He was then imbued with a new scheme and decided to remove his sons from the temptations of the city, and they travelled to Dakota Territory in May 1884.

The prairie lands of the Mid-west had previously been ignored, however there was a boom in wheat farming in the 1880s and most Indians were settled in reserves. The family then became pioneers of La Moure, a small township on the James River which was first established in 1882.

Some money was left in trust to his wife and sons in his father's will and this was held by his brothers Edward and George in England. As a result an agreement was reached between them and the Northern Pacific Railroad, thereby purchasing 480 acres (or three sections of land).

The farm was four miles southwest of the city on the Cottonwood Creek, and the family took possession but initially lived in La Moure City. In fact, during the first year they erected a fine barn and produced a crop, whilst meeting local Indians and shooting wildcats which trespassed.

Their prospects seemed good and they planned to erect a large dwelling, whereas they fenced an entire section and aimed to introduce livestock the next season. However, this was not to be, and a man so important in terms of soccer history died in relative obscurity.

His obituary appeared in the *New York Times* on 4 April 1886: "Arthur Pember, formerly a writer on the New York press, died at La Moure, Dakota yesterday morning aged 50 years. He was an Englishman by birth." - the cause of death being a carbuncle in the lumbar region &c.

Much of the population of La Moure turned out for his funeral which was carried out by Rev. Ely of the Presbyterian Church. He had achieved much in his life, firstly as a founder of soccer and then as a journalist with social conscience, but the move to Dakota suggests that in later years his main interest was regarding his five sons.

Meanwhile, his family saw no future in farming and left La Moure soon after his death, once arrangements were made in England. The farm was eventually sold in 1900, when the youngest son was aged twenty-one.

Of his sons, Cyril was briefly a photographer in Fargo and an artist in Syracuse and Manhattan. St. John died of tuberculosis in St. Paul in 1888, whilst Herbert was a stationery salesman in Brooklyn and Manhattan, but left his family and spent many years in California.

The two youngest sons initially attended an Episcopal boarding school in Maine, an arrangement made by Frederick their uncle, whereas Gilbert was later a minister in Pennsylvania and Godfrey moved to Poughkeepsie and worked for the American Express Company.

Arthur Pember left a considerable legacy and Jacob Riis one of the first photojournalists produced "How the Other Half Lives" a title taken directly from his book, and Theodore Roosevelt then shut down lodging-houses. In fact, the *New York Chronicle* stated that he was the prototype for George Plimpton who competed in sporting events as an amateur.

The F.A. Presidents

1863-67	Arthur Pember
1867-74	Ebenezer Cobb Morley
1874-90	Major Francis Arthur Marindin
1890-1923	11th Lord Arthur Fitzgerald Kinnaird
1923-37	Sir John Charles Clegg
1937-39	William Pickford
1939-55	Alexander Cambridge, 1st Earl of Athlone
1955-57	Prince Philip, Duke of Edinburgh
1957-63	Prince Henry, Duke of Gloucester
1963-71	George Lascelles, 7th Earl of Harewood
1971-2000	Prince Edward, Duke of Kent
2000-06	Prince Andrew, Duke of York
2006-	Prince William

CHAPTER 4

Alcock and the Oval

When the F.A. began it was strictly a regional organisation and only gained national significance with the arrival of professionals in the 1880s. Morley had done a good job getting things going, but the F.A. now needed a new kind of official - in particular, someone who could organise its affairs and take them forward over a number of years.

The ideal man for the position soon arrived in the form of Charles W. Alcock, who was secretary from 1870-95. He had a privileged education, played sport at the highest level, and had some excellent organisational qualities, although his origins were in fact less auspicious.

Samuel Alcock married Barbara Hopper at St. Nicholas, Newcastle on 29 December 1770 and was proprietor of the *Cannon P.H.* and a hackney horse-keeper. His younger sons remained in Newcastle as brush makers and grocers, but the story moved forward with John born in 1773.

John Alcock married Elizabeth Preston at St. George's Hanover Square, London, on 4 March 1797; then worked as an upholsterer and shipbuilder at Bishopwearmouth in the east of Sunderland. The area was important for coal and shipbuilding, attracting mariners and other allied trades, whilst vessels perused the coast southwards to London.

One of the main thoroughfares was Low Street close to the River Wear and its docks. Indeed, there were over 400 shipyards by the river but most of these went bankrupt or were taken over in the late 19th century, whilst the Alcock family lived there for over one hundred years.

John Alcock was an upholsterer and ship owner and had several children including Samuel (1798), John Thomas (1799), and Charles (1806), then married Hannah Crawhall and had another son Thomas (1818).

He died in 1838 and left Tavistock House, Tatham Street with garden and outhouses to his wife, also his workshops situated between Sunniside and Nile Street and his other freehold property. He bequeathed his share and interest in the business of upholsterer and cabinet-maker to Samuel (who was already a partner), and, "his ships, vessels, monies and other personal estate," in trust, the rents etc. to be paid to his wife Hannah.

Indeed, an advert in the *Sunderland Herald* in 1838, stated: "Owing to the recent death of Mr. J. Alcock his son Samuel will carry on the business, cash sale etc...." Further to this, several family members were ship owners and Samuel was twice Mayor of Sunderland.

Meanwhile, John Thomas and Charles Alcock entered ship building in a big way and established their own shipyard in 1835-42. This was situated at the western end of Low Street near an area called Pann's Bank, and the company first built ships of 200-300 tons; although the partnership was dissolved by 1842 and the partners then went separate ways.

The brother John Thomas ran the shipyard with "A building yard, patent slipway and hard" at 1 Low Street from 1842-65. He was a member of the Shipbuilder's Association, whilst the company eventually built vessels of up to 800 tons which the family also owned (it was sold by 1870).

Charles Alcock married Elizabeth Frances the daughter of John Forster a ship owner and initially lived at 10 Norfolk Street, Bishopwearmouth where they had two sons, namely John Forster (1841) and Charles (1842), both of whom had an important role within soccer.

They had several other children and resided at 10 Fawcett Street in 1847 and 17 John Street in 1851, whilst Charles was a shipbroker and merchant at 54 Sans Street from 1847-55. Alcock & Smith were also secretaries to the Albion Premium Insurance Association at this address.

Due to such affluence the eldest sons attended Harrow viz. John Forster (1855-57) and Charles (1855-59), both being members of "Druries House" at Church Hill and the High Street (near Football Lane). Concurrent with this there were business opportunities in the capital and the family moved to "Sunnyside," Chingford, beside Epping Forest, by 1857.

The house overlooked the valley towards Edmonton, and had extensive grounds with a tree-lined avenue and a lodge on Kings Head Hill. Of the brothers, William died at Chingford in 1858 and it seems likely Charles then took this as a middle name, whereas Edward and Arthur attended Forest School in 1857-62 and this had a material effect on soccer history.

Charles Alcock & Co. initially traded as ship and insurance brokers at "Colonial House," 155 Fenchurch Street, whilst John and Arthur joined the business at 42-43 Ethelburga House, 70-71 Bishopsgate Street (within) in the 1860s. Indeed, their father was also a magistrate and had a notable residence at 14 Park Square East, Marylebone - next to Regent's Park.

Charles Alcock senior died at Chingford in 1881 and has a memorial at All Saints Church (a mile from his home), while his sons were shipbrokers at 98 Bishopsgate Street that year, and their brother Edward went to sea as a mariner. The business was at 21 Great St. Helen's in 1890, whereas Arthur Alcock died at Tetuan, Morocco in 1902. [1]

---

[1] "Sunnyside" was demolished in the 1930s and the drive was renamed Woodberry Way, whilst Sunnyside Drive is nearby. The only surviving building is "Sunnyside Lodge," a red brick cottage with slate roof and some later additions.

FOREST F.C.

John and Charles Alcock were introduced to football at Harrow and both played a significant role in its growth, although it was the latter brother who soon came to the fore. In fact, he eventually wrote a history of the game and provided the following commentary:

"It was the winter of 1859-60, that really saw the first game of the great football revival. Great things it is said, from trivial causes spring. The trivial cause in this instance was the humble desire of a few Old Harrovians, who had just left school, to keep up the practice at all events of the game, at which they had some considerable aptitude."

Indeed, "Under the shadow of the Merchant Seamen's Orphan Asylum at Snaresbrook sprang the Forest F.C." The team played football utilizing the Harrow School code, although they omitted the catch behind, and later became "a resplendent butterfly" as the Wanderers F.C.

Clearly the brothers deserve much of the credit for the side's formation however other factors also played a part, and there are two questions that instantly come to mind: Why were they called the Forest F.C.? Why did they play at the idiosyncratic Snaresbrook, Leytonstone?

The maritime Alcocks had no direct links to the asylum and at least two other factors were significant, in particular their brothers' presence at the Forest School and some important local residents. Regarding the general story, an orphan asylum was established at St. George in the East, Stepney in 1817 but had become too large by 1859; consequently a new seven acre site was purchased from Lord Mornington of Wanstead Hall. [2]

---

[2] Garrett Wesley (1735-81), 1st Earl of Mornington, was an Irish politician whose sons included: Richard Colley Wellesley (1760-1842) the Marquis and 2nd Earl, William Wellesley-Pole (1763-1845) 3rd Earl, and Arthur Wellesley (1769-1852) Duke of Wellington. William was heir to the estates of his cousin William Pole in 1778 and became Earl of Mornington in 1842 but died in 1845.

His son the 4th Earl had a notorious life and married Catherine sister and co-heiress of Sir James Tylney-Long. He then became William Pole Tylney Long-Wellesley and was remembered in a famous verse: "Bless every man possess'd of aught to give, long may Long Tylney Wellesley Long Pole live."

He used up most of his wife's fortune, lost his children in a Chancery dispute, and was sent to the Fleet Prison for contempt. Despite being a Tory and living off the bounty of his uncle, he helped to defeat the Wellington ministry in 1830. The 5th Earl of Mornington (1813-63) inherited his mother's estates and provided the land for the orphan asylum.

G.C. Clarke an architect designed the orphanage in the Venetian Gothic style on Hermon Hill (Chigwell Road) in 1861-62, and Prince Albert laid the foundation stone. The red brick building was three-storeys high and had a large tower with black banding and ogee arches. Indeed, it was an imposing structure with shipping scenes in a frieze above the entrance, and housed three hundred orphans of British merchant seamen.

This was a strange rural location for such a large building and an unusual backdrop for the emergence of soccer, but possibly Charles Alcock used a degree of artistic licence in his description. [3]

Meanwhile, his family resided at Chingford four miles away to the north so one can ask, "Why was the team at Snaresbrook?" Clearly there were some other inherent reasons for this unusual choice of location.

Forest School was formed as a 'private' or proprietary grammar school in a house beside the common near to Snaresbrook Road, Epping Forest, on 1 October 1834. The institution moved forward under Rev. John Gilderdale who became headmaster in 1848 and made it into a public school. Most of the masters were churchmen and football was encouraged on the common until 1865, whilst the school was a member of the F.A. in 1868.

According to the school there was no connection to Forest F.C., however Arthur Alcock was a pupil in 1859-62 and their students were in the side. No doubt the Alcocks and their friends adopted the school name, and in fact a school XI provided them with some early opposition. [4]

The second factor was that several Forest players were local to the area, whilst a picture of 1863 revealed only the Alcocks and John Pardoe from Harrow. Indeed, the latter had other old boys' teams such as the Chequers and Harrovians, so this local factor appears to be pre-eminent.

In the first instance John Pardoe (1839) came from Leyton and attended Harrow in 1853-58 then lived at the vicarage in 1861. His family knew Lord Mornington and possibly he arranged the venue, whilst his brother Charles William was a solicitor at 6 King's Bench Walk near to Morley.

---

[3] The orphanage became "The Convent of the Good Shepherd" in 1919 and was described as, "A home for girls in need of care or correction and readjustment of morals" - they worked in the laundry and on needlework. Essex County Council purchased the site in 1937 and planned a new hospital but the war intervened and it eventually became Wanstead Hospital. More recently it was listed and became private apartments in 1996.

[4] The school is situated a mile from the orphanage, and at the centre are five ivy-clad two/three storey Georgian houses by the common. Some modern buildings and a games field are located to the rear.

The Tebbuts were shipbuilders at Limehouse and Wapping and lived at Leytonstone and Whips Cross. The brothers Charles M. (1839) and Arthur M. (1841) played for the side, whilst they moved to Hampstead and the former represented the No Names Club in the London team of 1866.

Alfred Cutbill (1836) was born in Hackney and resided at Blackheath, but attended the school in 1851 and became a barrister at 7 King's Bench Walk. His cousins meanwhile also had further connections.

Walter John Charles Cutbill (1843) whose father was a railway secretary in Hackney was educated at Forest School in 1857-60. He joined Forest F.C. but his family moved to Sydenham and he played for Crystal Palace, and was on the F.A. committee from 1864-70. Indeed, he represented the latter side at the county matches, while his brother Arthur Lockett Cutbill (1847) was at the school in 1858-64 and also played for Forest F.C.

William Standidge & Co. were artists and lithographers to H.M. Stationery Office at 36 Old Jewry, London, whilst the family lived at Debden Green, Loughton, Essex in 1861. This was not far from Chingford and they then moved south to George Lane, Wanstead in 1871-81 - indeed the orphan asylum could be seen clearly on the hillside beyond.

A son William John B. Standidge (1831) attended King's College School and played for Forest F.C., whilst his brother Charles Watson (1834) went to Winchester College which was also a pioneer of soccer. [5]

With such facts to hand it seems inconceivable that Forest F.C. did not have an association with Forest School. Both the Alcocks and the Cutbills were old boys of the school, whilst the local connection clearly outweighed any more distant affiliations to Harrow.

The club then played significant fixtures against Barnes and Richmond, and although the origins can be debated, it was John and Charles Alcock who took them forward as the Wanderers in 1864. Indeed, at the latter date the club moved to Battersea and attracted top players of the day.

Regarding the Association's emergence it was the elder brother John who led the way, representing Forest at the first meeting in 1863, and sitting on the committee until 1866. However, he then stepped down and made way for his sibling, who provided the more significant contribution.

---

[5] King's College and School were founded in 1829 as an answer to the 'Godless' University College. The Duke of Wellington was a patron but there were stormy debates over such issues, hence he fought a duel against Lord Winchelsea at Battersea Fields. The college could not confer degrees and had eleven feeder schools by 1836, including the Forest School and its own school in the Strand. Indeed, the latter was moved to Wimbledon in the late 19th century, and of the feeders only the Forest School still survives.

CHARLES WILLIAM ALCOCK

The younger brother lived with his family at Chingford, and left Harrow School in 1859, thus he began to play soccer with the Forest F.C. Initially he worked as a shipbroker in the city, and married Eliza Caroline daughter of Francis W. Ovenden, an artist, at St. Phillip's in Islington in 1864. After the marriage, Alcock lived near to the church as an insurance agent, but soon embarked on several important changes.

Through the Wanderers he became associated with some of the leaders of the game, thus he replaced his brother John on the F.A. committee. As a result he was then involved in the rule changes, and appeared for London against Sheffield at Battersea in 1866 and for Middlesex in 1867. He also played against the No Names Club during this period.

In addition, he was a good cricketer and played for several teams such as the Harrow Wanderers, Gentlemen of Essex, and Incogniti, and for some reason captained France v Germany in Hamburg: "He was a steady bat, a fair change fast bowler, and an excellent long stop or long field."

With such sporting interests, Alcock gave up the family broking business to become a reporter and writer, thus he published his first *Football Annual* in 1868 (in fact, the last actually appeared in 1905).

Meanwhile, he sat on the committee for four years, but replaced Graham as secretary in 1870, a time scale coinciding with several significant events. The family moved to a new home at West Dulwich, whilst Billy Burrup (secretary of Surrey C.C.C.) arranged for the Wanderers to transfer their games to the Oval at Kennington - both that year. [6]

---

[6] The Montpelier Club was formed at Walworth in 1796 and played at Lorrimore Square and Chapter Road (near Kennington Park). They moved to land owned by the Duchy of Cornwall in 1844 viz. "A nursery and garden ground in extent about ten-acres called the Oval with buildings thereon."

They became Surrey C.C.C. the next year with William Dennison as secretary whilst John Burrup took over in 1848 and his brother William in 1855. The two lived locally and were stationers and printers and may have met Alcock in this capacity. The club had assistance from Prince Albert, whilst William Burrup built the pavilion in 1858 and remained until Alcock took over in 1872.

Indeed, Burrup negotiated a new lease with the Otter family the next year, and they then dealt directly with the Duchy of Cornwall - this secured the club's future and provided a stage for Alcock. The cricket club experienced a fall in membership in the early 1870s, and the arrival of soccer was a partial remedy to the resulting financial problems.

In fact, Alcock contributed to the *Sportsman* and *Field*, and published a cricket calendar as well as his football annual from the 1870s. Meanwhile, the F.A. utilised his connections and held meetings at the Oval, and at the Sportsman and Cricket Press Offices, off Ludgate Hill, then made one of their most important decisions under his guidance.

A meeting took place at the Sportsman Office on 20 July 1871 and those present were Morley (president), Alcock (secretary), Captain F.A. Marindin (Royal Engineers), M.P. Betts (Harrow), Alfred Stair (treasurer, Upton Park), C.W. Stephenson (Westminster), J.H. Giffard (Civil Service), and D. Allport (Crystal Palace).

Alcock played in a house knockout competition at Harrow and believed such a contest could work equally well for members of the Association. The idea appeared a good one on paper; although some were concerned that it might lead to heated competition (and were clearly correct).

However, despite any such apprehensions the members were unanimous and agreed: "It is desirable that a Challenge Cup should be established, in connection with the association, for which all clubs belonging to the association should be invited to compete...." As a result the F.A. Cup was started in 1871-72 - and from small acorns come great oaks.

Meanwhile, Billy Burrup agreed to stage the Cup semi-finals and finals at the Oval although it was Alcock who usually receives the credit. Indeed, the first final was played on 16 March 1872, whilst Alcock replaced Burrup as the secretary of Surrey C.C.C. at the Bridge House Hotel, London Bridge on 6 April that year.

He then adopted a multiple role and was F.A. treasurer in 1872-77, clearly with many balls in the air. In fact, he helped to start international football and played in an unofficial game against Scotland at the Oval in 1870, and ran the line at the West of Scotland Cricket Ground on 30 November 1872 and at the Oval on 8 March 1873.

Concentrating efforts on his official capacity he promoted the Oval with several representative matches i.e. North v South, London v Sheffield, and Oxford v Cambridge. Indeed, the Cup Final took place there up until 1892, and it was also a venue for the Rugby Union from 1872-78.

However, he was less settled in his home life and resided at a number of addresses in south London including Tulse Hill, Brixton, and West Dulwich whilst he had a large family at this time.

He remained extremely busy thus he published *Football, Our Winter Game* in 1874, was captain of England against Scotland on 6 March 1875 (2-2) - scoring the second goal, and refereed the Cup Final (and replay) on 13 March 1875, when his rivals the Royal Engineers ran out as victors.

He also refereed the Cup Final between the Old Etonians and Clapham Rovers in 1879. Indeed, he had great energy initiating many innovations, including the first test match against Australia in 1880, whilst he was the managing official at the first Ashes game two years later.

However, there was then a serious crisis at the F.A., and it was Alcock and Major Marindin who were obliged to resolve the problem. There was much debate about the arrival of "allegedly" paid teams in the Cup, and several northern clubs were brought to account, however the professional game was finally sanctioned at Fleet Street on 20 July 1885.

Alcock was the first paid secretary two years later, and his son William was a clerk at the F.A. offices (but died at that time), whilst the F.A. was based at 28 Paternoster Row (1881-85) and 51 Holborn Viaduct (1885-92).

The family lived briefly in Streatham and he published *Association Games* (G. Bell & Sons) in 1890, revised 1906. He then had a permanent home at "Heathlands," 212 Kew Road, Richmond from 1891-97, which was a large property facing Kew Gardens and next to Eversfield Road. [7]

Charles W. Alcock, author, journalist, and employer lived there in 1891 with his wife, four daughters, and three servants, whilst he became a J.P. for Richmond and some local fields provided him with an idea.

He presided over the phenomenal growth of the Cup and 15 entrants in 1872 had risen to 163 in 1892, while crowds grew exponentially and he took the final to Fallowfield in 1893 and to Goodison in 1894. Meanwhile, he arranged an international at the nearby Richmond Athletic Ground in 1893, the referee being J.C. Clegg who was later the F.A. president.

Alcock was a prolific writer at Richmond and edited *The 'Oval' Series of Games* in 1894 (George Routledge & Son Ltd., Ludgate Hill). The book had a section on the Rugby Union by Charles J.B. Marriott and another on The Association Game by C.W. Alcock.

In particular he discussed the rules and history of soccer and the arrival of the professional game, their aim, "the protection of the genuine amateur by the legalization of professionalism." Like Major Marindin, however, he did not approve of such changes, and added, "It was under conditions which certainly must be described as onerous, rather than otherwise."

Indeed, he noted that soccer had spread around the Empire to Canada, India, Australia, and New Zealand, whereas the book was re-printed until 1920. Meanwhile, his other works included: *Famous Cricketers and Cricket Grounds* (1895), *Management of a Club, cricket etc.* (1900), and *Surrey Cricket its history and associations* (1902).

---

[7] Paxton Close is on the site of the house and only a boundary-wall remains, while the nearby Thornycroft Court was named after an adjacent property.

Apart from this he continued to do football annuals and edited *Famous Footballers* & *Athletes* and a *Handbook of Rugby Union* (1895-96). The F.A had offices at 61 Chancery Lane in 1892-1902 and he took the Cup Final to the Crystal Palace in 1895, but stepped down as F.A. secretary in August of that year and was the vice-president from 1896.

He held the latter post and secretary of Surrey C.C.C. up until his death and had a contact address at the Oval in 1898-99 and at York Mansions, Battersea Park the next year. He resided at 16 Ennerdale Road, Richmond in 1901 with his wife Eliza, daughters Florence, Helen, and Violet (who was also an author and journalist), and two servants.

The latter house was near to Heathlands at the other end of Eversfield Road and he remained there for six years. This was a substantial two-storey red brick building with central gable, ornate wooden porch, and tiled roof but was hard to identify due to some unusual numbering. [8]

Charles Alcock died at 7 Arundel Road, Brighton on 26 February 1907 and was buried with his young son at West Norwood Cemetery. An obituary appeared in the *Times* stating he was one of the 'real' founders of soccer, however there was no will and his wife Eliza administered his effects in London which came to £3,186.

The family remained at "Hazelwood," 16 Ennerdale Road for many years but moved to Worthing in the 1930s. His daughter Violet (1878) was an author, and with members of the Writers Club helped to form the Lyceum Club for women in 1903 - she eventually received the M.B.E. [9]

Alcock made a major contribution to cricket and soccer and has a room at the Oval, whereas the family memorial was restored in 1999 with an image of the F.A. Cup and states proudly: "C.W. Alcock an inspiring secretary of the F.A. 1870-95 and of Surrey C.C.C. 1872-1907."

---

[8] Ennerdale Road ran as follows: 2,4,6, Holmesdale Road, 8,10, Branstone Road, 12, Hatherley Road, The Avenue, 14, 16, Eversfield Road then fields, whereas the East Side went directly from 1-57. The property is now 68 Ennerdale Road, whilst the large white house on the corner is not to be confused with it.

[9] Constance Smedley, Christina Gowans Whyte, Elsa Hahn, and Jessie Trimble an American were the other founders. The former had support from her father W.T. Smedley (a film producer) and the first clubhouse was at Piccadilly in 1904. Lady Frances Balfour (sister-in-law of the P.M.) was chairman for fifteen years.

CHAPTER 5

The Wanderers

The Cup contest started by Alcock was initially a limited affair and only fifteen out of fifty F.A. members took part, since the gentlemen players feared that such games might lead to excessive rivalry.

The preliminary participants came mainly from London and the south viz. Barnes, Civil Service, Clapham Rovers, Crystal Palace, Donington Grammar School, Hampstead Heathens, the Harrow Chequers, Hitchin, Maidenhead, Marlow, Queen's Park (Scotland), Reigate Priory, Royal Engineers, Upton Park, and the Wanderers. [1]

In the first round both Donington and Queen's Park had a bye thus they met in the second, but the Scottish side had a walk-over and the school never entered again. Queen's Park received another bye in the third round and reached the semi-final without kicking a single ball.

Meanwhile, Alcock and the Wanderers had a walk-over against the Harrow Chequers in the first round, and M.P. Betts (of the latter) changed sides, which came within the rules - and was to be a significant decision.

In the second round they played Clapham Rovers and marked out their intentions by winning 3-1, whilst in the third they drew 0-0 with Crystal Palace. Both the teams progressed, as there were only three quarter-finals. They then met Queen's Park and the Scottish side travelled to the Oval for a 0-0 draw. In fact, they could not afford another journey and withdrew hence the Wanderers reached the final through a walk-over.

The Royal Engineers or Sappers had a successful run and were favourites. They had a bye against Reigate Priory, beat Hitchin 5-0 at the top field and Hampstead Heathens (victors over Barnes) 3-0 at home, then met Crystal Palace in the semi-final at the Oval with no score. However, they humbled their opponents 3-0 in a replay thus cementing their position.

It was a time of optimism and Gladstone a Liberal was in power, whilst the Reform Act (1867) extended voting rights and the Education Act (1871) established state education. Darwin published *The Descent of Man* that year causing a crisis of faith, and Stanley found Dr. Livingstone (I presume) on the shores of Lake Tanganyika in November.

---

[1] Donington Grammar School was situated between Boston and Spalding, whilst Queen's Park were unable to find opposition north of the border and entered the English contest. Only Maidenhead and Marlow have entered the Cup every year since it was started.

The first Cup Final took place at the Oval on Saturday 16 March 1872. The weather was bright with a just slight breeze, and Charles Alcock and Captain Marindin led the teams onto the pitch. The players wore striped jerseys, ringed socks, and long trousers, whilst the 2,000 excited spectators included men in top hats and ladies in long white dresses.

Morton Peto Betts of the Wanderers scored the only goal and played as A.H. Chequer, a synonym for "A Harrow Chequer" - the team he started with. There were several reports in the press including one in the *Sportsman Newspaper* on Tuesday 19 March 1872 (see Chapter 10); but who were the players who joined Alcock in this pioneering contest?

MORTON PETO BETTS

Peto and Betts were at the forefront of railway development, and William Betts was born at Charing, Kent in 1790. He married Elizabeth Hayward Ladd in Buckland, Dover in 1814 and was initially a millwright, whilst he had eleven children including Edward Ladd Betts on 5 June 1815.

A company William Betts & Sons were formed in 1820, and their first contract was the Town Bridge, Weymouth (1821-24), while the family lived in the town and initially attended the local Wesleyan chapel. [2]

Meanwhile, the country was gripped by railway mania after the Rainhill Trials in 1829, and George Stephenson and his son Robert won with their *Rocket* at a steady gallop. The Liverpool and Manchester Railway was then opened on 15 September 1830 and the steam-age had begun!

The Betts family soon jumped on the wagon and moved to Gosport near Portsmouth at the time. William Betts remained there for the next five years and thus carried out important work as an architect, surveyor, and engineer. Several children were baptized there, initially at the Methodist chapel, and then in the parish church at Alverstoke (Gosport).

Meanwhile, his son Edward was apprenticed to a builder Mr. Richardson in Lincoln and showed an aptitude for mechanical pursuits, constructing a working model of a steam engine. In addition he worked on the Black Rock Lighthouse at Beaumaris, North Wales, under his father's guidance.

The Stephensons employed Betts to build the Dutton Viaduct, part of the Liverpool to Birmingham, in 1833, and Edward aged 18 was in charge of some work. The firm also built the Royal Pier, Southampton and Betts was at the opening with the Duchess of Kent and Princess Victoria.

---

[2] Weymouth Bridge was rebuilt in 1880 and was finally demolished in 1928. It was then replaced by an opening bridge.

The Itchen Bridge Company was then formed in August 1833, with Hugh and James McIntosh (London) as main contractors, and William Betts as their local agent and foreman. They began to build the floating bridge and access roads the next year, whilst the crossing opened in 1836.

However, their most significant work was the London and Southampton Railway (1834), where they met future partners Brassey and Giles. They also consulted with McIntosh's regarding culverts on the project, and again worked with them on the North Midland Railway linking Derby to Leeds under the Stephensons. During the building of the Clay Cross Tunnel vital minerals were found and the Clay Cross Co. was formed in 1837.

William Betts then combined with Thomas Brassey and constructed the Gosport branch line of the Southampton Railway from 1839-42. Indeed, Sir William Tite designed Gosport Station with its Tuscan columns; however the journey from Portsmouth to London was notorious, since it took an hour to reach the station by both ferry and foot. [3]

Betts & Sons then initiated a new project and worked on the Midland Railway, including the Rugby Viaduct, in 1839. To facilitate this work the family moved north and lived at Regent Street, Southfields in Leicester in 1841, the son William Betts (20) also being listed as a contractor.

Of the daughters, Elizabeth Meadows married George Giles, and Mary Wicking married Frederick James Rowan the next year. Both these men were civil engineers and worked on railway projects with Betts & Son. [4]

The company then took on the S.E. Railway from Reigate to Dover and Paddock Wood to Maidstone - one of the first lines into Kent. Peto and Grissell were building a line from Ashford to Folkestone and Betts took over their work, especially the Saltwood Tunnel contract, in 1843.

---

[3] Queen Victoria used the station to reach Osborne and had a separate terminus at Royal Clarence Yard therefore important people came through Gosport. Indeed, a party in 1844 included the King of France, Prince Consort, Duke of Wellington, Duc de Montpensier, and Mr. Gladstone. The long trek ended when the London to Portsmouth line was finished in June 1847 although the harbour extension was only built in 1876. The Gosport line built by Betts was closed in 1953 however the station became a listed building.

[4] George Giles (1810-77) worked on the London-Southampton Railway in 1834, especially the section to Winchester. He was then employed by Betts-McIntosh on the Midland Railway and Rugby Viaduct, and was an engineer on the Hamburg to Bergedorf Railway and sewage system in 1839-46. He helped stop a great fire in the city with gunpowder, and worked on the Great Northern and Paris-Marseille line in 1850-56, and lines in Austria. He retired to "Westfield," Bonchurch, Isle of Wight a former home of Queen Adelaide (wife of William IV).

They also worked on mineral railways in Glasgow and North Wales, the latter with Robert Stephenson. Due to such success Betts purchased Bevois House, Southampton in 1844 and erected the Stag Gates at the entrance with the motto "Ostendo Non Ostento" or "I show not boast."

However, the firm were dissolved by mutual agreement and his son took over all the contracts, whilst Betts sold his house to J.H. Wolff a shipping agent in 1856 and moved to Sandown Terrace, Deal, dying nearby in 1867. In fact, he owned numerous properties around the country and his effects were valued at a little under £30,000.

Meanwhile, Samuel Morton Peto was born at Woking in 1809 and was apprenticed to his uncle Henry Peto a builder of 31 Little Britain, London, in 1823. He worked on Raymond's Buildings, Gray's Inn, and inherited the business with his cousin Thomas Grissell in 1830.

Their work then included Hungerford Market at Charing Cross, contracts with the Great Western, Great Eastern, and South Eastern Railways, and designs for two Birmingham stations in the 1830s.

Brunel was chief engineer of the Great Western to Bristol from 1833 and employed Peto and Grissell, who constructed the section from Hanwell to Langley in 1835. In fact, Peto was obliged to meet Brunel to discuss the accounts over dinner on numerous occasions.

The partners also built large parts of the South Eastern Railway including the viaduct, tunnel, and martello towers from Hythe to Folkestone, during 1841-43. In addition, they had contracts for several London buildings and clubs, and constructed Nelson's Column in 1843.

There was then a significant match and Edward Ladd Betts an engineer of Sandgate married Ann Peto (1821) the sister of Samuel at Cookham, Berks on 6 July 1843; the witnesses William Betts, Maria Reece Betts, William Peto, and Elizabeth Grissell. [5]

Peto consulted with George Stephenson on the Eastern Co. Railway, but his partnership with Grissell ended in 1846 and the latter took the contract for the Houses of Parliament (started in 1840). In fact, Peto and Betts were both members of the I.C.E. and promptly formed a new partnership.

Their work involved most major railways in England and many foreign contracts, while they built a Government troop-line in the Crimea and also parts of the Grand Trunk Railway, Canada in 1852-59. Indeed, Sir Samuel Morton Peto had a mansion at Somerleyton and a house at 12 Kensington Palace Gardens, being a Liberal M.P. from 1847-68.

---

[5] The Peto family had a farm at Cookham beside the Thames, and the village was opposite to "Cliveden House," later owned by the Astors. The latter attracted politicians and other notaries before the Second War (see Lubbock).

Edward Ladd Betts initially lived at 29 Tavistock Square, St. Pancras but purchased "Preston Hall," Aylesford, Kent in 1848. He then employed J.E. Thomas the architect of Somerleyton to design a Baroque mansion, whilst the opulent interior included *Scene in Braemar* by Landseer.

However, Peto and Betts then associated with Thomas Russell Crampton on the London, Chatham, & Dover Railway in 1860 and this was to be their downfall. There was a serious financial crisis in the City in 1866, and the partners were declared bankrupt the following year.

Samuel Peto lost his seat in Parliament but received tributes from Disraeli and Gladstone, whilst Betts had to sell Preston Hall and moved to "The Holmwood," Bickley Park Road near Bromley in Kent. He was exhausted by all the stress and died at Assouan during a trip to Egypt in 1871. [6]

Morton Peto Betts was born at 29 Tavistock Square on 30 August 1847 and attended Harrow in 1862-65. He was a civil engineer and represented West Kent and the Old Harrovians on the F.A. committee in 1871-72. He was also secretary of Bickley Park Cricket Club near the family home, and played a few innings for both Middlesex and Kent.

He went to South America on business in 1873-76 and was thus absent from the sporting scene, but as a member of the Old Harrovians played for England v Scotland at the Oval on 3 March 1877 (losing 3-1).

Meanwhile, he rejoined the Bickley Park committee and despite having work in Copenhagen, he married Jane Bouch at St. George's, Bickley on 17 April 1879. Indeed, the trustees of a marriage settlement were John Bouch junior and Reginald de Courtenay Welch of Hyde Park (see later).

The couple lived at 1 Plaistow Road, Bromley in 1881, near the Kinnairds at Plaistow Lodge, and Betts was again on the F.A. committee in 1881-82. In fact, he remained on the F.A. council for over 20 years.

He then had addresses in Streatham and Wanstead, and played cricket for Essex before they were a first class side, being their secretary in 1887-90. He also lived briefly at Leytonstone with his wife Jane and two daughters, but his partner died at Penge in 1892.

Betts was secretary of the Church of England Young Men's Society at 3 St. Bride Street near Ludgate Circus and gave this as a contact address; whilst he went to Swansea regarding work, thus he married Jane Eva Morgan at Croydon Registry Office on 6 July 1901.

---

[6] Thomas Brassey (1805-70) also worked with Stephenson and Locke; and on the London to Southampton and Great Northern - his sons including Baron Thomas Brassey and Henry Arthur Brassey who purchased Preston Hall from Betts. When he died in 1870 his estate was valued at a staggering £3.2 million, however Peto had no probate record and Betts effects came to just £16,000.

Her father was Rev. Rees Herbert Morgan, but her family were not very wealthy and spoke the Welsh language. Betts retired to the Villa Massa, St. Anne, Garavan near Mentone in the Alpes Maritimes, France in 1911, and died there on 19 April 1914. Clearly his assets were abroad since his estate in England amounted to just £40 8s 8d.

CHARLES HENRY R. WOLLASTON

The next sporting family emanated from an academic tradition and William Wollaston (1660) was born in Stafford, but was educated at Sidney Sussex, Cambridge. He then inherited the noble estate of Shenton near Leicester and also the motto "Ne Quid Falsi" or "Nothing False"

With great expectations he settled his affairs and married Catharine the daughter of Nicholas Charlton, a London draper, in 1689. They moved to Charterhouse Square and he became a moral philosopher with many papers, including *The Religion of Nature Delineated* which sold 10,000 copies.

His son Francis attended Sidney Sussex and continued to live there, being a member of the Royal Society. Indeed, the local church was St. Botolph's and the conversion of John and Charles Wesley took place nearby.

A grandson Rev. Francis Wollaston was married to Althea Hyde at the church in 1758, having no less than seventeen children! He initially held the vicarage of East Dereham in Norfolk but moved to Chislehurst, Kent by 1769. In fact, he also became rector of St. Vedast, Foster Lane in London and held all three parishes until his death in 1815.

His sister Mary married William Heberden physician to Queen Charlotte and Dr. Johnson, daughter Althea married Thomas Heberden a canon of Exeter, and his son Francis J.H. (1762) practiced as an eminent chemist and philosopher at Cambridge University.

Another son, William Hyde (1766), was a physician and member of the Royal Society, and engaged in chemical research at 14 Buckingham Street near Fitzroy Square. He discovered important properties of platinum with some commercial value, thus making a fortune of £30,000, and published fifty-six papers covering every aspect of science.

"His predominant principal was to avoid error," while he did experiments with electricity from 1801-21 and patented the *Camera Lucida* in 1807, which led to the discoveries of William H. Fox Talbot (see Marindin).

In addition, he adopted the wave theory of light and gave evidence on the imperial gallon in the Commons, whilst he was acting president of the Royal Society after the death of Sir Joseph Banks in 1820. However, he stepped down in favour of his friend and colleague Sir Humphrey Davy.

Despite such friendships, Wollaston lost out to some degree when Davy and Faraday developed the electric motor ahead of him in 1821. Indeed, he left donations to several societies and died at 1 Dorset Street, Marylebone in 1828 (the home of Charles Babbage, mathematician, 1829-71).

His brother Henry Septimus Hyde (1776) took a different path in life and was a merchant of Clapton, east London who had three wives. He married his second wife Frances Buchanan in 1813 and by her had six children, then traded in Exeter and Bristol. In later years he married Frances Monro and died at Little Danson, Welling in 1867 - his estate worth £16,000.

His son Charles Buchanan Wollaston was born at Clapton in 1816 and initially attended Exeter College, Oxford from 1834-38. He then became an honorary canon, and was married to Eleanor the daughter of Henry Revell Reynolds at All Souls, Marylebone on 30 July 1846. [7]

Rev. Wollaston also became the vicar of Felpham near to Bognor Regis, Sussex from 1847-70 and had six children, whilst he was a prebendary of Chichester and subsequently vicar of St. Mary Amport near Andover. He was staying at 35 Westbourne Place, Sloane Square with his brother-in-law Rev. Henry R. Reynolds in 1881, but then lived at 8 Bloomfield Terrace, Pimlico and died at Reading in 1887. [8]

His brother William Monro Wollaston was a fellow of Exeter College and the conduct of Eton in 1863. He was then vicar of Merton, Oxfordshire and chaplain of St. Paul's, Cannes from 1874-1910, whilst he wrote several letters to the *Times* regarding local issues. His first wife Constance died in 1888, and he married Mary Arabella Brodie of the Waldegraves in 1890, who was related to Samuel Whitbread and more distantly to James II.

---

[7] Henry Revell Reynolds (1745-1811) came from Gainsborough and then studied medicine at Edinburgh, being elected to Middlesex Hospital in 1773-77 and St. Thomas's in 1777-83. He first attended George III in 1788, and was physician extraordinary in 1797 and physician in ordinary from 1806.

His son Henry Revell (1775-1854) and grandson Henry Revell (1800-66) were both barristers with rooms at Wimpole Street and Harley Street respectively. The latter had children Eleanor (1824) and Henry Revell (1827) a minister, and later on Herbert Edward (1847) a long-time cathedral librarian at Exeter.

[8] 8 Bloomfield Terrace was a two-storey cottage for the gentry on the north side near St. Barnabas, Pimlico, and Orange Square. W.A. Mozart lived nearby at 180 Ebury Street in 1764 and the area was mostly fields until the 19th century.

His daughter Clare St. George married Arthur C. Bartholomew in 1874, who was the headmaster of Prospect House School - a Georgian property at Tilehurst near to Reading. Sutherland Stracey Wollaston (1859) was also a tutor there.

William had a London address at 99 Cambridge Street, Pimlico, and also resided at the Villa Montboissier, Cannes and was the Canon of Gibraltar. He died in Cannes in 1910 and his probate went to widow Arabella and to C.H.R. Wollaston, his estate being valued at £22,567. A marble tablet with brass plate was erected to his memory in Chislehurst Church.

Charles Henry Reynolds Wollaston was born at Felpham Vicarage on 31 July 1849, and was educated at Lancing College in 1862-68, being school captain. Like his uncle William he attended Trinity College, Oxford and received a B.A. in 1871, then was employed as a solicitor.

He played for the Wanderers in the Cup Final victories of 1872, 1873, 1876 (& replay), 1877, and 1878. Indeed, he scored a goal at Lillie Bridge on 29 March 1873 to help secure a 2-0 win over Oxford University.

His international career was also important and he played for England at the West of Scotland Cricket Ground, Glasgow on 7 March 1874 in front of 7,000 spectators. He was then in the return match at the Oval on 6 March 1875 in front of 2,000, and scored after five minutes to put England 1-0 ahead, although the game finished as a 2-2 draw.

He appeared for England at the Oval on 3 March 1877 in front of 2,000 and England lost 3-1, and was on the F.A. committee in 1879-82, whilst he refereed an international at the Oval on 5 April 1879 in front of 4,500 (5-4). The return game was at the 1st Hampden Park, Glasgow on 13 March 1880 and Wollaston captained England, but they lost 5-4 in front of 12,000.

He remained unmarried and was secretary for the Union Bank of London, 2 Prince's Street from 1878-98, whilst he resided at 14 Coleshill Street near Sloane Square in 1881, near to his father (now 51 Eaton Terrace).

In later years he was a bank director and lived at 63 St. George's Road, Pimlico near St. Gabriel's, Warwick Square in 1900-01. Indeed, he spent his leisure time in Switzerland and left money to his guides, whilst he died at 46 Belgrave Road, Pimlico on 22 June 1926 - his estate valued at £22,946.

THOMAS CHARLES HOOMAN

During the 1872 final both Hooman and Vidal attracted special notice due to their 'skilful dribbling.' However, the former had his origins away from the capital, his family being prominent manufacturers in Kidderminster.

James Hooman (1759-1827) was initially an attorney-at-law then made a significant match to Elizabeth Pardoe in 1781, and had ten children. Her brother Joseph was a weaver and established a company at this time, whilst the Hoomans followed his lead and were carpet manufacturers by c.1795. In fact, this was the town's principal occupation.

Hooman and Pardoe merged in 1805, the second partner being Thomas Pardoe (son of Joseph) who married his cousin Parthenia Hooman (1787) the next year. There were also some London connections and the couple had their children baptized at St. Pancras Church.

James Hooman junior (1784) joined the firm in 1809 and they then traded as Hooman, Pardoe & Hooman with a main office at New Road by the River Stour. The former then married Jane Carpenter and had a family of eight children who included James (1813). Meanwhile, the town grew rich on its carpet wealth and St. George's was consecrated in 1824, whilst Jane Hooman died in 1825 and her father-in-law two years later.

Joseph Bowyer a competitor was ruthless in his approach to business, and during a serious strike in 1828 he stood outside his house "The Copse," and brandished a gun at the impoverished weavers. The weavers returned to stone his property although he was compensated by parliament.

Meanwhile, James Hooman junior listened to their concerns, despite being very ill, and volunteered to be an arbitrator although his efforts came to nothing. Indeed, the strain was too great and he also died in 1829.

His children then became orphans and their upbringing was entrusted to Thomas Pardoe (1783) and his brother George Hooman (1797), the senior partners in the firm. However, Thomas Pardoe junior joined in 1829 and they then traded as Pardoe, Hooman & Pardoe.

There was severe competition and a trade slump meant Joseph Bowyer went bankrupt in 1830, whereas Pardoe-Hooman remained successful at their Oxford Road works with 130 looms in 1832 and 170 in 1836.

In fact, their growth was exponential and George Hooman was Mayor, whilst the business expanded to 172 Brussels looms and 70 Kidderminster-Ingrain looms by 1838, with 360 employees. Meanwhile, Thomas Pardoe junior died and his brother James succeeded him at the company.

In addition, James Hooman (1813) joined the business as a merchant and married Mary Ann Hemming at Great Alne in 1839, then purchased "The Copse" near to Hoo Lane and Back Brook by the railway. A sale brochure described it thus, "There is a handsome entrance hall, seven bedrooms, a conservatory, coach house, and three acres of land…."

The company were the largest in the town by 1840 and their main office was in Worcester Street, where they had a 36-loom factory. Further to this they had three spinning mills - one adjacent to the offices in Oxford Road, one at nearby Caldwall, and a third which they leased.

George Hooman was appointed Mayor of the town again in 1845, whilst as an innovator they introduced new methods and purchased a licence for Wytock's "Tapestry-Brussels" process in 1847.

As a result they built a large factory called "The Sling" in a narrow lane by the River Stour in 1848. This dominated the town and had 110 tapestry looms and a yarn-printing department (Pitts Lane car park is on the site). Indeed, James Hooman was listed as "carpet manufacturer firm of eleven employing about 700 persons, 400 males 300 females."

However, dark clouds loomed on the horizon, since companies generally made a "fatal mistake" when they rejected the power-loom. With this in mind the Hoomans installed a steam engine and looms at the Sling factory which were in operation by 1852, and had 800 employees including those who worked in their spinning mills.

They appeared to be in a strong position and therefore sold the Brussels handloom factories to concentrate on tapestry carpets. However, this was a fatal misjudgement since the market for the latter collapsed by 1857, and severe financial problems developed due to the level of investment in plant. Indeed, they were declared bankrupt in September 1858: "We regret to announce, the eminent firm Pardoe Hoomans & Co., carpet manufacturers of Kidderminster, are unable to meet their engagements."

"The firm and their individual members have for many years occupied the highest position in the trade, with honour to themselves and satisfaction to their connection, and the regret we feel will be shared by all ranks of the community. It is rumoured that debts amount to from £80,000 to £100,000 part of which is secured. Their assets are very large, but in so much as they consist of trade erections, plant and machinery, it may be considered doubtful, whether means may be taken to effect liquidation, whether the operation of the firm will be continued to the extent heretofore."

Some of the debts resulted when the firm converted to power looms and included £18,450 owed to the London Life Assurance Co. In fact, the loan was secured on life assurance policies on the four partners - George and James Hooman and Thomas and James Pardoe and through mortgages on their houses, property, and factory buildings!

The situation was clearly most serious and the Pardoe-Hooman works closed, whereas a large number of mill-workers became unemployed, and Kidderminster was literally devastated. Most of the owners left the town forever and James Pardoe was then works-manager and a director of John Crossley & Sons, Yorkshire, whilst George Hooman retired to Prittlewell, Essex. The town itself recovered when new firms took over. [9]

---

[9] Richard Smith & Sons of Kidderminster erected new power looms in the Sling factory, whereas The Copse was at the focus of manufacturing in the 1880s, with several large factories nearby. Kidderminster Harriers played at Aggborough just to the west from 1886, and the house was demolished in the 1950s.

Thomas Charles Hooman was born at The Copse on 28 December 1850 and was seven when his family left, but his father James was established as an agent at 71 Wood Street, Cheapside, London, by 1862.

Indeed, the former was educated at Charterhouse near the City in 1863-68 and played cricket and football for the school XI - he headed the batting averages, and also took part in boxing and rifle shooting. On leaving the school he joined his father in business in London. [10]

The family lived with three servants at 6 Holly Terrace, Highgate in 1871 whilst their trading address was at 10 Basinghall Street. The house was a notable stucco villa on West Hill with a balcony and colonnade looking out over the valley to Hampstead Heath. To the rear was a front entrance with grand portico, pilasters, and black double doors - of an unusual design and joined to the house by a short passage (now No. 87).

However, they lived at 2 Fitzroy Villas, 7 Hampstead Lane, Highgate, in 1873-76. The property (No. 19) was one of two, beside Park Villa, and although modernised has a slate roof and old brickwork to the rear. [11]

Meanwhile, Thomas Hooman continued to play soccer and took part in some major games. The school records state that he played for England v Scotland in 1870-72-73, but most likely he just played in the unofficial game at the Oval - since no other evidence has been found. He then appeared for the Wanderers in the first Cup Final, and later claimed that he scored the only goal. The records do not agree with this and he possibly confused it with another contest, however he added:

"There was no referee, only a timekeeper, and the captains were the sole arbiters. The game was not stopped once for a foul. The teams changed goalkeepers several times, changed ends after scoring a goal, and played six forwards with two half-backs and two backs."

He also appeared in North v South games and London v Middlesex in 1872-73, whilst he represented England in the sprint in 1872, rowed for Kingston in The Grand at Henley, and played some amateur golf.

As a merchant of Highgate he married Louisa Holt of Somerset Court, South Brent (near Weston Super Mare) on 10 September 1879. Her father William Skinner Holt was a brewer and may have been related to William Skinner the partner of Henry Goodwyn (see later).

---

[10] Charterhouse School was relocated to Godalming, Surrey in 1872.

[11] No. 1 Fitzroy Villas, 17 Hampstead Lane has grey-yellow brick on three-storeys with roof gables and a coat of arms above the door; Park Villa is now divided into Park Cottage and West Cottage in the Georgian style. Samuel Taylor Coleridge (1823-34) and later J.B. Priestley lived nearby at 3 The Grove.

Hooman was described as a merchant-shipbroker and lived at 53 High Street, Sevenoaks in 1881 with his wife, mother-in-law, and two servants. His father was away travelling and Mary Ann Hooman was at 6 Hermitage Villas, West Hill, Highgate, in 1881-86. This was part of a terrace of grand properties next to Millfield Lane at the bottom of the hill (No. 21).

There was then a change of direction after his father died and Thomas was a manufacturer of Portland cement residing at "Fernleigh," London Road, Ditton in 1891-1901, whilst his mother lived at Orchard Road, Malvern. However, the family then removed to Torquay and resided at "Frogmore" in Higher Warberry Road from 1904-10.

A son Charles Victor Lisle attended Charterhouse and played in fifteen matches for Kent County including the championship season of 1910, and was an amateur golfer for England against Scotland in the Walker Cup. His parents lived at Parkstone near to Poole by 1918, however Thomas died at 6 Marine Parade, Hythe on 22 September 1938.

ROBERT WALPOLE SEALY VIDAL

Vidal was likewise complimented for his skilful play and preceded the likes of Stanley Matthews, being dubbed "The Prince of Dribblers."

Edward Sealy Esq. resided at Friarn House, Bridgwater, Somerset, and married Elizabeth Urch the daughter of Rev. Lewis of Cannington in 1815. Their only son Edward was born at Bridgwater the next year, and went to Westminster and Christchurch, Oxford (B.A. 1838), then was a barrister at Middle Temple in 1842 and practiced on the Western Circuit.

In fact, he had "Great Expectations," and befriended Robert Studley Vidal a gentleman of "Cornborough House," Abbotsham, which was an isolated hamlet near to Bideford - some fifty miles west of Bridgwater. [12]

Captain Robert Studley his great grandfather was married to Anne King at Temple Church, London, in 1692, and Christian V of Denmark helped him attain his sea-skills, hence he was made captain of the "Experiment" by Prince George of Denmark in 1707. [13]

He also commanded the "Weymouth" and received silver mementos from Frederick IV of Denmark, and from the people of Naples for repelling the Algerine Corsairs. Meanwhile, Peter Vidal attended Westminster School and St. John's, Cambridge then entered the church.

---

[12] Charles Kingsley's novel of 1855 gave rise to the local name of Westward Ho!

[13] Prince George was the Lord High Admiral of England and also the husband of Queen Anne (1702-14).

The latter married Mary Studley at Lincoln's Inn Chapel, Holborn on 4 May 1733, and had a son Robert Studley Vidal who was a solicitor, and married Elizabeth Blinch at St. Clement Danes on 10 April 1768.

Their son Robert Studley Vidal (1770) was a barrister at Middle Temple, and a noted antiquarian who wrote several papers including one on nearby Kenwith Castle. He kept a pack of hounds and left land to William Kelly his hind and money to Mary Ann Kelly his "confidential" servant.

He also established two scholarships of £20 p.a. for boys to attend St. John's College, the students to come from Exeter Free Grammar School. Meanwhile, the house and estate at Abbotsham were placed in trust for Edward Urch Sealy, but with some stringent qualifications:

(1) The Mansion House and Edway's farmhouse being 40 acres, to be kept whole and in good repair.
(2) He should be in residence for two months each year although the period need not be continuous.
(3) The house must be constantly occupied or inhabited.
(4) Edward Urch Sealy and his successors must use the surname and arms of Vidal.
(5) They can use no other surname and must take the name Vidal within one year by an Act of Parliament.
(6) However, if the property is let, or they do not reside there, or do not take the name, or resume their old name then the whole reverts to the trustees for the masters and fellows of St. John's, Cambridge, forever.

These conditions were to control the life of Edward Urch Sealy and his descendants, since if they broke any of them they would lose everything. In fact, his benefactor died in 1841 and he inherited the estate and silverware, and as a kinsman his name was changed by Royal licence the next year.

Further to this, Edward Urch Vidal married Emma Harriet Eyre at St. Mary's, Bryanston Square on 19 May 1842 with E.C. Sealy, Alethea S.H. Eyre, Walpole Eyre, and Septimus Burton as the witnesses. [14]

---

[14] The church with semi-circular colonnade was at the end of Wyndham Place, whilst the Eyres lived at 22 Bryanston Square. Walpole Eyre came from Burnham, Bucks and his family were the largest landowners east of Edgware Road in the 1790s. They laid out the Eyre Estate, St. John's Wood to the designs of James Burton, whilst his brother Decimus designed London Zoo. The Haliburton family came from Dryburgh on the River Tweed and were related to Sir Walter Scott, whilst the latter's cousin James Haliburton trained as a builder but after a family dispute took the name of Burton.

Indeed, this was a match concurrent with his new status and the couple took up residence at Cornborough, whilst they entered into the spirit of the will and had fifteen children in the name Vidal from 1843-67. The house was a rugged two-storey building above a lawn with woodland behind, and the fields of the estate reached right down to the sea. Meanwhile, several sons attended Westminster and entered into the church.

Robert Walpole Sealy Vidal was born at Cornborough on 3 September 1853, and attended Westminster in 1867. He enjoyed football at Vincent Square and outplayed his seniors in games against teams like the Crusaders, and was also appointed the school captain in 1871.

Naturally he preferred Battersea to any other ground (or so he said), and was the youngest player in the Wanderers side in 1872, when he carried out some "judicious middling" to bring about the only goal. He spent a brief period on the F.A. committee, but then left the capital and matriculated at Christchurch, Oxford on 23 May that year.

He represented England at the Oval on 8 March 1873 (4-2), and played for the university in the Cup with an impressive march to the final: Palace 3-2, Clapham Rovers 3-0, Royal Engineers 1-0, and Maidenhead 4-0, however his side then lost to the Wanderers at Lillie Bridge on 29 March.

There was soon more success and Vidal won the Cup with Oxford, when they beat the Royal Engineers 2-0 at the Oval on 14 March 1874. It was a good year and he was on the F.A. committee, an Oxford blue, founder and first president of the university golf club, and a good oarsman.

However, he then concentrated on the spiritual, and trained as a priest at Cuddesdon College, being ordained at Salisbury in 1877. Initially he was a curate at Sarum and a vice-principal of Ely College, but married Lucy C. Carter the daughter of a mariner at Cotterstock on 2 June 1881.

He then received the ideal appointment and became vicar of Abbotsham in 1881, however his wife died in 1883 and his father one year later, whilst the Cornborough estate was valued at just £4,594.

Rev. Vidal then married Gertrude Molesworth at Abbotsham on 15 July 1885, and lived at the vicarage with four children and three servants in 1891. His mother Emma and sister Alethea remained at Cornborough House at this time, whilst there were soon some further developments. [15]

The conditions of Robert Vidal's will had weighed on the family for fifty years, thus his kinsman altered his name by deed poll on 26 May 1892, and was thereafter known as Rev. Robert Walpole Sealy.

---

[15] Hickman Molesworth was an officer in the Royal Artillery in India, and his daughter Gertrude was born at Bangalore on 11 September 1862. He lived with his family at "Kenwith House" in Abbotsham in 1881.

It is unclear if there was any direct correlation, but the family then left Cornborough forever and Emma Harriet Vidal died nearby at Bowood in 1897, whilst daughter Alethea lived at 7 Taw Vale Parade, Barnstaple (see Morley). Rev. Sealy then entered into the spirit of village life and ran at the local sports day, whilst he played cricket for Devon and was a member of the Royal North Devon Golf Club.

He worked on several committees and was a local patron with a prebendal stall at Exeter Cathedral, but died at Abbotsham on 5 November 1914. He was laid to rest beside his church, and many have since passed by, but few know that "The Prince of Dribblers" once walked the same path.

CHAPTER 6

Eton and Harrow

The Wanderers side consisted mainly of players from two schools in 1872: Bonsor (20), Lubbock (25), and Thompson (23) of Eton; and Alcock (29), Betts (24), Bowen (35), Crake (20), and Welch (20) of Harrow.

The other players were Hooman (22) of Charterhouse, Wollaston (22) of Lancing, and Vidal (18) of Westminster, thus confirming the dominance of the former colleges in the side. A few of these gentlemen, who were mainly defenders, are considered in the following discussion.

EDWARD ERNEST BOWEN

Despite being slightly older, Bowen secured a place in the side through his keen interest in sport, while some of his students were also players. His family had Anglo-Irish descent with Welsh origins, and Christopher Bowen married Eliza Miller and had eight children at Hollymount, Mayo.

Their son Christopher was born in 1801 and educated at Trinity College, Dublin, achieving a B.A. in 1824. He trained as a minister at Killaloe near Limerick in 1825, then married Catherine Emily daughter of Richard Steele of Fermanagh on 17 January 1834.

Rev. Bowen was curate of Bath Abbey in 1838-43 then perpetual curate of St. Mary Magdalen, Southwark in 1843-55. He resided at Park Villa, Priory Lane, Lee Road near to Blackheath at the time, thus his sons Charles S.C. and Edward E. were educated at Blackheath Proprietary School.

Meanwhile, his brother Charles was born in 1804 and married Georgiana Lambert at Crossboyne, Galway then had seven children. They lived at Lee Park, Blackheath from 1845 but sailed on the *Charlotte Jane* to Lyttelton in New Zealand in 1850. This was the first ship to arrive in the Canterbury Colony and Godley the founder was there to greet them.

Charles Christopher Bowen their eldest son soon became prominent and was secretary to Godley, and also owner and editor of the *Lyttelton Times*. However, he sold the paper to William Reeves in 1859 and travelled to the Andes with Clements Markham, then sat on the Legislative Council, held some senior posts, and lived at Middleton Grange, Riccarton. [1]

[1] Clements Markham his brother-in-law was president of the Royal Geographical Society; hence Bowen entertained Scott and Shackleton at his Middleton Grange home before their expeditions of 1901-04 and 1910-12.

Meanwhile, Rev. Bowen was rector of St. Thomas's, Winchester in 1855-69 but retired to Totland, Isle of Wight, and lived at "Heatherwood" and "Glenheadon" looking across the Solent. Indeed, he owned much land in the area and provided a school and founded Christchurch, Totland, whereas a memorial at the church states he died at Bordighera, Italy in 1890.

A son Charles Synge Christopher was born at Woolaston, Gloucestershire in 1835, then became a barrister in 1861. He was friends with Edward H. Pember and Horace Davey who all became prominent legal gentlemen. In fact, he married Emily Frances daughter of James Meadows Rendel (related to the Wedgwoods), and was later a Lord of Appeal in Ordinary.

His brother Edward Ernest Bowen was born at Glenmore, Co. Wicklow on 30 March 1836 but was educated at Blackheath Proprietary, the school being a prominent pioneer of early soccer.

He then attended King's College School in the Strand and matriculated at Trinity, Cambridge in 1854. The latter had many notable students including Bacon, Byron, Thackeray, Tennyson, and Macaulay, whereas Kinnaird and Thompson were also students there.

Bowen excelled in his studies and was a Bell and Prizeman Scholar and president of the Union in 1856, then received a fourth class B.A. in the classics in 1858 and also an honorary fellowship.

Initially, he was an assistant master at Marlborough College, but went to Harrow a year later then made an unselfish contribution over many years. He was just twenty-three when Dr. Charles Vaughan the headmaster gave him the position, not much older than his students, amongst them being Betts (1862-65), Crake (1866-70), and Welch (1864-71).

Meanwhile, Bowen was not just a pioneer of soccer at the school but was also a good skater, a noted mountaineer, and a middle-order right hand batsman and wicket keeper, with two innings for Hampshire in 1864.

In addition, he was a founder of the "modern side" at Harrow with Rev. W.D. Bushell and Rev. R.H. Quick in 1869, and was deeply involved in the movement until 1893. Its upper two forms had some of the most inspiring and original masters, who taught modern subjects like French and German, and perhaps carpe diem was in vogue.

Bowen was a notable author and constant contributor to the "Saturday Review," at the height of its reputation; whilst he had a detailed knowledge of campaigns and battlefields - being an expert on Napoleon, and also on various elements of modern history.

Indeed, he took such strategies onto the pitch and played for England with Alcock in the unofficial international at the Oval in 1870, and for the Wanderers in their victories of 1872 and 1873 (when 37 years old).

Parker's Piece - The Cambridge Rules were tried out in 1848

Freemasons Tavern, Holborn

Location of the first six F.A. meetings in 1863

The Eton Wall Game - The Collegers played the Oppidans from 1844

Ebenezer Cobb Morley (1831-1924)

His home at 26 The Terrace, Barnes

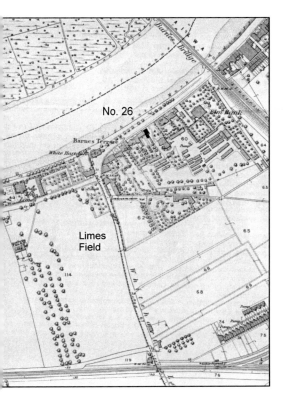

Richmond Green - Football was played on the restricted pitch in 1862

Barnes (1867) - Limes Field, the venue for Barnes F.C.

Left: St. Alban's Bank - The Graham family abode from 1881

Right: 5 Beverley Villas - Residence of R.W. Willis in 1867-72

Arthur Pember (1835-86) - The first F.A. president 1863-67 - adventurer, reformer, and undercover journalist (as a costermonger in New York)

1233 Third Avenue - His home from 1872-77

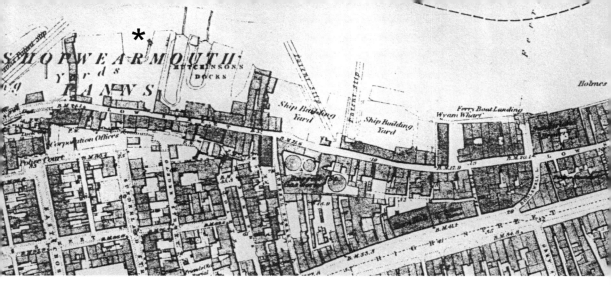

Bishopwearmouth (1855) - The Alcock shipyard at Low Street and Pann's Bank

Sunnyside Lodge, Chingford and 14 Park Square East

Charles Alcock senior (1806-81), a shipbroker in the city, resided at "Sunnyside House" and near to Regent's Park

Snaresbrook, Essex - "Under the shadow of the Merchant Seamen's Orphan Asylum sprang the Forest F.C... they became a resplendent butterfly as the Wanderers"

Charles W. Alcock (1842-1907) - F.A. secretary 1870-95
He began the F.A. Cup competition in 1871-72, and was commemorated at West Norwood

Edward Ladd Betts (1815-72)

With Sir Samuel Morton Peto, he built many major railways

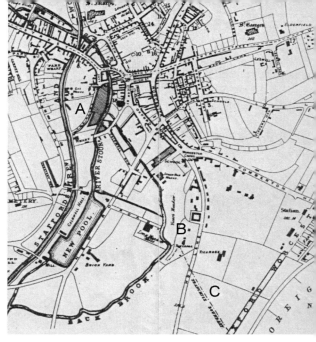

Kidderminster (1859) - Hooman

(A) The Sling, (B) The Copse, (C) Site of Aggborough football ground

Edward E. Bowen (1836-1901)

A pioneer of soccer, and master at Harrow from 1859

The Grove, Harrow - The "house" of Sheridan, and E.E. Bowen from 1881

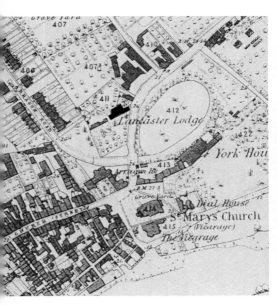

Lancaster Lodge, Twickenham

Welch family home in 1854-64

The Army College, Heath End

Reginald de Courtenay Welch (1851-1939) was the principal from 1895

These were his only major appearances and he then concentrated his time at Harrow, living at Small House on Grove Hill from 1864-81, a property once held by the Bishop of Durham. In the 19th century masters often lived alone and took in boys as lodgers to earn extra income, and this was the origin of the school house system.

Bowen organised the 'cricket field bill' from 1879, which was a method of calling five hundred names in one and a half minutes. This saved the boys walking up the hill from the playing field to answer and Mr. Bowen did this every half holiday, of each summer term, from its inception.

He was a Liberal politician and reformer who contested Hertford against the First Lord of the Treasury in 1880, but without any success, whilst he resided at Peterborough Road the next year with nine pupils aged 14-17, a housekeeper, a butler, and two servants. [2]

Some notable boarders resided with him, among them Viscount Pears A. Vallelort (15) born London, and Prince Emich E.C. Leiningen (15) born Osborne, Isle of Wight. However, the job of housemaster could be most harrowing and one story states the prince set fire to his house. [3]

By late 1881 Bowen was living at The Grove located at the top of Church Hill, just beyond the old school and next to St. Mary's. In fact, he altered the house so that all the boys had single rooms, whilst at least ten servants were required. He also continued his interest in politics, but he could not accept "Home Rule" and thus had no active part after 1885.

He was well known for Latin and English verse and especially for school songs like "Forty Years On," many of which became classics. These were published as "Harrow School Songs" and showed a religious feeling seldom seen in public, as he was generally a most reticent man. In 1901, he lived at The Grove with his mother Catherine (aged 94), 30 boarders, and 14 servants. Indeed what a cacophony of noise! [4]

---

[2] This was possibly Small House and today Peterborough House with plain grey-yellow façade, Gayton House, and Elmfield with its portico entrance and brick extension '1892' are on Grove Hill (just behind is Peterborough Road).

[3] Queen Victoria was the daughter of the Duke and Duchess of Kent. Her mother previously married Prince Charles Emich of Leiningen, and grandson Ernest was a favourite nephew of the Queen - he was captain of the Royal Yacht in 1858 and later an admiral. His son Emich was born at Osborne in 1866.

[4] The Grove was once the vicarage, whilst Richard B. Sheridan was a pupil at Harrow in 1762-68 and resided there in 1781-84. The old property burnt down in 1833, but the Georgian house with stucco façade remains today. Just below the house is a plaque, "These form rooms embody the walls of Sheridan's stables."

Bowen made a great contribution and ruled the boys with a strictness of discipline, tempered with gaiety, humour, and sympathy; whereas holiday afternoons always saw him out on the cricket or football field.

However, he went on a cycling tour with Professor Bryce in 1901 and reached Moux ten miles from Saulieu near Dijon in the Côte D'or, France. He seemed in good health, but whilst mounting his bicycle he fell to the ground and died shortly afterwards - on 8 April 1901.

The *Times* stated, "Few men have been more consulted on important educational questions; no one ever gave more conscientious care than he did to the formation of his opinion upon all subjects concerning life and conduct." A wreath from the boys of his house marked his vacant seat in the chapel, and the school cricket-field flag covered his coffin, while Rev. W.E. Bowen and several other family members were present.

The nearby churchyard of St. Mary's had been closed for many years, but the vicar and local board made a dispensation, thus there is a memorial just beside the south wall. The Grove then passed to the Harrow Governors, whereas his mother died at Totland the following year.

His estate was valued at £68,052 in July 1903, the executors Rev. William E. Bowen nephew of 119 Barkston Gardens, Earl's Court (see Leitch) and C. Colbeck Esq. However, both of his brothers had died thus the former inherited Glenheadon and lived there until 1938.

There are family memorials at Totland, whilst the one at Harrow states: "From Strength to Strength: Edward Ernest Bowen assistant master at Harrow for 42 years" - clearly a fitting tribute to this great man.

WILLIAM PARRY CRAKE

The Wanderers Cup Final side included four players from Harrow, thus Edward Bowen was supported on the field by his protégé William Parry Crake. The latter came from a family of merchants who were engaged in the lucrative East India trade for many years. [5]

William the son of John and Mary Crake was born in the new suburb of Marylebone in 1787, and married Mary Ann Mason in 1809 then had nine children. Initially he worked as a builder (like Adam), but soon became involved in design and was also a property speculator.

───────────────

[5] The East India Company (John Co.) traded in India from the 17th century and controlled much of the sub-continent, however after the Indian Mutiny there was direct rule under the Government from 1858-1937. They made a large investment in infrastructure and the Royal Engineers undertook much of the work. Trade was also enhanced with the arrival of the Suez Canal in 1869.

He was well sited for such progression since there were some large scale developments nearby. To the north was the Eyre Estate (discussed under Vidal) and to the west was a development between Edgware and Bayswater Roads in Paddington. The latter was a speculative venture which aimed to compete with Belgravia and was thus dubbed 'Tyburnia.'

The aim was to provide leases of 95 years, and maintain high standards by giving them to individuals rather than a developer. However, the trustees found this approach impractical and much of the land went to speculators, namely builders who acquired large plots in different streets.

William was a plumber, painter, and builder at 18 Old Quebec Street near to Portman Square in 1820-43, with a residence at Notting Hill. However, his son John then joined the business as an architect, and they took on new contracts which changed the family's fortunes forever.

Paddington was slow to develop with just a third of the site covered by 1828, whilst St. John's was built with Gloucester and Sussex Squares to the west. There was more development near the Grand Union Canal, whereas the Great Western and its terminus gave a further boost in the 1830s.

William Crake then took leases on the first 'mansion houses' in Hyde Park Gardens in 1837, acquiring most of the terrace and some properties nearby. The original plan was to build a crescent, but presumably due to the costs his son John Crake eventually designed two straight terraces. [6]

Indeed, Crake retired on the proceeds in the 1840s and was a magistrate for Middlesex and Sussex at 10 Stanhope Street, Paddington in 1851 living with his wife Mary Ann, one daughter, and five servants. However he died at St. Leonard's in 1861 - his effects under £140,000, and his wife Mary Ann remained at Stanhope Street until 1879. [7]

The family had ascended the social scale, and Vandaleur Benjamin Crake (1816) was a barrister at 6 King's Bench Walk, and his son went to Eton. Edward Neville Crake (1826) attended Kensington School and was curate of Knightsbridge, and the dean and vicar of Battle in Sussex. He retired to Hans Court, Kensington and died there in 1909 (see Lubbock).

Meanwhile, William Hamilton Crake was born at Notting Hill on 22 May 1824 and baptized at Marylebone Church. He may have worked briefly in the family business and resided at Paddington, but became a merchant in the East India trade and met his wife through such business links.

---

[6] Arthur Fitzgerald Kinnaird was born at 35 Hyde Park Gardens in 1847.

[7] The house was between Hyde Park Crescent and Gloucester Square, and may have been one that he built. The family lived in the Paddington district for nearly eighty years, and Stanhope Street was re-named Southwick Place.

Indeed, he married Jane the daughter of George Wood Esq. by licence at Ealing on 10 December 1850. Her family owned Hanger Hill House a three-storey Georgian property from the 18th century, and had 500 acres in the 1840s-60s, whilst they had connections to the local Hamiltons. [8]

After their marriage William and Jane Crake spent a brief time in England but then went to Fort St. George, Madras, on the southeast coast of India. William operated there as a merchant, but these were turbulent times, and this was the period just before the Indian Mutiny.

Three children were born in Madras: William Parry (1852), George (1854), and Edith Hamilton (1855), but the revolt had started by May 1857, with heavy fighting around Delhi and Lucknow to the north. There was much fear amongst Europeans therefore the Crakes returned to England.

A daughter Ada Jane was born at Wadham Lodge, Ealing in 1858, whilst the mother lived there with her children in 1861, and the father resided at 7 Elgin Crescent, Notting Hill. After the crisis passed two sons were born in Madras namely Arthur H. (1863) and Douglas H. (1865).

However, the family then lived at 34 Gloucester Square, Paddington, on a permanent basis and a child Lawrence H. was born in 1868. The father then continued to work as an East India merchant and four of his sons went to Harrow School; whilst his daughter Edith married Alfred George Lucas at Kensington in 1877 and lived at Kirkley near Lowestoft. [9]

Crake remained at 34 Gloucester Square with his wife and seven servants and was a partner in Crawford, Colvin & Co. at 71 Old Broad Street, but he died in 1883 and his effects were valued at £209,820.

Jane Crake then lived at the family home but died at Borrowstone near to Aberdeen in 1895, and William Parry Crake, George Crake of the Tamar Brewery, and Arthur Hamilton Crake proved her will in London. [10]

---

[8] The Hanger Hill estate became a golf course in the 1900s and still remains, but the house was demolished during the 1930s.

[9] Charles Thomas and Sir Thomas Lucas had an agreement with Samuel Morton and James Peto to build 21 dwellings at Kirkley in 1852. Lucas & Aird worked on the Metropolitan Railway, Albert Hall, and Exhibitions in 1862/71, whilst John Aird & Co. built the Crystal Palace football ground in 1894. C.T. Lucas promoted painter David Roberts and lived at Warnham Court and 9 Belgrave Square.

[10] Gloucester Square is situated beside Radnor Place, but the area is much altered and only a few buildings survive. An L.C.C. blue plaque was placed at No. 35 in 1905: "In memory of Robert Stephenson (1803-59) engineer who died here," but was moved when the property was rebuilt in 1937. Indeed, the Crake family home was also demolished just before the Second War.

William Parry Crake was born in Madras on 11 February 1852 and grew up in India, but was a pupil at Harrow in 1866-70, playing in the football and cricket XI. He also appeared for England at the Oval in 1870 and for the Wanderers in 1872, but then concentrated on his business career. [11]

He most likely spent time in Madras which explains his absence from any other soccer games, and he married Emily Noble Chase there in c.1882. Her father Thomas resided at Masulipatam (Bandar) in the 1850s, two hundred miles north of Madras, and was possibly a civil servant - having children Georgiana, Emily Noble (in 1856), and Anne Hall Chase.

The Crakes remained in Madras and had sons Ralph Hamilton (1884) and Eric Hamilton (1886), but the connection to India ended in the late 1880s. William continued as a merchant, but had retired to 31 Norfolk Crescent, Paddington by 1892, and his sons then attended Harrow School.

He had three servants in 1901 and his son Eric immigrated to Kenya in 1912, whilst the father died at 31 Norfolk Crescent on 1 December 1921. The house was near to St. John's Church, but no trace remains, whereas Emily resided at Langham Hotel, Portland Place and died in 1935.

EDGAR LUBBOCK

The Wanderers victory in 1872 was largely due to their backs, and indeed, "the certainty of kicking displayed by Lubbock and Thompson throughout enabled the forwards of the victors to attack without fear."

The family, meanwhile, had a prestigious ancestry and William Lubbock was the rector of Lamas, Norfolk by the River Bure. His son John became a successful London merchant and was made a baronet in 1806, whilst his son William remained in Lamas and had offspring John William (1774) who joined his uncle as a merchant and banker in London.

The latter married Mary the daughter of James Entwisle at Manchester in 1799, and they had a son (also) John William born at Duke Street, Piccadilly on 26 March 1803, and baptized at St. Margaret's. Due to their financial successes the family purchased "High Elms," Downe, Kent in 1808.

Initially, they remained in the capital and the estate was used for mixed farming, whilst Sir John Lubbock died at St. James's Place in 1816, and the baronetcy went to his nephew and partner. Lubbock, Forster & Clarke were bankers at 11 Mansion House Street in 1817-29, whilst Sir J.W. Lubbock M.P. lived at 23 St. James's Place and High Elms (and died in 1840).

---

[11] Henry M. Butler of Gayton, Northants was headmaster of Harrow in 1881 and his boarders included Arthur H. Crake (18) and Howard E. Betts (16).

Meanwhile, his son had an eminent life and was educated at Eton and Trinity, Cambridge. He was an excellent mathematician and after travelling entered his father's bank and engaged in a life of arduous enquiry. He was on the committee of the *Society for the Diffusion of Useful Knowledge* and joined the Astronomical (1828), and the Royal Society (1829), producing learned papers on astronomy, tides, climate, and banking probabilities.

Indeed, he was treasurer of the Royal Society from 1830-35 and married Harriet, daughter of Lieut. Col. George Hotham from Beverley, in 1833; then lived at 29 Eaton Place, Belgravia and had eleven children. [12]

Lubbock was the first vice-chancellor of London University in 1837-42 and vice-president of the Royal Society in 1838-47, and as the third baronet inherited 23 St. James's Place, but mostly led a retiring life at High Elms. Indeed, the estate was landscaped with some Italian gardens.

However, he guided the bank through several commercial panics and was a treasurer of the Great Exhibition in 1851, and effected an amalgamation of Lubbock, Forster & Co. of 11 Mansion House Street with Robarts & Curtis of 15 Lombard Street in 1860.

High Elms was a huge estate and thirty-eight people were resident on the night of the 1861 census including twenty servants; however the father died there in 1865 and his estate was valued at £120,000.

All of his eight sons went to Eton and had a high profile, whilst the first son progressed from John Lubbock (1834), to Sir John Lubbock (1865), and ultimately to the 1st Lord Avebury (1900).

The latter was initially inspired by his father, then Charles Darwin who encouraged him to have a microscope and a love and respect for nature and science. He became fourth baronet and head of Robarts, Lubbock & Co., whilst he was a fellow of the Royal and Geographical Societies, a member of the Royal Academy, and president of the Linnean Society.

Indeed, he received several honorary degrees and wrote on plants and the origins of man and civilisation. He was a Liberal Unionist for West Kent in 1865/68 and Maidstone in 1870-80, passing the Bank Holiday Act (1871) resulting in August Bank Holiday otherwise "St. Lubbock's Day."

He represented London University in Parliament in 1880-1900, and passed the Ancient Monuments Act in 1882; then married his second wife Alice Augusta Laurentia Lane, daughter of General Augustus Henry Lane Fox-Pitt-Rivers, the "Inspector of Ancient Monuments."

---

[12] The ground floor was red-brick with white stucco and pilasters above, whereas the Bonsors lived at 51 Eaton Place (see later). The couple had six children there, all baptized at St. Peter's, Pimlico; and there is a blue plaque stating - "Sir John Lubbock Baron Avebury 1834-1913 Born Here."

In addition, he passed several acts to protect open spaces and wild birds, and was chairman of the London bankers and other commercial bodies. As a result he was rewarded for his sense of duty and became Lord Avebury in 1900, whilst he lived at 48 Grosvenor Street, Mayfair and 2 St. James's Square near Nancy Astor (4) and Lord Kinnaird (10). He died at Kingsgate Castle, Broadstairs in 1913 and his estate was valued at £315,137. [13]

Many of his brothers worked in the bank, and Henry James (1838) lived at 8 Upper Belgrave Street in 1886 (see later). Frederic Lubbock (1844) married Catherine daughter of John Gurney of Earlham Hall, Norfolk in 1869, and was a West India merchant who lived at 19 South Audley Street and at "Emmetts" near Ide Hill in Kent.

The latter's son Percy Lubbock (1879) wrote *The Craft of Fiction* in 1921 discussed by E.M. Forster during the Clark Lectures at Cambridge, and his most notable work was *Earlham* written in 1922. [14]

Meanwhile, two of the family were sportsmen of note. Alfred Lubbock was born at St. James's in 1845, then had eight innings for Kent in 1863-75 and was present on the Fitzgerald tour of North America. He also played for the Old Etonians in the Cup Final replay on 16 March 1875.

His brother Edgar was born at 23 St. James's Place (still present) on 22 February 1847, and baptized at Piccadilly, then grew up at High Elms and attended Eton from 1859-66 - at the same time as A.F. Kinnaird.

He played in the cricket XI for three years and was captain in 1866, being a good middle order, right hand batsman and fast under-arm bowler, but lost out to Harrow at Lord's. He also appeared for the Gentlemen of Kent, and had two innings for Kent C.C.C. in 1871 scoring 65 runs.

In addition, he played for the Wanderers in the first Cup Final in March 1872, and went on the Fitzgerald tour (with W.G. Grace) in summer of that year. He also played for the Old Etonians in the Cup Finals of 1875 (both games) and 1876 (replay) - although they lost on both occasions.

---

[13] Robarts, Lubbock & Co. amalgamated with Coutts in 1915 at 15 Lombard Street and 440 The Strand. The Lubbocks lived at High Elms for 150 years but the estate was sold to Bromley Council in 1965 for a nurses training centre, and the land was designated a green-belt area and golf course. A disastrous fire destroyed the house on 'August Bank Holiday' in 1967 whereas a blue plaque states: "Lord Avebury - scientist, politician, author and banker lived at High Elms."

[14] The Gurneys of Norfolk were Quakers, bankers, and social reformers. John Gurney married Catherine Bell and had a daughter Elizabeth (1780) who married Joseph Fry cousin of J.S. Fry (chocolates). She was a prison reformer and visited Newgate, whilst the Bells were related to both Barclay and Wakefield.

His nephew John Birkbeck Lubbock (1858) son of Lord Avebury went to Eton and Balliol, Oxford, and was a blue in 1881. He played for the Old Etonians against Clapham Rovers in the 1879 final winning 1-0; and for Oxford University against the same opponents in 1880 (losing 1-0).

Edgar Lubbock, however, turned to business in a big way, whilst like Bonsor and Kinnaird his concerns were multifarious and he had a hand in several pies. Indeed, with some general business training and a hint of legal knowledge he became a partner in the Whitbread Brewery in 1875.

The latter was established at Chiswell Street south of Bunhill Fields (near to the present day Barbican) in 1750, and through innovation became a highly lucrative venture with a degree of Royal patronage. [15]

Meanwhile, he resided with his brother Beaumont a banker at 7 Clarges Street, Mayfair, and married Amy Myddelton Peacock at Greatford near Stamford on 23 June 1886. She was the daughter of Gilbert Peacock who was also a banker and resided at "Greatford Hall."

In addition, Lubbock was a director of the Bank of England and lived at 14 Berkeley Square, Mayfair in 1891 - the other residents John B. Lubbock banker, Henry W. Whitbread brewer, and two army gentlemen, whilst his wife sojourned at 13 North Parade, Grantham with several guests.

Indeed, the couple enjoyed a dynamic social life and had a country estate Caythorpe just to the north of Grantham, and Lubbock was master of the Blankney Foxhounds. Further to this he had two daughters: Nancy (1897) born at Eton and Bridget Gian (1901) born at Westminster.

With such resources he was a man of influence and power who moved in notable social circles, meeting people of consequence, and was residing at "North House," 13 North Parade, Little Gonerby near Grantham in 1901 with his eminent guest Waldorf Astor and five servants. [16]

---

[15] Samuel H. Whitbread (1720-96) began as a clerk, but soon owned the largest brewery in the country and purchased Cardington Manor, Bedford, in 1769. He visited Goodwyn's at Lower East Smithfield and approached Boulton and Watt in 1784, thus Smeaton built some handsome buildings and a rotative engine was set to work in 1785. George III and Queen Charlotte visited in 1787.

His son Samuel was born in 1758 and inherited a 5/8 share - then married the daughter of Earl Grey, and spoke frequently for the Whig cause in Parliament but was often criticised for verbosity. He helped to rebuild Drury Lane Theatre from 1809, but died at Dover Street in 1815. The Chiswell Street engine was gradually enlarged and the brewery passed to his sons William and Samuel.

[16] William Waldorf Astor married Mary Dahlgren Paul and had a son Waldorf in 1879. The father was created 1st Viscount Hever and owned the "Waldorf Astoria Hotel" in New York and also Hever Castle in Kent (continued).

Meanwhile, his wife Amy lived at "The Court," Caythorpe & Frieston, just to the north - the residents being her daughters, father Gilbert Peacock a banker, her brother Hugh Peacock a brewer, and twenty servants. She had several guests including Bache Edward Cunard of the shipping family.

A daughter Marigold R. Stella was born at their new property Essendon Place, Hatfield in 1903, and Lubbock made an extensive will leaving the latter to his wife, and 838 ordinary shares in Whitbread's to his daughters with £10,000 going to each. In addition, he also left money secured on his other two properties at Caythorpe and Grantham.

Cosmo Bonsor resigned as Deputy Governor of the Bank of England and Edgar Lubbock replaced him in the post in April 1907. In fact, he received no preliminary training for the position, but due to his business knowledge soon had a complete mastery of his difficult duties.

He appeared in good health and was a keen rider, but died at 18 Hans Court, Knightsbridge on 9 September 1907. His funeral was at Caythorpe but a service was also held at St. Peter's, Eaton Square for those who could not travel, including the Whitbreads - his effects £208,171. [17]

His wife Amy was left comfortably off but married John Henry Trollope (Lord Kesteven) at Stamford in 1914. The latter owned 10,000 acres and he resided at Casewick Hall, but died soon afterwards and the estate passed to a nephew and then to a relative. Baroness Kesteven died in 1941.

The son was educated at Eton and New College, Oxford, and married Nancy W. Shaw in 1906. He was an M.P. for Plymouth in 1910-19 and owned the Observer whilst Nancy was the first woman M.P. (Countess Constance de Markiewcz was elected for Sinn Fein before her, but refused to sit in London).

The couple owned "Cliveden House," Cookham a meeting place for politicians known as the Cliveden Set, and entertained German diplomats leading to charges of appeasement; although Lady Astor helped Churchill to power in 1940.

[17] The Whitbread Brewery at Chiswell Street was used until 1976 with premises at 26 Wharf Road, by the Grand Union Canal. The Georgian architecture was then restored as a conference centre. The main entrance is on Chiswell Street and to the right is a red brick Georgian house with plaque recording the visit of George III. There is an extensive cobbled courtyard and in the southeast corner is Watt's two-storey engine house of 1784. Opposite the entrance is a clock tower building dated at 1887 and 1912, whilst a notable feature is the grand brick chimney.

ALBERT CHILDERS THOMPSON

There was a degree of difficulty in tracing the ancestry of "Thompson," since his father changed the family name; whilst his heritage extended to 1066 with some notable links to Sir F. Fleming master of the ordnance under Edward VI, and General James Wolfe of Quebec.

The family resided at Kirby, Yorkshire in the early 18th century and were merchants in Oporto, whilst John Thompson married Elizabeth Croft and Mildred Childers and was also related to the Hothams and Walkers.

Richard John Thompson was born at Kirby Hall in 1771 and was baptized at Little Ouseburn. He married Elizabeth the daughter of John Turton in 1803, whereas her mother Mary was daughter and co-heiress of Richard Meysey and a descendant of the De Meyseys of Brittany.

The couple had ten children at Kirby Hall whilst their son Harry Stephen (1809) married Elizabeth Ann, daughter of Sir John Croft of Doddington Hall, at Maidstone in 1843. The latter couple then resided at Moat Hall near to Little Ouseburn, and they had several children, but the father removed to Kirby Hall upon receiving his inheritance in 1853.

Harry Stephen Thompson was a J.P. and High Sheriff in 1856 and M.P. for Whitby from 1859-65 (in place of Robert Stephenson the engineer). He maintained a contact address at Thomas's Hotel, 25 Berkeley Square from 1858-61, this being a notable hostelry with a fascinating history, and was also listed at the Traveller's Club in 1860-65. [18]

Meanwhile, he was described as a farmer with 368 acres at Kirby Hall in 1861, whilst the household included his five sons - all of them "Etonians," and the estate had a carpenter, gamekeeper, farmer, and farm bailiffs. The family also had an address at 3 Mansfield Street near Cavendish Square in 1862-65, but then moved to No. 18 and held this property until 1884.

The father Harry Stephen was to be made a baronet thus he changed the family name to Meysey-Thompson (by deed poll) on 19 February 1874. In fact, he became a baronet the next month, but then died at Kirby Hall on 17 May following, his effects being valued at nearly £180,000.

---

[18] The hotel was opened between Jones Street and Bruton Place in c.1798, whilst the Duke of Wellington called on Mrs. Porter at Berkeley Square, hoping for a meeting with courtesan Harriette Wilson: "If you have good news to communicate, address a line to Thomas's Hotel."

Many prominent people stayed in the 1850s, whilst P. Coles was the manager at 25-26 Berkeley Square in 1900-03, and it was Thomas's Hotel Ltd. in 1904; but it was rebuilt as luxury apartments the following year.

His wife Lady Elizabeth Anne Thompson resided at 18 Mansfield Street from 1876-84, and at 45 Lennox Gardens, Pont Street by 1890, however she died at Holme Priory, Wareham in 1910.

Of their family, daughter Elizabeth Lucy (1844) married Walter Stafford Northcote, 2nd Earl of Iddesleigh, in 1868, his father Stafford Henry being a Tory and both the Chancellor and Leader under Disraeli.

Henry M. Meysey-Thompson (1845) was second baronet at 2 Hamilton Place, and a Liberal Unionist M.P. for Knaresborough in 1880, Brigg in 1885-86, and Handsworth in 1892-1905. In addition, he was a director of the N.E. Railway and Barrow Steel Co. and 1st Baron Knaresborough.

Charles Maude (1849) played for the Old Etonians in the 1875/76 finals with A.G. Bonsor, A.F. Kinnaird, and E. Lubbock, then married Emily Walker of Sand Hutton and lived at 31 Tavistock Square (see Betts).

Ernest Claude (1859) was appointed aide-de-camp to the Earl of Onslow, Governor of New Zealand, in 1889-92, and represented Handsworth from 1906-22. The latter owned Clandon, Surrey, and after the Mount Tarawera eruption (1886) transferred a Maori meeting-house to his estate.

Meanwhile, Albert Childers Thompson was born at Moat Hall on 13 July 1848, and attended Eton in 1862-65 then Trinity, Cambridge from 1867-71. In fact, he attended both of these colleges with Arthur Kinnaird.

Having played in the first Cup Final in March 1872 he became a barrister and special pleader three months later, with chambers at 9 King's Bench Walk and 4 Paper Buildings, Temple; his work being on the Midland and North East Circuits in Yorkshire and at the Leeds Borough Sessions.

His name then changed to Meysey-Thompson and he lived at the family home 18 Mansfield Street in 1875-83, and married Mabel Louisa Lascelles (19) at Goldsborough on 9 August 1882. The church was near to Kirby Hall and her father James Lascelles was the rector and a canon of Ripon. [19]

The couple had one son Hubert Charles the next year and resided at 12 Montagu Square, Marylebone from 1884, whilst the father had chambers at 1 King's Bench Walk and also at 41 Parliament Street.

He was a well-known parliamentary counsel, but became ill and spent the winter on the west coast of America. His intention was to resume work on his return, however he died at Montagu Square on 20 March 1894 - and his wife at Sevenoaks in 1941.

[19] The Lascelles family made their money from sugar plantations in Barbados, and purchased the Harewood estate north of Leeds in 1748. Rev. Lascelles was the son of the 3rd Earl of Harewood, whereas his son Cecil Henry was the brother-in-law of William Pember Reeves. The 6th Earl married the daughter of George V and the 7th Earl was the president of the F.A.

REGINALD COURTENAY WELCH

The last Wanderer to consider was the man 'under the tape' and had an important role in the early F.A. His grandfather John Welch was a Lancaster merchant who married Dorcas Walmsley in 1802, then had eleven children who were baptized at the High Street Chapel. [20]

The first son John Welch was born on 31 July 1803 and was educated at Lancaster School and Caius, Cambridge in 1823-26. He was then admitted to the Inner Temple and became a barrister in 1829, whilst he spent his life as a special pleader with a large practice and numerous pupils.

His initial chambers were at Hare Court opposite to Temple Church in the 1840s, whilst he married quite late to Henrietta Anne Ffowell, daughter of Richard Sprye, at St. Nicholas, Brighton on 2 November 1844. Her family had no links to the law and were in fact civil servants who spent many years in the sub-continent and beyond. [21]

John Welch was twenty years older than his bride, whilst the wedding was a society affair and the witnesses included Thomas Barrow and T. Stamford Raffles who was also a barrister. [22]

---

[20] There was a long tradition of nonconformity in the town and George Whitefield preached at the Friends Meeting House (of 1690) during the 18th century.

[21] Richard Samuel Mare Sprye (1798) was born at Crediton, Devon and married Henrietta Digby in c.1822. They sailed for the East Indies the next year, and a daughter Henrietta was born off the Cape de Verde Islands, but was baptized in Madras. Richard worked for H.M. Service at George Town on Pinang Island, by the Malacca Straits, Malaya and in Tamil Nadu, India and had six more children. However, he returned to Britain and lived in Kensington.

[22] Sir Thomas Stamford Raffles was born on the "Ann" off Port Morant, Jamaica in 1781 - then was educated in Hammersmith. He represented the E.I.C. and was sent to Pinang or Prince of Wales Island in 1805, then was Lieutenant Governor of Java in 1811 but returned to England in 1817, and discussed the creation of the zoological gardens with Sir Joseph Banks. He was also Governor of Bencoolen (Sumatra) in 1818-23, and purchased Singapore from the Sultan of Johore on 29 February 1819. His other legacies were London Zoo opened to members in 1828 and to the public in 1847, and the famous Raffles Hotel in Singapore.

Thomas Raffles (1788-1863) was his first cousin and a minister in Liverpool, and had a son Thomas Stamford Raffles who was a barrister and stipendiary magistrate of Liverpool. A grandson of the same name was educated at Rugby School and Cambridge in 1877 then lived at Langham Rectory, Colchester.

The couple initially lived at 6 Westbourne Place at one end of Westbourne Terrace in Paddington, and had five children who were baptized locally. In fact, the father had offices at 3 King's Bench Walk by 1851, and remained at this address until 1882 (see Morley).

Meanwhile, he moved to Lancaster Lodge, Richmond Road, Twickenham, in 1852, residing there ten years (near a home of J.F. Alcock), and clearly wished to assert his allegiance as York House was directly opposite.

A carriage arriving from Richmond saw the former on the right with its stables, outbuildings, and large garden, and an extensive carriage factory to the rear. It was between Arragon Road and Oak Lane facing southwards, whilst Richmond Road curved around into the narrow Church Street with St. Mary's, the Thames, and Eel Pie Island nearby. [23]

The couple had six children at Lancaster Lodge in 1853-62 and three of their sons attended Harrow. Indeed, education became a priority thus the family moved to Lancaster House, College Road, Harrow, with their eight servants, and stayed until the 1870s (now a main shopping street).

John Welch had retired to "Greenhill," Parkside, Wimbledon by 1882, but the next year lived with his son Reginald at 57 Cambridge Street, Edgware Road (now Kendal Street) and made his will there. He left all his estate in trust for the benefit of his wife and daughters during their lifetime, then afterwards for the benefit of his son.

His wife Henrietta died at Cannes on 4 February 1888 and he at 5 Alma Terrace, Kensington on the 16 May, and was buried at Kensal Green; but surprisingly had no executor and this held up the probate until 1904.

Reginald Courtenay Welch was born at 6 Westbourne Place on 17 October 1851 (the middle name coming from his uncle), whilst the appendage of de Courtenay appears to have been added later. He was educated at Harrow as a home boarder with W.P. Crake in 1864-71, and was joint-editor of *The Harrovian* in 1869-71 and played for the cricket and football XI's.

After leaving school he was goal-keeper for the Wanderers in the first two Cup Finals, played for England v Scotland in Glasgow in 1872/74, and was a member of the F.A. committee in 1873-75 and 1879-80. He was also honorary secretary of the Harrow Chequers and Old Harrovians from 1872-84, as well as being the editor of various Harrow magazines.

In addition, he was a trustee for M.P. Betts regarding two life assurance policies on the latter's marriage, and "a student of the Lower Temple and tutor (at Law)," lodging at 57 Cambridge Street, Paddington in 1881.

---

[23] Lancaster Lodge was un-named by 1896 and was demolished for road widening in 1914 - York Street and a tramway then replaced it. The house was located on Cornwall Road, whilst York House became the local council offices.

The house at Cambridge Street was owned by Thomas Halsey, a baker, and was on the corner of Portsea Place (but no longer remains). [24]

Welch was a school army tutor there in 1883, but moved to 6 Southwick Place, Paddington (Stanhope Street) opposite to St. John's, Hyde Park, and married Adeline Charlotte Compton at St. Jude's, Portsea on 22 December 1888 - she resided with her mother in Bayswater Road. [25]

However, the couple had just one son Walter George Frederick born at Paddington in March 1890, whilst the father an army tutor had moved to 1 Southwick Crescent by 1893. This thoroughfare was later renamed as Hyde Park Crescent and was near to the residence of W.P. Crake.

Meanwhile, Colonel Berdoe A. Wilkinson (1827-95) attended the Royal Military Academy, Woolwich and was a lieutenant in the Royal Engineers from 1846-76. After spending nine years as an army tutor at Darmstadt in Germany he established an army college at Heath End, Surrey in 1880. In fact, his sons helped to run it for a while, but at his decease Mr. Welch was appointed principal and also owned shares in the college.

Indeed, the latter was one of the first to ski in Switzerland (the sport came from Norway in 1900), and was the driving force behind the Aldershot Tattoo and organised the first two events at Government House.

However, his son Walter a lieutenant in the Royal Field Artillery died on the Western Front on 30 October 1914. Despite this his father produced a scheme for the working classes to invest in War Loans (adopted by the Central Committee), and he attended a recruiting rally at Farnham Picture Palace in October 1915, due to the large number of casualties.

He formed the Farnham branch of the British Empire Union at the local corn exchange to establish a war council, but "without regard to party" in December 1916, and erected a memorial to his son at Hale, stating, "He was the life and soul of our little mess, a keen and good soldier."

After the war he continued to run the college and trained thousands of officers for the army, but died there on 4 June 1939 and was buried at Heath End, his estate being valued at £16,593.

His wife was provided for in a marriage settlement, but he left property to Miss Emily Gunner matron of forty years, bequests to his three sisters of West Kensington, and £100 to an old female friend of his son's.

---

[24] This is now Kendal Street and the surviving houses go up to No. 56, and have white stucco ground floors with brown brick above. William M. Thackeray (1811-63), the novelist, lived nearby at 18 Albion Street (see Merriman).

[25] Her family emanated from the West Indies, but her father Abingdon worked in the Bombay Civil Service and Adeline was born at Poonah in 1855.

The estate was then placed in trust, firstly for his nephew and niece John and Madge Welch, and secondly for the trustees of the Royal Artillery War Commemoration Fund. The income was to provide scholarships of £75 for the sons of officers of the Royal Artillery (especially those at Woolwich), so they could follow their fathers; and to attend the Royal Military College, Sandhurst or the Royal Air Force College, Cranwell.

In the first instance the scholarships were available to boys who went to Charterhouse, Wellington College (Berks), and Stowe, while the income was also for non-commissioned officers and men of the Royal Artillery, to assist in their children's education, and to be called "The Walter George Frederic Welch Scholarship and Bequest." Indeed, it was to be a perpetual memorial for his son of the 117th Battery R.A. who died at Ypres.

His last request was that his trustees continue the Army College Ltd. and appoint a new principal, however during the war it was requisitioned by the Air Ministry and was put up for auction at the Bush Hotel, Farnham on 30 June 1948. There were 7-8 reception rooms, 26 bedrooms, 6 bathrooms, staff living and bedrooms, and domestic offices, attractive gardens and fine playing fields (and a garage) covering some 5½ acres. Indeed, it may have been suitable for flats but was demolished and replaced by housing.

The Wanderers were one of the first great teams at Battersea and fielded Alcock, Elphinstone, and Kinnaird against Sheffield in 1866 - the other players being from Barnes, the Crusaders, and the No Names Club. [26]

During the two county matches in 1867/68 they supplied four and three team players respectively - the others (as above) and from the Civil Service, schools, universities, and old boys clubs. Indeed, the Wanderers won the Cup four more times viz. Oxford 1873 (2-0), Old Etonians 1876 (3-0), Oxford 1877 (2-1), and Royal Engineers 1878 (3-1).

The competition changed with the arrival of northern professional outfits and the Wanderers were disbanded in 1881, whilst some players returned to their old boys clubs. Meanwhile, their opponents the Royal Engineers are discussed in the following three chapters.

---

[26] Battersea Fields were reclaimed from the Thames marshes in the 16th century and were a venue for fairs, pigeon shooting, and donkey racing. H.M. Office of Works took charge in 1846 and they were drained and levelled using soil excavated from Victoria Docks (built by Peto and Betts). 120 acres were sold for housing and 200 acres formed the park with boating lake, cascades, and Italian gardens, whilst there were three cricket/sports grounds by the river.

CHAPTER 7

The Royal Engineers

Chatham Docks lay just beside the River Medway, to the north of the main township, and became an important naval centre under Elizabeth I, being protected by strategic forts such as Upnor Castle.

The Royal Engineers established a significant presence there, and the School of Military Engineering was formed at Brompton Barracks near the docks, after a request from the Duke of Wellington, in 1812.

The Corps earned a reputation as leaders in engineering advance, and trained their officers to a high standard of both physical and mental fitness. Most of them attended public school and they helped construct the Albert Hall in 1867-71, whilst they designed the 'steam sapper' a traction engine that pulled vehicles across country. Much of their work was abroad, and they built both road and rail infrastructure throughout India.

Due to their public school connections many officers had a keen interest in sport and the Royal Engineers joined the F.A. at its inception. Indeed, Captain Marindin was posted to Chatham in 1866-74 and helped make the team one of the best in the country; whilst he sat on the F.A. committee, helped inaugurate the F.A. Cup, and eventually became the organisation's president (see later).

But who were the men who took on the Wanderers in 1872? All of them appeared in Hart's Army List that year, and Marindin was brigade major at the school, Merriman was assistant instructor in field works, and the others were lieutenants - four of them being new recruits. Some of these cadets had further postings, but all had recently attended the school.

HENRY WAUGH RENNY-TAILYOUR

The attack was led by Renny-Tailyour, Mitchell, and Rich and the first was the epitome of an officer, gentleman, and sportsman, his name having the very flavour of the British Empire. Indeed, he was followed by other bi-sporting greats such as Denis and Leslie Compton and Ian Botham.

Hercules Tailyour possessed the manor of Borrowfield, Montrose in 1615 and it passed to Hercules who married Catherine daughter of Sir William Ogilvy of Barras. Montrose itself was a prosperous town on the north east coast of Scotland with a large natural harbour, many Georgian houses on the High Street, and an ancient parish church beside the guildhall.

Robert Tailyour their only son died unmarried and the estate passed to his sister Elizabeth Jean Tailyour, the wife of Robert grandson of Patrick Renny Esq. of Usan, Co. Forfar (married 1773). The couple had twelve children and three of their sons entered the British Army. [1]

Alexander Renny was born at Montrose on 31 January 1775 and succeeded to Borrowfield on his mother's death in 1806. In her will she directed that he took the surname Tailyour as well as the family crest and coat of arms, but he apparently omitted to take certain legal steps.

He married Elizabeth Bannerman the daughter of Sir Alexander Ramsay at Edinburgh in 1808, and had eight children, whilst he owned the estates of Borrowfield and Newmanswalls in Montrose. Meanwhile, he declared that his descendants would forfeit their land unless they took the name Renny-Tailyour, and he died in 1849.

His son Thomas Renny was born on 18 March 1812 and joined the army as a cadet with the Bengal Engineers in India. As a captain he married Isabella Eliza Cook the daughter of Major Adam Atkinson of Lorbottle (a village near to Alnwick) in 1847.

Upon his father's decease he applied to the Royal Court, requesting that he and his heirs might use the surname and coat armorial Renny-Tailyour of Borrowfield. Such a request was granted by Victoria at St. James's on 16 November 1849, although the petitioner was then overseas.

Thomas Renny-Tailyour was stationed at Mussoorie near the Punjab high in the foothills of the Himalayas, which was infamous as a holiday retreat for officers. It had a mountain road connection to Dehra Dun and a rail link to Roorkee, a military settlement forty miles to the south, the latter being the site of a premier engineering college (established 1847).

The couple had three children in India and the father was promoted to major, however he retired as a lieutenant colonel in 1856 and returned to Montrose just before the Indian Mutiny.

He lived at Dubton House on the Borrowfield estate, two miles north of the town, and was a local benefactor, whereas he had three more children there and all of his sons were educated at Cheltenham College.

Indeed, he supported the volunteer force and was a captain of the rifle-company, worked as a local J.P., followed the Whig cause, joined the Montrose Natural History and Antiquarian Society, and sat on various local boards with regard to the infirmary and roads.

---

[1] Hercules Renny was a lieutenant colonel in H.M. Army, and Charles Renny a captain in the 40th Regiment died during the storming of Montevideo, Uruguay in 1806. There are memorials at Montrose Presbyterian (Ch. of Scotland) to Robert Renny who died in 1787, his wife Elizabeth Jean, and his son Alexander.

The census recorded him at Dubton House with his wife Isabella and daughter Louisa, but he died in 1885 and was buried at Rosehill Cemetery just north of the town. In fact, he was greatly respected and lived by the maxim, "What thy hand findeth to do, do it with all thy might."

Henry Waugh Renny-Tailyour was born at Mussoorie on 9 October 1849 and spent his early years in India, then attended Cheltenham College from 1859-67, at the same time as R.G. Graham and G.W. Addison. Indeed, the latter joined him in Boyne House, and this association was to pay great personal dividends in the future (see below).

Meanwhile, his sporting prowess came to the fore and he played for the cricket XI and scored a century against Newnham College, then entered the Royal Military Academy at Woolwich in 1868.

He joined the Royal Engineers as a lieutenant and went to the School of Military Engineering in 1870-72. Indeed, he was a confident character with an irresistible smile and was much in demand for his sporting ability, thus he played in the 1872 Cup Final and rugby for Scotland the same year.

After a posting to Portsmouth in December, his sporting career really took off and he appeared for Scotland at the Oval on 8 March 1873, the team including seven members of Queen's Park and Kinnaird of the Wanderers. This was the second such contest and Scotland lost 4-2, whilst his team mate Goodwyn also played for England.

He then returned to the School of Military Engineering in 1873-76, and much happened during this time. He played with Addison, Marindin, and Merriman in the Cup Final on 14 March 1874, losing 2-0 to Oxford, but played a major role in the final the following year.

His team took on the Old Etonians and they initially played out a 1-1 draw on 13 March 1875. The side included Merriman and Wingfield-Stratford however in the replay on 16 March the Engineers won the Cup 2-0. In fact, Renny-Tailyour scored in both these matches, and may have had a third, although this was usually accredited to W.F.H. Stafford.

Due to his posting he made several appearances for Kent C.C.C. and for the Gentlemen v Players, being a middle-order right hand batsman, a right hand fast round-arm bowler, and also a good cover point.

Renny-Tailyour was a dashing soldier and eligible gentleman who lived at Gillingham, thus he met and courted the sister of a colleague. As a result he married Emily Rose daughter of John Wingfield-Stratford at Addington, Kent on 9 September 1875, the witnesses including their two fathers, his brother Edward, and her sister Florence.

The Wingfield-Stratford family had some notable antecedents in Ireland, and her father was a landowner with 200 acres in Addington, a local J.P., and had no less than seventeen servants. Her brother Cecil Vernon played for England at the Oval on 3 March 1877 (1-3), and married Rosalind Isabel Bligh that year and resided at Norton, Isle of Wight (see below). [2]

Meanwhile, Renny-Tailyour and his wife had ten children over the next twenty-two years and most were registered in the name Tailyour, although his wife remained at home during most of his sojourns.

Indeed, he then received a significant posting as aide-de-camp to James Hamilton, the Lord Lieutenant of Ireland, in February to December 1876 and spent this period residing in Dublin. In fact, he departed on the same day as Hamilton and was sent to Gibraltar for most of 1877, at the same time as his team mates Bogle and Mitchell. [3]

He was ordered home soon after and was acting instructor of telegraphs at the S.M.E., Chatham until 1881. This gave him a new sporting opportunity and he scored some large innings, including 331 not out against the Civil Service in 1880 (a run a minute!). Three children were born during this period, all of them being baptized at Addington Church.

Meanwhile, he was instructor in fortifications at the R.M.A., Woolwich in 1881-84, and had lodgings at 38 The Common near the town. Indeed, he played further games for Kent C.C.C. in 1881-83 and his career total was 818 runs, with a high of 124 runs; whilst he was promoted to captain and two sons were baptized at the Garrison Church, Woolwich.

---

[2] Richard Wingfield, the 1st Viscount, built "Powerscourt," Co. Wexford in the Wicklow Mountains in 1731. His son then married Amelia Stratford the daughter of John who was the 1st Earl of Aldborough in 1760.

Clontarf Castle, Dublin was the stronghold of King George but Sir Charles Coote took it for the Puritans, and it passed to John Vernon quartermaster of Cromwell's army. Charlotte Vernon married Gen. Sir John W. Guise and their son John C. fought at Sevastopol, Lucknow, and Secundra Bagh earning the V.C.

John Wingfield-Stratford (1810) married Jane E. Guise his sister at Rendcomb, Cheltenham in 1844, and had children Edward John (1849), Cecil Vernon (1853), Emily Rose (1855), and Florence Mary (1858) born at Addington.

[3] The Lord Lieutenant was the Viceroy or King's representative in Ireland and was at the Viceregal Apartments, Dublin Castle in the social season January to March (from the 1780s), and the Viceregal Lodge, Phoenix Park, at other times.

James Hamilton (1811-85), 1st Duke of Abercorn (Ireland), attended Harrow, Christchurch (Oxford), and Dublin. He held the post in 1866-68 and in 1874-76 being succeeded by John Winston S. Churchill, 7th Duke of Marlborough.

In the 19th century real power was with the Chief Secretary of Ireland although the Unionists supported the Lord Lieutenant, a post that survived up until the end of British rule in 1920.

He was then assistant instructor in field fortifications at the S.M.E. from 1884-88, and lived nearby at 16 Kingswood Villas, Gillingham. During this time he continued to play cricket for the Engineers and amassed a total of 307 innings with 12,291 runs by 1888, whilst he was promoted to major and shortly returned to Gibraltar.

His brother-in-law Captain Cecil V.W. Stratford R.E. (37) resided at the Cracknells, Norton near Yarmouth on the Isle of Wight in 1891. Indeed, a daughter Rosalind Lilian Renny-Tailyour was born at Braxton Cottage, Norton near to the property on 11 September 1890 - although the mother gave her home address as (19) Dubton House, Montrose.

The cottage, with its whitewashed walls and red tiles, was situated upon Yarmouth Road at the junction with Westhill Lane, whilst Major Cecil V. Wingfield-Stratford resided at the notable Norton Lodge from 1894-99, and Braxton was located just beside his estate. [4]

Renny-Tailyour never returned to India but he had "special duties" in the colonial employment (local forces) at Sydney, New South Wales in 1891-94, and was made commander there. Indeed, a son Henry Frederick Thornton was born at Homebush, Sydney on 31 July 1893.

The father then returned home and was briefly in the Thames district in 1895, but was a lieutenant colonel commanding the 4th Battalion (Training Division) at the S.M.E. until he retired on 4 October 1899. In total he had thirty years service and was entitled to a pension of £300, whilst his last two children were baptized at Rochester Cathedral.

Lieutenant Colonel G.W. Addison retired on the same day and the old boy network then came into play. The Earl of Iveagh contacted both parties and they became directors on the Guinness board soon after, although Renny-Tailyour was the most active representing the Earl of Iveagh in Dublin, whilst Addison was mainly a consultant in London. [5]

---

[4] Norton Lodge was a plain two-storey stucco property, with bow windows and a conservatory on the east side. It was on a small coastal-ridge looking towards the Solent (with West Hill nearby), and became Norton Grange a holiday retreat.

[5] Arthur Guinness opened the St. James's Gate Brewery in 1759 and as Protestants the family were against independence. They were sole owners by 1825, being the richest family in Ireland, whereas Edward Cecil Guinness (1847) was the largest shareholder in a public company in 1886. He became the 1st Earl of Iveagh in 1891 and purchased the "Elveden Estate," Thetford, Suffolk from the Maharajah Duleep Singh in 1894. He was generally in England from 1900, and was host to Edward VII, whilst his son Rupert married Lady Gwendolen F.M. Onslow in 1903 (see Thompson), and became 2nd Earl and chairman in 1927.

Renny-Tailyour lived at Shrewsbury House, Merion near to Dublin and worked at St. James's Gate, whilst his wife died at 30 Devonshire Street, Marylebone in 1904. Her funeral was at St. Mary's Episcopal, Montrose, with many in attendance including her family from Kent, whereas a son Cecil Ramsay died in Northern Nigeria in 1911.

However, the father was promoted to managing director of Guinness in 1913, and then had a prominent role in decision making, thus authorising many influential and strategic corporate actions.

The Dublin 'Lock Out' was a strike by dockers, seamen, and carters in 1913-14, and caused severe disruption to overseas distribution hence the company purchased two ships at his direction. Meanwhile, 800 employees went to fight in the First War and he guaranteed them half-pay and jobs on their return, whilst he had to deal with the restrictions imposed by Lloyd George and his Government during the war.

He retired from the company in early 1919 and moved to Newmanswalls, a family property just south of the Borrowfield estate, and was a J.P. and member of the local asylum board. However, he died there soon afterwards on 15 June 1920 and has a memorial at Rosehill Cemetery.

Of his brothers, Edward Ramsay (1851) was a captain in the Gaika and Galeka Wars (9th Kaffir), south of Natal, in 1877-78. This was a time of great unrest and the Zulu and 1st Boer Wars followed soon after, whereas large gold deposits were uncovered at Witwatersrand in 1887. As a result he moved to Barberton in the Transvaal and was in business at Port Elizabeth, then was a gentleman of Johannesburg. [6]

At this time he became friends with King Lobengulu of Matabeleland and secured a concession, his company gave up mining rights elsewhere. In fact, he returned to England to finalize matters in 1893 and was sent to select a territory, but died at Mangwe in Matabeleland soon afterwards. [7]

---

[6] Cape Colony was established on 8 January 1806 whilst the Boers moved north in the 1830s and established Transvaal in 1856. The first diamonds were discovered some ten years later, whilst the British annexed the Transvaal in 1877.

[7] King Lobengulu ruled this part of Rhodesia from 1868 and had an agreement with Cecil Rhodes regarding Mashonaland in 1888. The latter then came under the jurisdiction of Dr. L. Jameson, and after trouble with the Matabele he chased Lobengulu into exile, whilst he raided the Transvaal in 1896.

The South Africa Co. had to pay large compensation and Edward H. Pember debated the matter, whilst more than anything this led to the 2nd Boer War. The Boers were defeated by May 1902, and the Transvaal and Orange Free State were part of the Empire. The Union of South Africa a dominion was formed in 1910, and it became an independent republic in the Commonwealth in 1961.

His brother Thomas Francis Bruce (1863) attended the R.M.A., Woolwich and joined the Royal Engineers, then was involved in the Burmese War in 1885-89, joined the Chin-Lushai and Chinese expeditions in 1889-93, and was on the Sino-Burmese Boundary Commission in 1897-1900. He retired to Newmanswalls as a lieutenant colonel in 1920 and died in 1937.

John Wingfield Renny-Tailyour of the Royal Artillery inherited the family estates and resided at Dubton House until 1969. Indeed, the property with its white-washed walls and large chimneys remains across fields to the north of the town, and was once an ancient farmhouse.

Borrowfield Farm was located to the south on Borrowfield Lane, whereas Newmanswalls a 19th-century property with extensive gardens had a main entrance in Brechin Road, and another to the north. It was demolished in the 1940s leaving just a boundary wall, while Renny and Tailyour Crescents are new developments situated nearby.

HENRY BAYARD RICH

This was another family with Irish connections since John Sampson Rich was born at Woodlands, Limerick in 1800 and married Amelia Whitfield at Manchester in 1821. He became a captain in the Royal Artillery, and his son Frederick Henry was born at Woodlands on 8 March 1824.

The latter joined the Royal Engineers as an ensign in 1843 and had brief periods at Chatham, Woolwich, Dover, and Devonport. In fact, he went to Ireland as a 1st lieutenant in 1845, and then to Canada the next year and the West Indies in 1847-51, where he moved in some prominent circles.

The exact sequence of events is unclear however he married Elizabeth daughter of Richard Henry Bayard at St. Stephen's Church, Philadelphia on 2 August 1848 - the officiating minister being Henry W. Ducachet. [8]

---

[8] Samuel Bayard a French Huguenot and merchant of Amsterdam married Ann Stuyvesant, sister of Peter the last Governor of New Amsterdam. She moved with her four children to what became New York in 1647, and lived at Bayard Mansion in the Bowery. The family moved to Bohemia Manor, Maryland on Chesapeake Bay in 1698, and Col. John Bayard (1738) was a Philadelphia merchant and also a leader of independence. His nephew James Asheton Bayard (1767) was a senator, and had two sons and a grandson in the Senate.

The Carrolls came to Annapolis from England in 1688 and Charles Carroll (1737) signed the Declaration of Independence and was the oldest surviving signatory in 1826. Richard H. Bayard (1796) married his granddaughter Mary Sophia Carroll a great beauty at Howard, Maryland, and the couple had a daughter Elizabeth in Delaware in 1828.

The Sappers and Miners had several companies in America in the 19th century and were based in Halifax (Nova Scotia), Quebec, Bermuda, and Barbados, but also had old links to Philadelphia and worked on boundary commissions, building the Rideau Canal, Canada from 1826-32.

Indeed, Rich and his company had some important links to history, and during his time in the West Indies, he was stationed at Berbice in British Guiana (renamed Guyana after independence).

Britain occupied the area in the Napoleonic Wars, in 1814, and acquired Berbice, Demerara, and Essequibo around rivers of those names, whilst it became a colony in 1831 with Georgetown (Demerara) as the capital.

The couple had two children at this time: Henry Bayard (1849) born in Berbice and Charles Carroll (1850) born in the West Indies. However, the father received a posting to Ireland in 1851-59 and became a captain, then had three children at Athlone, Co. Westmeath by the Shannon, and another child at Curragh, Co. Kildare in 1856.

Captain Rich was stationed on Malta from 1859-61 and a daughter Agnes was born there, then he pre-empted Major Marindin and was seconded as an Inspector of Railways at the Board of Trade from April 1861.

Clearly he had his sons' future in mind thus he leased a large property "Woodlands" on Dulwich Common from the College Estates that year. The house and stables were situated on the north side near to Thurlow Park and College Roads, with common land to the south. Indeed, four of his sons attended Dulwich Grammar School in the village during 1861-68, however there were soon some considerable changes in the area. [9]

Peto, Betts, and Crampton began building the London, Chatham & Dover Railway in 1860, and purchased large areas of land from the school in 1863. The company went bankrupt, but Dulwich College was built on the sale profits in the Baroque style (opposite to Woodlands) in 1866-70.

---

[9] Philip Henslowe owned the Rose Theatre in Southwark and was a rival to Shakespeare, thus he formed a partnership with Edward Alleyn (1566-1626) and they established the Fortune Theatre at Golding (Golden) Lane, Cripplegate in 1600. In fact, Alleyn married Henslowe's step-daughter and purchased the Manor of Dulwich for £4,900 in 1605, then moved there in 1613.

Soon after he became reformed and established *The College of God's Gift* on 21 June 1619, which was a charitable institution to educate twelve poor scholars, with a chapel and almshouses. The theatre burnt down and was demolished in 1661, and there is a plaque in Fortune Street just north of the Whitbread Brewery.

The almshouses were at the junction of Gallery and College Roads, whilst new properties (like Woodlands) were built on Dulwich Common in the 1800s. Indeed, Sir John Soane added Dulwich Picture Gallery from 1811-14, and the Grammar School was constructed just opposite in 1842.

Meanwhile, the father was seconded to the railways and became a major and lieutenant colonel. He was briefly at the War Office in 1872, however retired as an honorary brevet colonel (on full pay) on 1 February 1873, having served in the army for over thirty years.

After his retirement he continued to work as an Inspector of Railways (junior) with the Board of Trade in Whitehall, and a daughter Louisa was born in 1875, whereas he moved to a substantial house in London.

17 Queen's Gate Terrace, Kensington was a fashionable Regency property with imposing six-storey stucco façade, grand portico entrance, and carved cornices above all the windows. Indeed, it was a mirror of Victorian society since behind there was no garden, and the austere brickwork looked down upon the lowly stables and mews.

His wife died there in 1885, but he continued as a railway inspector and knew Marindin in this capacity; whilst he lived with his son Frederick an R.N. commander, two daughters, and nine servants in 1891.

Meanwhile, some former connections came into play, and Frederick H. Rich a retired colonel of 17 Queen's Gate Terrace married Cecile D'Olier Gowan of 20 Courtfield Gardens at Kensington Church on 18 June 1891, the witnesses being Leila Gowan and John Rich. [10]

This was a most auspicious match and the couple resided at 17 Queen's Gate Terrace with six servants in 1901; but he died at Oareford, Oare, Somerset on 22 August 1904 aged 80. This was a remote location north of Exmoor near the Doone Valley made famous in *Lorna Doone*. Frederick St. George Rich captain R.N., Carlisle Howard Rich C.E., and Vincent Frisby Esq. obtained his probate, the estate being worth £98,759.

Regarding his sons, Charles Carroll Rich (1850) was in the Royal Horse Artillery and spent time in India, but died at Heidelberg in 1902; and Frederick St. George (1852) was a commander in the Royal Navy and also aide-de-camp to Edward VII in 1906-07.

---

[10] The Edict of Nantes (1598) was revoked in 1685 and many Calvinist Huguenots emigrated. Isaac D'Olier went to Dublin and fought in the Battle of the Boyne in 1690 - William was victorious over James II and many Catholics left Ireland.

Jeremiah D'Olier (1746) a merchant helped establish the Dublin City Plan and a daughter Cecilia was born in 1796. She married Philip Gowan there in 1814, then moved to Dulwich and had ten children - some baptized in the college chapel.

George D'Olier Gowan a stockbroker married Sarah C. Bowie at Anne Arundel, Maryland in 1838, and Cecile D'Olier Gowan was born in Virginia in 1842. Her father died at "Woodlawn" in Dulwich, whilst brother Bowie Campbell married Leila Davidson in Maryland in 1875. The family lived at 20 Courtfield Gardens, and Rev. Charles Voysey resided at "Woodlawn" in 1884.

His daughter Louisa Maud (1854) married Frederick James Crooke who was educated at Winchester and had a notable cricket career for Lancashire, Gloucester, and the M.C.C. - his figures 35 innings and 573 runs.

Meanwhile, Henry Bayard Rich was born at Berbice, British Guiana on 14 June 1849 and grew up in Ireland, but was educated at Dulwich in 1861-64 and also at Marlborough College in 1864-66. He then attended the R.M.A., Woolwich and was a lieutenant at the S.M.E. from 8 January 1870.

After taking part in the first Cup Final he was posted to Aldershot with his team mate Mitchell in 1873, and went overseas to Hong Kong in 1874-76. During his time there he served on an expedition against the Malays in Perak in early 1876, and was mentioned in despatches receiving a medal with clasp. The region was beside the Perak River on the Malacca Straits, 120-miles north of Kuala Lumpur on the Malay Peninsula.

Rich returned to Aldershot with C Troop in 1877-79 and witnessed the marriage of H. Mitchell (see Chapter 8), but was then placed in charge of signalling for Telegraph Troop, 1st Division in the Cape of Good Hope. He served under 1st General Lord Chelmsford and Sir Garnet Wolseley C.I.C., and saw action in the Zulu War from May-November 1879.

As a result he received a medal with clasp and remained with C Troop in South Africa until 1880, but was posted to Colchester the next year where he was re-acquainted with William Merriman.

Henry Bayard Rich lieutenant R.E. of St. Giles, Colchester married Ada Melvill Simons of "Tyersall," Sydenham at St. Stephen's, South Dulwich on 3 May 1881. She was born in Singapore and her father was Henry Minchin Simons an East India merchant, and her mother was Caroline Melvill. The couple no doubt met in Dulwich, since the bride's family lived just south of the village at Crescent Wood Road in Sydenham Hill.

Indeed, Rich was promoted to captain in Colchester then served with A Troop in the Egyptian Campaign in 1882, again under Sir Garnet Wolseley. Soon afterwards he was sent to India, and with the risks in mind made his last will on 2 September 1882: "My last Will, I Henry Bayard Rich do hereby leave everything I have (or am likely to have) in the world, to my wife Ada Melvill Rich signed *H.B. Rich* Captain R.E."

Initially he was stationed at Roorkee in September 1883, however he then travelled to Rawalpindi near the frontier, and during a game of polo had a serious collision dying there as a result on 17 November 1884.

His widow was granted administration at a court in Rawalpindi, whilst his obituary was in the *Times* on 19 December: "Many brother officers will regret the loss of Captain Henry Bayard Rich, whose death, the result of an accident at polo, occurred in India last month…."

She then returned home and resided at "Tyersall" whilst his effects came to just £5,162 in 1885. Meanwhile, Francis Slater Picot a lieutenant in the 2nd Wiltshire of 72 Courtfield Gardens married Ada Melvill Rich at St. Jude's, South Kensington on 16 July 1888. The Picot family had many links to Jersey, whilst Courtfield Gardens appear later on (see Addison).

HERBERT HUGH MUIRHEAD

The Muirhead family are traced to Scotland, and unlike some of the other families had an academic background of some considerable note.

Initially they lived at Dunipace, Stirling and George Muirhead (1715) was minister of Dysart, Fife in 1747-52 and a professor at Glasgow University; whilst his brother Patrick (1717) married a cousin Elisabeth Muirhead and became the next minister of Dysart. [11]

They had eight children including Lockhart (1765) a doctor of law who married Anna Campbell in 1804. He was principal librarian and professor of natural history at Glasgow from 1809 until his death in 1829.

His son James Patrick was born at The Grove, Hamilton on 26 July 1813 and attended Glasgow College in 1826 and Balliol, Oxford in 1832-35, but preferred Alpine expeditions and only achieved a third class degree. His grandmother Elisabeth Muirhead was a cousin of James Watt the engineer, and such connections soon had a major impact on his life.

Indeed, James Watt senior was born at Greenock in 1699, and with his father made mathematical instruments. He was a ship owner and merchant and married Agnes Muirhead (the aunt of Elisabeth) at Hamilton in 1729, whilst they had a son James Watt junior born at Greenock in 1736.

The latter was educated at the local grammar school and made models in his father's workshop, then lived with his mother's relatives in Glasgow in 1754. During that time he trained as an instrument maker, then set up a workshop at the university and met some eminent scientists.

He married his cousin Margaret Miller at Glasgow on 15 July 1764 and had a small family, whilst he became familiar with lecturer Joseph Black and his concepts of latent heat. He also received a model of a Newcomen steam engine and realised that the design incorporated a serious flaw.

There was a large boiler, but this failed to drive the piston due to a loss of heat. His answer was a separate condenser/pump which sent steam directly to the piston, thereby reducing the loss of energy through cooling.

---

[11] Dysart was on the northern outskirts of Kirkcaldy, this being the birthplace of economist Adam Smith (1723-90) and architect Robert Adam (1728-92).

His discovery took place in 1765 but the concept was not developed due to his limited means and some incorrect legal advice. However, he made an arrangement with John Roebuck of the Carron Works and built an engine at Kinneil, Linlithgow although this aroused little interest. As a result he had to work as a surveyor to make ends meet, and replaced John Smeaton as engineering advisor at the Carron Foundry.

Meanwhile, Matthew Boulton was born in Birmingham in 1728 and joined his father's business, becoming sole owner by 1759, and married Anne Robinson at Lichfield the next year. The marriage contract included a large dowry thus he established the Soho Works at Handsworth in 1762.

At the works they produced good quality metalwork and pottery, and he built the elegant Soho House there in 1766. This became the meeting place for the "Lunar Society," an intellectual group which included patrons such as Erasmus Darwin, John Whitehurst, and Josiah Wedgwood.

The most significant event was when Benjamin Franklin joined the group and introduced them to his colleague Dr. Small. In fact, Roebuck was a friend of the Boultons who were likewise working on the steam engine, and Small contacted Watt who then visited the Soho Works in 1767/68.

Initially, the latter remained in Scotland, although he was encouraged to take out a new patent in 1769. Unfortunately, this was based on amateur advice and the specifications were later contested.

Roebuck was in severe difficulty by 1772, so Boulton offered to purchase his two-thirds share in the engine, and also to pay a £1,200 debt. The offer was too good to miss thus the inventor moved south and Boulton & Watt formed their partnership by 1775. Indeed, Watt had the inventive capacity and Boulton had the necessary capital and also the desire.

Watt's original patent was for fourteen years and six had expired, thus Boulton asked Parliament to extend the agreement to 1800. Meanwhile, the experimental engine was moved from Kinneil to Soho and there was soon interest from the Cornish mines, thus Watt was dispatched southwards.

He had a torrid time in Cornwall disliking the climate, the company, and the lack of research, however several single action engines were installed but to pump water out of the mines - not to drive machinery.

James Watt was married for a second time to Ann MacGregor in 1776, whereas Joseph Priestley joined the "Lunar Society" and discovered oxygen which he initially described as dephlogisticated air.

There was, however, a slow return on the investment (with much capital tied-up in the machines) and Watt wilted under the financial pressure, thus Boulton had to use all his energy and business talents to encourage him to continue his efforts at this time.

As a result the inventor worked with renewed vigour and developed a cranked engine with a rotary motion, although one of his employees leaked the designs. Despite this they established several patents for the "sun and planet" wheel, converting reciprocating to rotary motion, culminating with their rotative engines produced during 1784-85.

The first of these were installed in London breweries and in particular at H. Goodwyn, Lower East Smithfield and S. Whitbread, Chiswell Street. Watt also built on the work of Priestley and discovered the composition of water viz. two parts phlogiston to one part dephlogisticated air. With such triumphs he became a member of the Royal Society in 1785, and took up residence at Heathfield House near to the Soho Works.

Boulton was totally committed to the project and was taken to the verge of bankruptcy regarding the innovative engine. In fact, Watt received a profit by 1787, but Boulton had to wait longer due to his considerable investment. However, there were a number of similar patents, and the partners were involved in extensive litigation at a cost of £6,000 from 1792-1800.

In addition, a steam-press was installed to produce copper coins in 1788 and the first patent came out two years later. Large quantities were made for the E.I.C., foreign governments, and colonies and a new coin for Britain in 1797, whereas a press was supplied to the mint at Tower Hill (1805).

The partners retired in 1800 and the business passed to their sons James Watt (j) and Matthew Robinson Boulton. The latter married Mary Ann Roul and had six children at Soho including a daughter Katherine Elizabeth born in 1819. He also purchased a second home at Tew Park, Great Tew, just north of Oxford (a former centre of learning under Lord Falkland).

Meanwhile, James Watt junior was caught in the French Revolution and fled to Italy, but returned to England in 1794. He was imbued with his father's talents and fitted out the "Caledonian" in 1817, which was the first steamship to leave a British port and sailed up the Rhine.

He resided at Aston Hall above the Aston Lower Grounds (see Villa) and began to write the lengthy memoirs of his father, but this proved a difficult business and he became ill. As a result he decided to entrust them to a younger man, and contacted his distant cousin James P. Muirhead who was then at Oxford (1835). The latter soon became involved in the task which was ultimately to be a life-long occupation.

Muirhead became an advocate in Edinburgh in 1838 and also published some legal works at the time, whilst he resided with his mother at 26 Heriot Row, on the north side of Queen Street Gardens. These also formed his chambers and were situated in the new town near to Princes Street, whilst the shadow of the castle fell upon them.

In fact, he put all of his energies into the life of James Watt and used a manuscript from his youth, left to the family by Elisabeth Muirhead. After consulting a work by Arago, he went to Paris in 1842, and continued to investigate the claims of Cavendish that "he" discovered "water."

Muirhead also travelled down to Birmingham and was given free access to the papers of Boulton & Watt, and met with Boulton at Soho House and Watt at Aston Hall. In fact, he was taken in by the academic atmosphere pervading these rooms and became well acquainted with the families.

Katherine Boulton grew up in the shadow of the Lunar Society and had a keen interest in literature and the classics, making her an ideal partner; thus it was no surprise that Muirhead an advocate of St. Stephen's, Edinburgh married her at Handsworth Church on 27 January 1844.

Initially, he continued to practice at 26 Heriot Row and a son Lionel Boulton C.L. was born in 1845, whilst he secured conclusive evidence on his research and published: "The correspondence of the late James Watt on his discovery of the Theory of the Composition of Water." [12]

However, his wife found such a climate uncongenial and he was forced to give up his career at the bar, and moved to Haseley Court, Oxford in 1847. This was a suitable environment for study however James Watt junior died in 1848, and five more children were born at Leamington, Hastings, and Brighton. The family then lived at Haseley Court in 1851 with his sisters-in-law Anne R. and Mary A. Boulton, and nine servants.

Indeed, three quarto volumes were published in 1854 being the memoirs, correspondence, and patent specifications with engravings: "The Origin and Progress of The Mechanical Inventions of James Watt," which formed the basis of a more expansive work "The Life of James Watt" in 1858-59.

His labours regarding the famous engineer were finally completed, thus the couple concentrated on their children's education and three sons went to Eton (1859-65). The father also continued to write and led a retired life on his estate, receiving letters of compliment from Longfellow.

He was a regular contributor to "Blackwood's Magazine" from 1882 and did several translations of verse, whilst he died there in 1898. Lionel and Francis (two of his sons) and Napier George Sturt lieutenant colonel R.E. obtained his probate, the estate being valued at £74,979.

Regarding his family, Lionel attended Eton and Balliol, Oxford, but was taken prisoner by the Turks at Palmyra in Syria in 1868. He had a narrow escape then was an artist/writer at Haseley Court (until 1925). His brother Francis was a successful barrister of Lincoln's Inn, and Bertram became a

---

[12] Many advocates had chambers at Heriot Row (as they do today), and Robert Louis Stevenson resided at No. 17 from 1857-80.

lieutenant in the Royal Navy. Of the sisters Eleanor Annie was at home, and Beatrix Marion married Napier George Sturt (son of Charles) in 1876, the latter's family providing a fascinating history.

Charles Sturt was born in Bengal in 1795, his father a judge with the E.I.C., and attended Harrow then joined the army in 1813. He was involved in the Peninsular War and Waterloo then sailed to Botany Bay in 1827.

Being a favourite of the Governor, Ralph Darling he was acquainted with explorers John Oxley and Hamilton Hume, and went on expeditions to the Darling and Murray Rivers in 1828-29. He was a man driven by courage, faith, and prayer and always slept with a Bible under his pillow.

Indeed, on one occasion he disposed of everything including a gas lamp, but kept the Holy book, stating, "Something more powerful than human foresight or human prudence appeared to avert the calamities and dangers with which I and my companions were so frequently threatened."

He returned home in 1833 and wrote, "Two Expeditions into the interior of Southern Australia," which influenced Wakefield and colonisation. He then went with his wife Charlotte to N.S.W. and received a large estate at Mittagong for helping to establish Adelaide, whereas he failed to find an inland sea during a major expedition to the interior in 1844, and was in fact marooned at a waterhole for six months. He was then appointed colonial secretary but retired to Cheltenham in 1853.

Herbert Hugh Muirhead was born at 3 Oriental Place, Brighton on 10 December 1850 and was initially educated by his parents, but went to Eton College at the same time as A.G. Bonsor in 1865. He attended the R.M.A., Woolwich as a gentleman cadet then became a lieutenant in the Engineers with Cotter and Goodwyn on 2 August 1871.

Initially he was stationed at the S.M.E. Chatham in 1871-73, and through school connections played in the first Cup Final, but was soon posted to Curragh and Cork Harbour in 1873-75. He spent a short time back in Chatham but was then stationed in Bermuda and went to Gibraltar in 1878. He was present at the latter with both Bogle and Cotter, and was described as a single officer and C. of E. residing at Engineer's Lane.

Returning home on 1 June 1881 he spent six months at the Royal Military College, Aldershot then was a captain at Curragh from 1881-83. Thereafter he spent ten years at the Royal Arsenal, Woolwich, and was an assistant of building in the ordnance factory, becoming a major in 1889; although he was briefly posted to Waltham Abbey. [13]

---

[13] Royal Arsenal F.C. was founded at the Dial Square workshop of the Woolwich Arsenal in 1886. They became Woolwich Arsenal F.C. in 1891.

There was then a significant posting to Esquimalt, Canada at the southern tip of Vancouver Island, some ten miles from Victoria. This was one of the best natural harbours in the Pacific and was a colony from 1849, whilst the Royal Engineers constructed roads and defences in the area.

A hospital was built there during the Crimea and gold was discovered in 1858-63, thus many of the Engineers became settlers, whilst the Admiralty moved the Pacific Fleet from Valparaiso, Chile in 1865 and new defences were built in 1887. Major Muirhead was a lieutenant colonel employed on special duties regarding the defence works from 1893-98. [14]

He was then at Pembroke Docks until his retirement in 1902, but died of pneumonia at 32 Seymour Street, Marylebone on 4 March 1904. A plaque to Edward Lear appears on the adjacent property (No. 30), and nearby is Old Quebec Street; whilst Muirhead has a memorial at Great Haseley with a distinctive Greek inscription upon it.

ADAM BOGLE

John the son of Adam Bogle and Janet Lamey was born in Glasgow on 29 December 1808, and became a prominent merchant in the city. He traded as Bogle, Alexander & Co. at 30 Gordon Street (opposite the main station) in 1834-35, although his postal address was at 100 Queen Street and his mother resided at 169 West George Street that year.

Meanwhile, he became aware of profitable trading opportunities in the antipodes and travelled to Van Diemen's Land (Tasmania) on business, or perhaps to start a new life, in the late 1830s. [15]

He was not the only one with such aspirations and the Du Terreau family were already settled there. The latter were of French Huguenot extraction and initially lived around Soho and Westminster in the 18th century. They almost certainly worked as watchmakers, and were partners with a family who had auspicious timekeeping connections.

---

[14] The Royal Navy abandoned the Esquimalt site in 1905, and it was then home to the Canadian Pacific Fleet from 1910.

[15] Robert Hobart sent Captain David Collins to the Port Phillip region south of Melbourne in 1803, due to concerns about the French. However, the settlement failed and settlers and convicts moved to Van Diemen's Land in May 1804.

Hobart Town was established on Sullivan's Cove and became profitable thus they exported to Sydney by 1817. Mansions were built near Queen's Domain and a botanical gardens established, whilst Battery Point gave protection from 1818. In fact, Port Phillip and Melbourne were not settled until 1834-35.

François Perigal lived at Hungerford Market and was a watchmaker at the Royal Exchange in c.1741, then master of the clockmakers by 1756. He moved to Twickenham and his son Francis continued in the trade.

Another Francis Perigal married Mary Du Terreau (1746) at St. Martin in the Fields in 1765, and was a watchmaker to King George III at 57 New Bond Street from 1770-94, then traded as Perigal & Duterreau from 1794. The latter company were also watchmakers to the king, and his son was likewise the master of the clockmakers in 1806.

A brother John Perigal was head of the third branch and married Jane Grellier at St. James's, Piccadilly in 1780, then had four children including Elizabeth (1782). He was a watchmaker and goldsmith at 11-12 Coventry Street and at 55 Princes (Wardour) Street, Soho from 1807-11.

In fact, Jacques Du Terreau and his wife Mary had six children including Benjamin and Mary in the years 1741-55. Their son resided in Soho and Marylebone, whilst a grandson Benjamin (1767) worked as a watchmaker with the Perigals, and became an engraver of some note.

However, this was not his only work and he was an insurance broker at Lloyd's Coffee House in 1807-09; whilst he married Elizabeth Perigal by licence at St. Martin in the Fields on 7 May 1811 - the witnesses being J. Perigal, Mary Perigal, and Sarah Moon. [16]

Benjamin Du Terreau an insurance broker lived at 9 Buckingham Street, Charing Cross near to the Adelphi (Adam) and Hungerford Market (Peto), and a daughter Jane Sarah was born there and baptized at St. Martin in the Fields on 9 January 1813. In fact, the Embankment was yet to be built, and a water-gate with landing place was situated at the end of the street.

There was then a complete change of direction and the fates were decided when Benjamin immigrated to Hobart to work as an engraver in 1832. Soon after there was a new connection and John Bogle married Sarah Deutereau [sic] at St. Andrew's (Presbyterian), Hobart on 8 February 1838.

Their daughter Jane was born later that year, but the couple returned to Glasgow, and Bogle, Alexander & Co. traded as merchants at 21 Renfield Street, just north of Buchanan Street. In addition, the *Cornwall Chronicle* in Tasmania announced: "Mrs. John Bogle of Glasgow, a son, husband in firm at Hobart of Kerr, Alexander & Co."

Meanwhile, Benjamin Du Terreau became a colonial artist and his work "The Conciliation" was produced in 1840. It showed George A. Robinson posing with some Aborigines in a mood of friendship and peace.

---

[16] Edward Lloyd established a coffee house at Tower Street in 1687, and dealings took place at the Royal Exchange. It was a base for marine underwriters, whereas 79 brokers subscribed £100 to form Lloyd's Society (of insurers) in 1771.

This is now considered to be the first Australian painting, otherwise the *National Picture*, and helped to perpetuate a lie about the treatment of the native peoples. In fact, Robinson who was "Protector of the Aborigines" was responsible for their forced eviction and betrayal.

John and Jane Sarah Bogle had daughters Janet and Mary in Glasgow, whilst Bogle, Kerr & Co. advertised in Tasmania as late as 1843. However, such connections soon ended and they lived at 19 Woodside Crescent near the university and traded at 11 Moore Place, West George Street; whereas two sons were born: John Du Terreau (1845) and Adam (1848).

Due to considerable financial success John Bogle moved to "Woodside," Braddon's Row, Tormoham (Torquay) in 1850 and had a son Benjamin (*infant*) and daughter Anne, then retired and lived off his dividends. At his death in 1879 his estate was worth £70,000, and today the site is occupied by Woodside Drive situated on Braddon's Hill Road.

John Du Terreau Bogle attended Harrow from 1860-61 and excelled at shooting, then was a lieutenant at Chatham in 1866. He married Blanche Eleanora B. Savile (a twin) whose family lived at Cleveland House, Dawlish in 1869, and a sum of £11,000 was settled on their marriage.

Bogle was sent to Portsmouth in 1870-71 and then to Paget, Bermuda but was at York Town near Sandhurst and its military college in 1874, and at Shorncliffe in Kent from 1876. As a captain he was assistant instructor in surveying at the S.M.E., Chatham in 1879-83, and resided at 1 Gillingham House near to both Church and Christmas Streets.

He commanded the 20th Company Engineers in Bermuda in 1883-84 and was an instructor in surveying at 2 Staff Quarters, Brompton Barracks from 1885, but was posted to Mauritius in 1889-93. Thereafter he was promoted to lieutenant colonel and commanded at Weymouth in 1894, whilst residing at Aberdeen House, The Esplanade. He also held a similar position in the Straits Settlements, Singapore in 1895-97, but then retired after 32 years of service and like many other soldiers resided in Bath.

It is unclear what happened to his wife Blanche however he lived at 30 Ouseley Road, Wandsworth in 1915. Indeed, he banked with Cox & Co. at Charing Cross and left all his money to Madam Emmy Wisnowska (shades of Edith Wharton), whilst his father's gold watch by Abraham L. Breguet and his microscope went to his sons, and he died in 1917.

His brother Adam was born in Glasgow on 21 June 1848 then spent his childhood in Torquay, and went to Harrow in 1862-65. After attending Woolwich he entered the Royal Engineers as a lieutenant on 15 July 1868 and was at the S.M.E., Chatham until 1870, no doubt playing football with Marindin and the others at this time.

He had a temporary posting to Cork the following year and was stationed at the Royal Arsenal, Woolwich in 1871-74, but then rejoined the soccer team at Chatham and appeared in the first Cup Final.

Like Muirhead and Rich this was his only major game, thus players so important in terms of soccer history only received a brief stage. He followed his brother to Bermuda in 1874 and was at Line Wall, Gibraltar in 1876-79, and a stone tablet on a building in Secretary's Lane backing onto Line Wall Road, states: "Offrs Barracks No XVI."

Bogle then spent a year at Curragh in Ireland, but became a captain and commanded the 37th Company of Engineers at the S.M.E., Chatham in 1880 and the 25th Company at the Staff Quarters, Aldershot in 1881.

He was appointed instructor in fortifications at the Royal Military College, Sandhurst on 1 February 1882, and married Ethel Glossop at St. Matthias, Ilsham near Babbacombe on 20 July that year. Her father John J. Glossop was a J.P. of the Royal Fusiliers and lived at "Lunesdale," Torquay.

Bogle stayed in Sandhurst and was promoted to major in 1887 then was briefly in Jamaica in 1890, but spent his last two years at Dover and retired after 23 years with a pension of £250 p.a. He died at "Collyers," Petersfield on 3 March 1915 and left his house, carriage, and yacht to his wife, whilst a marriage settlement went to his nieces and nephews. His estate was worth £24,707 and his wife Ethel died at Bramshott Chase in 1945.

CHAPTER 8

Gibraltar Connections

The Royal Engineers lost the Final of 1872 but there were extenuating circumstances. Creswell one of their best players broke his collarbone ten minutes in and could do little thereafter, indeed, "Too much praise cannot be accorded to him for the pluck he showed in maintaining his post, although completely disabled and in severe pain until the finish."

AGENT FOR THE PACKETS

Edmund Creswell was born at Funtington in Sussex in 1776, and married Susannah Drawbridge (of Heathfield) at St. Mary Aldermary in 1802. They then lived in the small parish of Kingston near Lewes in the shadow of the South Downs. Most of the village was situated along The Street and the father was a corn merchant, but he may have had duties in the post office since the latter building was also a granary store.

The couple had several children and Edmund became a yeoman at nearby Falmer in 1818, whilst the regular postal service from Brighton to Lewes ran past the village. Such associations may have led to his appointment as Agent for the Packets in Gibraltar in November 1822. [1]

---

[1] The Moors settled in Gibraltar in 711 and the name came from Gibel Tarik or Tarik's Hill. They built a castle above the town and only lost control to Spain in 1462, while the British came in 1704 and cemented sovereignty with the Treaty of Utrecht in 1713. The Moorish town was demolished in 1731 and replaced by the Casemates, which connected with Landport Gate - the only land entrance.

The Company of Artificers was formed there after a Royal Warrant on 6 March 1772, and dug long tunnels into the limestone rocks above the town with gun openings. There were several sieges including the "Great Siege" in 1779-83.

As a result the Corps of Military Artificers were formed at Woolwich, Chatham, Portsmouth, Gosport, Plymouth, and Channel Islands in 1787, plus Gibraltar in 1797; with units in Malta, Nova Scotia, and the West Indies from 1800.

Gibraltar had two units in 1806 and three in 1811, while the S.M.E., Chatham was founded in 1812 and the Corps was the Royal Sappers and Miners in 1813. After Napoleon's defeat there were 12 companies at Woolwich (3), Chatham, Gibraltar, Corfu, Bermuda, Halifax, Cape (and Mauritius), and three for surveying. This increased to 22 in 1849, whereas the Royal Sappers & Miners were joined to the Royal Engineer (officers) in 1856.

By the time of his appointment the volatile situation with regard to Spain had settled down, and Gibraltar then became an important centre of trade due to its pivotal position in the 19th century. Indeed, the Fortress Felipe V which protected the Spanish side was demolished at the end of hostilities, and the town of La Linea eventually replaced it.

The walled town of Gibraltar was established along Main Street below the rock, and had several gateways with a harbour on the Bay of Algeciras. It had two places of worship viz. King's Chapel (1704) near the Governor's Residence and Holy Trinity Cathedral (1838) built in the Moorish style - in fact the former was used by the army and the latter by the townsfolk.

John L. Cowell a merchant of the garrison married Harriet eldest daughter of Edmund Creswell in 1823, but there was an epidemic of yellow fever in 1828 and two daughters died, whilst the father Edmund died in 1831. All of them were buried at Sandpits (Withams) Cemetery near to Rosia Road.

His son Edmund (1813) was educated in England and became a clerk in the Ordnance Dept. and Military Secretary's Office in Gibraltar in 1830-31. However, he then took over his father's role at a salary of £50 p.a. and was basically the postmaster but under a different name, whereas there was an overland post via the colonial secretary.

The family had important connections but in particular to William Carver who was a farmer at Ingarsby (a deserted village) near Hungarton, Leicester. The latter's sons were merchants in Manchester and established some vital links to both Alexandria and Gibraltar.

In fact, his brother John was a merchant at Waterport Street, Gibraltar by 1823, and William Carver (1813) junior married Emma Louisa Drinkwater at Holy Trinity in 1842, and his brother John Carver (1814) junior and his wife Ann Rickards joined them just two years later.

Meanwhile, Thomas Creswell a brother of Edmund and a merchant of Gibraltar married their sister Martha Carver (1818) at Hungarton in 1844, and several of the witnesses travelled there from the colony.

Initially, the couple went to the Philippines and a daughter Martha H. was born in Manila in 1849, but they settled in Lisbon and had several children including Frank Stenhouse in 1853, whilst James Fforde son of a clergyman and a civil engineer was married to their daughter Martha.

William and John Carver also had several children, some of them being born in Gibraltar, but both had moved to College Road, Whalley Range, Manchester by 1858, whereas the firm Carver Brothers & Co. traded in the city at 7 Lower Mosley Street from 1855-91.

William Carver of "Broomfield House," Halliwell Lane, Cheetham died at Heckfield, Hampshire in 1868, and has a faded memorial by the church; in fact his brother-in-law Rev. James Chataway was the minister. Meanwhile, Frederick Carver (son of John) was a merchant of Knutsford and married Isabella Maclaren a relative of Campbell-Bannerman (P.M.).

Benjamin Carver (1823) senior was born at Old Ingarsby and married Emily Frost at Manchester Cathedral in 1854, then went to Gibraltar as a merchant. He resided at "Polefield House," Prestwich by 1881 and worked in the family firm with a telegram address "Atlantic Manchester," but died there in 1912 and his estate was valued at £174,894.

Benjamin Carver (1834) junior the son of Robert of Queniborough was a cousin and was the last member to go to Gibraltar in the 1860s. Indeed, he married Emily Leonora Jane Power at Holy Trinity in 1864 and this caused a degree of confusion regarding the records.

The latter lived adjacent to the Cowells and at Library House, 6 Library Ramp from 1894-1907. In fact, he was connected to Holy Trinity for many years and has a gold-plated plaque with red and black lettering, whilst he was buried at North Front Cemetery situated towards La Linea.

Edmund Drinkwater Carver (1843) the son of William and Emma became a merchant in Alexandria and married Louisa Moberly Bell at Widcombe, Bath in 1866. Significantly, Rev. James Chataway and G.E. Tate (vicar of the parish) performed the ceremony. [2]

Meanwhile, Frank S. Creswell a merchant of Alexandria married Emily Scholes at Heckfield and resided at "Crumpsall," 17 Darlaston Road, in the leafy suburbs of Wimbledon, by 1887.

Indeed, several of the family followed him there and Emma L. Carver the widow of William lived at 2-4 Thornton Hill, Wimbledon and "Redstone," 1 Edge Hill, just around the corner from Darlaston Road, in 1887-99. The third family member to arrive was her son Edmund D. Carver who resided in a substantial property "Ingarsby," Edge Hill (formerly Charlton House) from 1890-1909.

---

[2] Thomas Bell (j) was the son of Thomas Bell and Elizabeth Moberly who married at Marylebone in 1789. His mother had links to St. Petersburg, George Moberly the headmaster of Winchester, and Rev. Henry E. Moberly of Heckfield.

He became a merchant in Alexandria and married Hester Dodd, whereas he had children Louisa M. (1843) and Charles Frederic M. (1847). Rev. James Chataway, meanwhile, married Elizabeth Ann Drinkwater (sister of Emma) at Holy Trinity in 1851 and was the vicar of Wartling, Heckfield, and Rotherwick.

Of his sons James Vincent and Thomas Drinkwater owned a sugar mill and newspaper at Mackay, Queensland, while his daughter Ethel married Charles F.M. Bell in 1875. The latter was foreign correspondent for the *Times* and managing director in London from 1890-1911.

This was one of three large houses namely Ivyhurst (21), Ingarsby (29), and Donhead Lodge (33) built opposite Brackenbury's School in c.1867, which was of great significance regarding the later story. [3]

In fact, Edmund continued to work as a merchant in the city and died at Buenos Aires, Argentina on 26 March 1909, his estate valued at £113,022. His wife Louisa Moberly Carver was at "Ingarsby" until 1926.

Regarding his brothers, Henry Clifton Carver worked as an engineer and married Mary Coates at Crumpsall in 1869. He lived at Birkenhead, Wales, and Wilmslow and traded as "Coates & Carver," but died at Bilbao, Spain in 1893. Charles William Carver was a cotton broker and Egyptian merchant of West Derby and Liverpool and married his cousin Mary Creswell Carver (daughter of John). Thomas Gilbert Carver attended Forest School and was a barrister in Liverpool until 1890, and then at Temple in London.

Meanwhile, Edmund Creswell and his brother Charles James spent their whole lives in Gibraltar, and Edmund in particular had a vital role in the community as Agent for the Packets.

He put regular adverts in the *Gibraltar Chronicle* for "The Packet Office" with times of the 'last post' regarding the packet ships, whilst he married Mary Margaret Ward Fraser in late 1844, and the couple arrived in Gibraltar on the "Royal George" from Marseille on 9 January 1845. [4]

The Creswells lived at Hargraves Parade between Town Range and Prince Edward's Gate in 1849, and had a family of thirteen including Margaret S. (1847), Edmund William (1849), William Rooke (1852), Mary C.E. (1857), John Edwards (1864), and Frederick Hugh Page (1866).

Edmund Creswell was honorary secretary of the Public School in 1838 and treasurer of the Garrison Library in 1853; indeed he held both positions until he died and the former passed to Benjamin Carver junior. Meanwhile some heroics actions were soon to be performed.

---

[3] Mary Arnold granddaughter of the headmaster of Rugby ran a school for young ladies at Donhead Lodge in 1880-1902. Meanwhile, John Matthew Brackenbury (1816-95) was a founder of Marlborough College in 1843, and ran Nelson House School as a military academy in Wimbledon High Street from 1849.

This became Brackenbury's by 1852 and prepared students for army exams at Sandhurst and Woolwich, whilst it moved to a new building designed by Samuel Teulon at Edge Hill in 1859. Land from the college was used to build Lower Edge Hill and Darlaston Road, but Brackenbury departed in 1882 and it closed in 1887. Wimbledon (Jesuit) College was started there in 1892.

[4] Mary M.W. the daughter of William Fraser (of Balmain) chaplain in the E.I.C.S. was born at Futtehpoor, north of Calcutta, in 1826. Her mother died soon after and her father remarried Mary Way then was vicar of North Waltham.

A heavy squall struck the Bay of Algeciras on 15 February 1854 at 7 a.m. and the guard-boat of the "Samarang" was overturned. The crew clung to the keel and shouted for help, thus Creswell hastened to the Ragged Staff Gates and jumped into a boat (calling for volunteers), then rowed to them. Four men were eventually saved and a report appeared in the paper, whilst much of the town was damaged by the ferocity of the hurricane.

The two postal services were amalgamated in 1857 and Edmund was made deputy-postmaster general, whereas a new post office was built at 7 Main Street (104) in 1858. As a result the family moved there, and the father was editor of the *Gibraltar Chronicle* from 1862-70.

During this time he reported on a case at Saffi, Morocco and brought the plight of the Jews to the government, leading to the mission of Sir Moses Montefiore to the Sultan with some beneficial results.

He was appointed surveyor of post offices in the Mediterranean in 1867 viz. Malta, Alexandria, Cairo, Constantinople, and Smyrna (Izmir), and lived at 7 Main Street with seventeen other people including eight of his children, Anne Fraser (an aunt), and four servants.

However, he had a severe setback when he was bitten by a barbary donkey in 1869, and suffered a severe hand injury with four amputations. Despite this he became superintendent of the Gibraltar Government Telegraph in 1871, at a salary of £800 p.a., and was a representative of the International Postal Congress with suggestions to the delegates in Spain and Switzerland. His health then deteriorated and he died at 7 Main Street in August 1877 and was buried at North Front Cemetery.

Margaret S. Creswell took over her father's duties at £500 p.a. and lived at the post office with her mother and brother Henry a merchant in 1890, but it was rebuilt the next year and ceased to be a family home. The women then resided at 6 South Barrack Road, while Charles James Creswell (1817) and his wife lived at No. 18 which was later a sub-post office.

Mary M.W. Creswell died at Campamento near La Linea on 31 July 1892, whereas Margaret remained at 6 South Barrack Road above Rosia Bay, and was awarded the I.S.O. She retired to 56 Main Street in Campamento, but due to the Spanish Civil War died at Rosia Steps in 1936. [5]

There is a memorial in North Front Cemetery to Thomas Drinkwater and members of his family viz. Henry Clifton Carver a grandson, and Emma Louisa eldest daughter and wife of William Carver of Manchester.

---

[5] Campamento on the Bay of Algeciras faces Gibraltar and was a popular summer retreat, and some old villas survive on the main street. The "Calle El Polo" leads to an open space, the site of the Polo Club, whilst Rosia Bay was a fortified battery and an anchorage for the "Victory" after Trafalgar.

EDMUND WILLIAM CRESWELL

The eldest son was born at Hargraves Parade, Gibraltar on 7 November 1849 and was baptized at Holy Trinity. In fact, he was a British subject and received his education at Bruce Castle School (with its postal connections), and also at Brackenbury's, Wimbledon in the mid-1860s. [6]

He attended the R.M.A., Woolwich in 1868 and became a lieutenant in the Royal Engineers on 8 January 1870, then was at the S.M.E., Chatham until August 1872 and was appointed secretary of the football team. He played in the first Cup Final and appeared for the Engineers at cricket, whilst he may have visited his relations during this time.

After some leave in late 1872 he worked on a major canal/government irrigation scheme in India, and was appointed assistant engineer 2nd grade. Indeed, he married a relative Emma Mary Carver (daughter of William) at Christchurch, Byculla near Bombay on 30 January 1875, the minister being Rev. A. Selehampton. The couple then resided in the Aligarh region to the south east of Delhi, and Emma made a will where she signed over dividends from her father (and his will) to her husband.

Creswell was assistant engineer at Kasganj east of Aligarh on the Ganges plain in 1875-79, and had children: Mary Drinkwater and Edmund Fraser, then was promoted to 1st grade on the Lower Ganges Canal, but sailed to Gibraltar in 1880 and a daughter Margaret E. was born there.

He was posted to the S.M.E., Chatham, but was a boarder in Bedford in 1881 and his family were at four locations - his wife with Hugh Mitchell in Enfield (see below), his two daughters at Mottingham with grandmother Emma Carver, and his son in Gibraltar with the Creswell family.

The father then joined the Ordnance Survey in 1881-88, and was a captain in Derby and Southampton having three children at the time. He also made several county cricket appearances but these were not first class.

He was stationed at Wynberg, Cape Colony near Cape Town in 1888-92 and a daughter Alison was born; whilst Mary was a scholar at Donhead Lodge, Wimbledon, and Edmund was at Wellington College, staying with his uncle Henry Clifton Carver at Wilmslow during the holidays.

---

[6] The Hill family were reformers in Birmingham, and started Bruce Castle School in a Tottenham manor house in 1827. They had a liberal system of education, whilst Rowland Hill reformed the postal service being secretary to the Postmaster General in 1846-64. His brother Edwin was a master and supervisor of stamps, and Arthur was headmaster - followed by his son in 1868-77. William Glasgow Cowell a cousin of the Creswells was a pupil there in 1861.

Indeed, the father remained itinerant and was in Liverpool in 1892 and Shoeburyness, Essex in 1894, where his last child John was born. He was promoted to lieutenant colonel and then received an ill-fated posting to the Military Works Department, Meerut, near to Delhi, in 1897-98.

In fact, his wife Emma Mary died at Mussoorie in the Punjab on 11 May 1899 (just before her mother). Despite this he continued in India, until his retirement after thirty years of service on 12 August 1900. Initially, he lived at "Spencer House," River Hill, Cobham, with five of his children, and for a time utilized his army training to work at the Land Registry.

He also stayed at 31 Cavendish Square and married Isabel Agnes daughter of Justin Vulliamy (a merchant) of "Hawksview," Cobham, at All Souls, Marylebone on 19 October 1907. They then resided in the village and just one child was born, Michael Justin on 21 September 1909. [7]

Meanwhile, daughter Agnes Cicely was married to her 2nd cousin Francis Creswell Fforde in 1907, and Ruth Leslie to Frank Eustace G. Talbot in 1909. The latter, a colonel in the 14th Sikhs, was a relative of the Earls of Shrewsbury, Dukes of Beaufort, and the Ponsonby family (see later).

During the war the father joined the Ordnance Survey and was in Ireland and Shrewsbury, whilst Alison married her cousin Edmund Clifton Carver (son of Henry) in 1915. The family then moved to "Copse Hill," Ewhurst in 1918, not far from Compton the residence of G.F. Watts - whose original benefactor was Charles Hilditch Rickards a Manchester paper manufacturer and brother- in-law of John Carver junior.

Edmund William Creswell died at Copse Hill on 1 May 1931, whilst of his sons Edmund F. (R.A.) married Ann Rickards Harrison daughter of Charles Carver, and Sir Michael Justin Creswell was the Ambassador to Finland, Yugoslavia, and Argentina from 1954-69.

Meanwhile, William Rooke Creswell (1852) joined the Royal Navy and had official thanks for his actions in the Laroot River in 1873. He immigrated with another brother to be a farmer in Queensland, but became 'Father of the Australian Navy' in 1885 and lived at Silvan, Victoria.

---

[7] François Justin Vulliamy a Huguenot was a watchmaker and his son Benjamin (1747) was clockmaker to George III. A grandson Benjamin Lewis (1780) joined his father at Pall Mall and was master of the clockmakers in the 1820s and worked for George IV, William IV, and Victoria. Barry approached him regarding the clock for Westminster but instead chose the design of Edward J. Dent.

A brother Justin Theodore (1787) moved to Nonancourt, Eure, France and had children including Justin (1832) and Theodore j. (1835) - then lived at Mickleham, Surrey in 1862. However, both of his sons were married in France, and Isabel Agnes the daughter of Justin was born there in 1868.

John Edwards Creswell (1864) a physician did important work on malaria &c. in Egypt, and resided at Charmouth but died at Campamento, whereas Frederic Hugh Page Creswell (1866) was engaged in mining in Venezuela, Asia Minor, Rhodesia, and Transvaal, and was a South African politician in 1910-38. Indeed, both of the latter attended Bruce Castle School.

HUGH MITCHELL

The Engineers had many connections in Gibraltar, whilst Hugh Mitchell senior was born in Scotland in c.1787 and was an ensign or 2nd lieutenant by 1803. He served with the Indian Army under the E.I.C. and joined the Royal Marines in 1820, being promoted to captain in 1826. In fact, he was married to Jessie McCaskill (21) the daughter of a colonel of the 9th Foot in c.1835, and returned to St. John's Wood soon afterwards. [8]

The area was mainly pasture until the arrival of the Grand Union Canal, but Thomas Lord brought cricket there in 1814, and the Eyre family had ambitions to build large villas in the 1820s. Meanwhile, a military barracks was established at St. John's Wood Farm.

Hugh Mitchell a major in the Madras Army lived at 17 Wellington Terrace in 1836; however a daughter Jessie Camilla was born at Cuttack on the delta just south west of Calcutta in 1839. The father became a lieutenant colonel in 1844, but then returned home and resided at "West Villa," 29 Cavendish Road (West) in St. John's Wood from 1846-51.

This was the last house in the street on the north side of Lord's Cricket Ground, and was part of the Eyre Estate. It was a substantial three-storey stucco mansion with ornate scroll work, roof cornice, and large chimneys looking out over extensive grounds. [9]

The couple had two children Mary (1845) and Hugh (3 December 1849), whilst the father was retired from the Royal Marines and the house had five servants. Indeed, he died at the Marine Barracks, Woolwich Dockyard in May 1851, but left his family amply provided for.

---

[8] Lieutenant Colonel Sir John McCaskill had two children Jessie (1813) and John Charles (1817), but died at Mudki near to Ferozepore part of the Sutlej Campaign (1st Anglo-Sikh War) on 18 December 1845, whilst the Battle of Ferozeshah was fought soon afterwards. His son had a similar rank and married Jane Agnes Smith at St. Thomas's, Ryde in 1867 then lived at Stoke near Guildford.

[9] The property remains at the end of Cavendish Avenue (3-19) and Close (21-29), in a private road part of the Eyre Estate. There are eucalyptus trees by the house which is impressive, but a new grandstand obscures the view.

His widow Jessie was possibly at 19 Devonshire Terrace, Notting Hill in 1862, but lived at 87 Kensington Gardens Square, Bayswater in 1871 with her daughter Marie and five servants. This tall property of white stucco had a grand portico entrance and cornice, but was probably speculative infill, since it was at the centre of the square (with a lawn behind) and obscured the view of the houses on either side.

Jessie Mitchell died at Beachfield Road, Sandown in 1887, whereas her daughter Jessie married William H. Wooldridge in London the next year. He was in fact a solicitor and clerk to the Isle of Wight Council for 35 years, and they resided at "St. Peter's" at Hill Street in Sandown.

Meanwhile, Hugh Mitchell junior attended Harrow from 1864-67 and was acquainted with Mr. Bowen, Betts, Crake, and Welch, and represented the shooting XI. He then went to the Royal Military Academy, Woolwich and became a lieutenant in the Royal Engineers on 8 January 1870 on the same day as Creswell and Rich, leading to some long-lasting friendships which were transferred to the soccer field.

Indeed, he was sent to the S.M.E., Chatham from 1871-72 and played in the first Cup Final in the attack, but this was his only major game. He spent the rest of the year in Aldershot and was in Bermuda in 1873-75, whilst he had a posting to Gibraltar in 1875-78. In fact Bogle, Cotter, Muirhead, and Renny-Tailyour were all in the colony in the late 1870s, whilst the Creswell family were long-term residents.

No doubt he was acquainted with the Creswells through a friendship with his colleague, and may have supported them when the father died in 1877. Indeed, whatever the series of events, he was engaged to Mary Catherine Edwards the sister of Edmund Creswell, and "ordered home" to Chatham in 1878 and thence to the R.E. Troop Depot at Aldershot.

He married his fiancé at White Notley, Essex located between Braintree and Witham on 22 August that year. In fact, William F. Fraser the vicar was her maternal uncle, and the witnesses were H.B. Rich who was stationed at Aldershot and William R. Creswell the brother of Edmund.

Mitchell was based at the Staff College, Aldershot in 1879-81 and lived at Frimley, but had moved to Fir Tree House, High Road, Enfield by 1881, and the household included Emma Mary the wife of Edmund Creswell. He also had a temporary posting to the Intelligence Department of the War Office, Horse Guards but retired as a captain on 11 March 1882.

Unlike his colleagues he only completed twelve years service, and despite a gratuity of £1,200 embarked on an entirely new occupation. He qualified as a barrister at 3 Elm Court, Temple in 1884, and initially worked on the South Wales & Chester Circuits and the Glamorganshire Sessions.

His address was 44 Hogarth Road in 1887 and 6 Douro Place, Victoria Road, Kensington in 1891-92, whilst he had five servants. The latter was a distinctive three-storey town house with portico entrance in a quiet cul-de-sac, but his wife died there of peritonitis in May 1892, and he was left with five young children to support. [10]

He then had an offer from overseas and moved to "Mount Pleasant," 7 South Barrack Road, Gibraltar in 1894. In fact, James and Martha Fforde his relatives lived there in 1891-93 and also in South Africa, Kingston, and Lurgan, whilst the Creswell family resided next door at No. 6. [11]

Hugh Mitchell was a barrister and solicitor there and in Tangier and was at Cloister Chambers, 77 Irish Town near to the junction with Cloister Ramp and Market Street. All three intersected by Line Wall Road, and Cloister Building a white-fronted property with shutters occupies the site.

He had four sons Hugh, Kenneth, Edmund, and Philip and made his will in Gibraltar in 1903, but left all of his estate to his eldest child Katharine. The money was to be used for the support of his younger children, and the will was put away in a drawer for the next thirty years.

He retired from practice in Gibraltar in 1926 aged 77 however he died at Brakpan, Pretoria on 16 August 1937. This was a gold mining centre to the east of Johannesburg, and his daughter Katharine of P.O. Box 265 Benoni or c/o the Manager, Government Gold Mining Areas Ltd., Brakpan proved his will, and retired to "Danny," Hurstpierpoint in Sussex.

Kenneth Grant Mitchell (1885) was an engineer in the Indian Service from 1909-46, and also a temporary captain in the Royal Engineers, then under secretary to the Punjab Government in 1919.

Sir Philip Euen Mitchell (1890) attended St. Paul's and Trinity, Oxford, then was in Nyasaland (Malawi) from 1912-19 and Tanganyika until 1935. He was the Governor of Uganda (1935-40), Fiji-West Pacific (1942-44), and Kenya (1944-52), but retired to Algeciras and died in Gibraltar in 1964.

---

[10] 6 Douro Place has a blue plaque: "Samuel Palmer (1805-81), artist, lived here in 1851-61." The latter did most of his work at Shoreham, Kent, whilst the property remains among several old houses at the west end of the street.

[11] Mount Pleasant a large white building occupies the site, and was previously the home of Telecom. Opposite there is a villa No. 20 dated 1891 which was recently used by the Gibraltar Broadcasting Company (G.B.C.).

CHAPTER 9

The Empire Builders

There was a definite correlation between sporting prowess and the major conflicts of the 19th century. Indeed, those who appeared on the playing fields of public schools, and at the Oval, were also involved in nearly every aspect of British history and its Empire building motives.

In fact, it was no surprise that sayings like "he had a good innings" or "it was rather a sticky wicket" were subsequently applied to the theatre of war. There have been several examples of the role of such players in the earlier chapters, and this fact is confirmed during the following dialogue.

THE CRIMEAN WAR

In general, the first soccer players came from the higher ranks of society however there was one example that went against this trend.

Edward Cotter was born as a Catholic at Youghal, Co. Cork in 1798 and came to London to work as a tailor in about 1820. He was not a wealthy man and married Isabella Wilkie by licence at St. Martin in the Fields on 9 September 1821. She was the daughter of John Wilkie of White's Alley, in the Liberty of the Rolls district near to Chancery Lane.

The couple continued to follow the Roman religion and were associated with the Sardinian Chapel, Duke Street near Lincoln's Inn Fields, and had several children baptized there, namely: John (10 August 1823), Edmund (1825), and Mary (1827). [1]

Three other children were born and they resided at Little White's Alley in 1841 with an apprentice, but the son Edmund a pawnbroker's assistant died of consumption in 1848 and they moved to 16 Dean Street, Fetter Lane. However, the mother died in 1853 and a son William in 1856, and all were buried at Chelsea All Souls Catholic Cemetery in West London.

Meanwhile, Edward a tailor lived at 16 Dean Street in 1861 with his son James a copper-plate printer, and shared their abode with Henry Dean (a tailor) and his wife Mary - three other families occupied the house.

---

[1] The Sardinian Chapel has the oldest Catholic registers in the country (dating from 1731). It was demolished during the building of Kingsway in 1904-05 and was then replaced by St. Anselm & St. Cæcilia (in Kingsway itself).

Despite such pecuniary depravation Edward was later called an esquire and after retiring from business, died at the Tailor's Benevolent Institution, Queen's Crescent, Kentish Town on 28 June 1875 aged 78.

His son John spent his early life in the confines of White's Alley and may have trained as a tailor, but enlisted with the 3rd Foot (1st Battalion) as a private soldier at London on 25 January 1840 aged 17. Indeed, their full title was the 3rd East Kent Regiment of Foot, otherwise "The Buffs."

He was initially posted to the Chatham Depot and spent the end of the year at Upnor Castle beside the Medway. The battalion then embarked for Bengal; however John was sent to Reading and was engaged in recruiting for almost four years, finally returning to Chatham in 1844.

He remained there the rest of the year and was briefly on guard duty at Sheerness, whilst the main battalion were stationed at Allahabad in India. He was also on recruiting duty in Leicester and Bradford in 1845 then spent time in Chichester, Gosport, and Winchester with a march from Bristol, and was promoted to corporal on 12 August 1846.

At this time the potato crop failed in Ireland and many troops were sent there to deal with the political and social unrest. The Irish Potato Famine lasted from 1846-50 and caused one million deaths, whereas large numbers of people immigrated to America and elsewhere.

Indeed, the 3rd Foot decamped to Dublin at the end of the year, and ironically received extra rations and 'three' hot meals on the march. They were stationed all over Ireland during the crisis including Belfast, Carrick, Limerick, Galway, and Cork, whilst Cotter was promoted to sergeant and married Joanna Gibson who was presumably also a Catholic. [2]

The 3rd Foot departed Cork on the "Athenian," a freight ship, with the 44th Regiment on 10 April 1851. Among the contingent were Colonel Sir J. Dennis, Captains Blair, Lobb, and Maude, other officers, five ladies, 290 men, 17 women and 17 children. Their destination was Malta. They sailed into Grand Harbour as the sun was rising on 2 May, with Fort Ricasoli to port and the ancient walled-town of Valletta to starboard. [3]

---

[2] The marriage could not be traced since Protestant records began in 1845, but central Catholic records did not start until 1864.

[3] The Knights of St. John (1099) arrived at Birgu, Malta in 1530 and removed to Valletta with its grid of streets, eight auberges, and main palace in 1565. Fort Ricasoli with seven bastions and 2,000 troops was added opposite to Fort St. Elmo in 1670, Napoleon arrived in 1798, and Nelson blockaded the town which became a colony in 1802. The opening of Suez increased its role, and there was a grand siege during the Second War and independence in 1964.

This was the first time that John Cotter had seen a foreign land and the 3rd Foot were initially based at Fort Ricasoli, on the south side of Grand Harbour (in mid-1851), but transferred to Fort St. Elmo at the east end of Valletta later that year. This was built in 1552 and was a notable four-pointed star situated at the end of Merchant Street.

The troops were presumably billeted in the barracks of the fort whilst the officers stayed in the city. Indeed, a son Edmond William Cotter was born in Valletta on 13 February 1852 and named after his father's two brothers. No record of the birth was found as registration had not started, and army chaplains' returns were poor; although another son George Michael was baptized at St. Dominic's on 21 November 1853. [4]

The father was then described as a colour sergeant and spent four years on the island, but there was soon a change of circumstances and he played a role in a far greater story. Much tension existed in Europe due to Russian expansion and their army was the largest in the world.

The Crimean Peninsula was annexed from the Turks in 1783, and the Russians built a formidable fortress and port at Sevastopol on the south west coast. This was the scene of a serious European conflict with many countries involved and others waiting in the wings.

It was the first major conflict of modern warfare with the introduction of the rifle, whilst it exposed the inadequacies of the British Army with its feudal hierarchy of officers.

A number of battles took place including Alma, Inkerman, and Balaklava with the infamous "Charge of the Light Brigade," whilst there were severe problems at Scutari Hospital with many soldiers dying of disease. As a result Lord Palmerston and the Whigs took control and Peto, Betts, and Brassey built a supply railway from Balaklava up to the front.

There were then three sieges at Sevastopol which was composed of Fort Malakhov and two redans, but there was stalemate with the British, French, Turks, and Sardinians being entrenched. This caused a build up of troops and the 3rd Foot arrived at Balaklava on 12 May 1855, whilst the allies prepared a decisive bombardment on 8 September.

The British had 11,000 troops and stormed the Great Redan three times but were repulsed by 7,500 Russians, whilst the French took Fort Malakhov Bastion (the main defence) and the Russians withdrew across the river, thus the allies took possession of the ruins of Sevastopol four days later.

---

[4] Valletta had just two Catholic parishes: St. Dominic's the original parish church and St. Paul's Shipwreck, a chapel for the cathedral. The Anglican pro-Cathedral (Queen Adelaide's Church) also called St. Paul's was built with Ionic columns and a Gothic spire, on the site of the Auberge d'Allemagne, in 1839-44.

This was the last major conflict of the campaign since the harsh winter was coming, and all parties had a desire to end the war. There was then some urgent letter writing and Lieutenant Colonel Maude (who led the attack on the Redan) asked that Cotter be promoted to an ensign. Due to losses, he was the only one who could keep the adjutant's department in order.

There was clearly some reticence on the part of his superiors however Viscount Hardinge finally approved his ensigncy without purchase on 24 January 1856. He then became a 2nd lieutenant (ensign) and Adjutant of the Corps, whereas the whole course of his life and that of his children were changed in this one decision.

The 3rd Foot left Balaklava on the "Adelaide" and "Imperador" on 10 May and sailed west to Corfu, making landfall six days later. Cotter lived there with his wife, son, and one servant, whilst he had a second child Francis Gibson on 12 June 1857. However, soon after the birth he left to join the 2nd Battalion who were without an adjutant, and he arrived at Limerick on 13 October that year. [5]

The bulk of the battalion sailed on "H.M.S. Vulcan," a large 6-gun troop ship bound for Valletta, on 16 April 1858. The ships complement included Lieutenant Col. Maude C.B., officers, Adjutant J. Cotter, 3 wives, 8 children, 3 servants, 546 rank and file, 30 women and 30 children. They stayed some four years and Cotter received £29 11s per quarter, paying £1 4s income duty, whilst his sons probably went to the army chapel school. [6]

---

[5] The Venetians purchased Corfu from Naples in 1402, and it became a haven for artists, scholars, and history when the Ottoman Turks ruled Greece. The French took over in 1797 but an Anglo-Turkish and Russian alliance removed them and it was a republic in the Ionian State in 1800. The French came back in 1807 and the British then ruled from 1814-64, up until the modern Greece was formed.

The Regiment consisted of soldiers returning from Holland in 1665, and was Prince George of Denmark's Regiment in 1689 and the 3rd East Kent Regiment of Foot or Buffs in 1782. The 2nd Battalion formed in 1803, disbanded 1815, and reformed at Limerick on 24 July 1857. They became the Buffs East Kent Regiment in 1881 whilst Cotter was always of "The Buffs."

[6] Two chapel-schools were built at Fort Verdala, Cospicua and Upper Barracca Gardens, Valletta by the Engineers from 1852-55. The latter was in classical style and there were also schoolrooms at Fort St. Elmo and Ricasoli. The 3rd Foot had 121 men and 21 children learning, although 21% of troops were illiterate with the R.E. 97%, R.A. 59%, and the Infantry 55% (literacy).

The school ceased in 1868 and it was used by the Methodists until 1883 then by the senior chaplain to the forces, but it closed when the troops left in 1950. It was briefly an army social club and mailroom, then a Stock Exchange in 1999.

The battalion left Malta in June 1862 and then sailed to Gibraltar where they stayed for over a year. It seems likely his wife died at this time as he had extended leave, whilst the Corps moved to Barbados in 1863-66 with some of their troops in Demerara.

They were then stationed in Belfast, Dublin, and south Britain in 1869 and Cotter headed the list of lieutenants, but he was afflicted with paralysis and retired as a captain on half-pay at Devonport on 5 January 1870.

Meanwhile, he married Mary Ann the daughter of Richard N. Martyn a brewer and gentleman at St. Stephen's, Saltash on 23 July that year. It was at this point that he described his father Edward as an "Esquire," whilst the witnesses included Alfred Crocker a surgeon major.

The couple resided at 1 Home Park Place, Saltash and had three children Harry, Isabella, and Bertram Wilkie, whilst his wife's parents lived next door and Brunel Terrace was situated nearby. John Cotter died there on 24 July 1882 aged 58 and his wife remained in the area until 1920.

His son Francis joined the Royal Marines in Plymouth in 1876 and took part in conflicts in Sudan in 1882-85, then married Rose M.A. Cartwright in 1891 - in fact her mother Rose Catherine was a sister of Alfred Crocker. He also joined the flag-ship in Australia and declined a position in Sierra Leone then retired to Johannesburg.

Harry J. Cotter was educated at Kelly College, Tavistock and joined the R.A., being on the Isazai Expedition in 1892 and in the First War, whilst Isabella K. married Sir William Wenmoth Pryn (of Saltash), a surgeon rear-admiral who wrote important medical papers. Indeed, these factors alone clearly reveal how the family were 'raised up' in society.

EDMOND WILLIAM COTTER

The eldest son was educated in both Malta and England and attended the R.M.A., Woolwich in 1869, residing there as a gentleman cadet in 1871. He then became a lieutenant (as a Catholic) and went to the S.M.E., Chatham on 1 October 1871, thus he appeared in the first Cup Final.

Soon afterwards he was involved in a more serious conflict and was sent to Cape Coast, a settlement on the Gold Coast, in November 1873.

Major General Sir G. Wolseley was in command and the Engineers built bridges and roads to aid the troop movements, whilst the 28th Company of Sappers arrived from Chatham a month later. An expeditionary force under Wolseley crossed the River Prah and headed for Kumasi, the Ashanti capital (seventy miles north), in early 1874; then camped at Eginassie and three columns attacked the stronghold at Amoaful on 31 January.

Cotter was part of the rearguard at "Amoaful" but the Ashanti outflanked them, and attacked the post at Quarman, some 2½ miles behind the main battle. He defended the position bravely with ten sappers until relieved by the rifle brigade, and as a result received a medal with clasp.

The force resumed their advance to Agemamue and the Ordah River, securing Ordahsu, then burnt Kumasi on 4 February 1874. Wolseley also took part in several other major conflicts, while Cotter and the Engineers joined the "Himalaya" on 21 March and returned to Chatham.

He then had a permanent stay in India and was an assistant engineer 2nd grade with the Sappers and Miners at Bangalore, Madras, and Nellore from November 1874. However, he returned to the Northern District and as a resident of Leamington married Jessie Tyeth daughter of Langford Frost, a captain of the 57th Regiment, at Saltash on 11 October 1876.

Having spent time in Warwick and Newcastle he was stationed at Town Range, Gibraltar in 1878, and then Britannia Road, Portsea in 1880, whilst after a brief period in Ireland he went to Roorkee, India in 1884.

He had a significant role as field engineer in the Zhob Valley expedition, and commanded the 4th Co. Bengal Sappers and Miners under General Sir O. Tanner. The valley provided a strategic link from the N.W. Frontier to Quetta, and the party were the first Europeans to explore the region. He was then in Madras in 1884-85 and was briefly at home in Chatham, but there were some further developments in Africa.

Due to the problems in Khartoum and Sudan, he was posted to Egypt on 1 April 1885 and served under Generals Lord Wolseley and Grenfell on the Nile expedition. In fact, he was station or district officer at Assouan and Shellal as part of the Nile Frontier Field Force.

He was then back in India and served with the Madras Sappers and Miners at Bangalore. The British annexed Upper Burma during the third Burma War leading to armed resistance from the Chin and Lushai tribes. Cotter helped raise the Burma Sappers and Miners and was on the Burma Field Force in 1887-88, thus he was awarded a medal with clasp.

He was then at Secunderabad and Allahabad by the Ganges and was made a major; whilst he resided at 3 Winsor Terrace, Saltash with his wife and three daughters in 1891, but was stationed in Egypt from 1892-97. He then became a lieutenant colonel and commanded the Royal Engineers at Cork until 1902, and was fully retired by 1904.

He spent some time in Yeovil and Weymouth but settled in Bournemouth and had a property "Esbekieh," 97 Cranleigh Road, Southbourne in 1930 (Esbekieh Gardens are in Cairo). He died on 23 August 1934 but his effects were only £470, and there is a memorial at East Cemetery, Boscombe.

GEORGE WILLIAM ADDISON

The cotton and wool industry brought considerable wealth to Lancashire and Yorkshire in the 18-19th centuries, with raw materials and waterpower in the Pennine valleys and a large work force. Indeed, the Addisons earned their wealth from wool and had their origins in the West Riding.

William Brook & Sons were successful wool-staplers in Meltham and the business included William, James, Joseph, and Charles, whilst they became Jonas Brook & Bros and founded a bank in Huddersfield. Indeed, the latter brother married Hannah Wilson in 1820, and they diversified at Meltham becoming manufacturers of cotton and silk from 1827-34.

George Wilson Addison was born in Halifax in 1788 and then married Elizabeth Brook (a sister) by licence at St. Luke's, Old Street on 3 January 1809 - witnesses John Addison and William Brook. Initially they had three children in Meltham but a son George was born in Chester in 1817.

Indeed, the father owned a business with Mr. Roper as a worsted spinner and wool-stapler at Bradley Mills, Bowling Gate, Bradford, in 1822-34; then traded as G.W. Addison & Sons at Hall Lane, Bowling in 1842-63 and the family resided at Hallfield. In addition, they owned the Bradford Woollen Yarn Warehouse, 15 Causeyside Street in Paisley (1844).

George Addison worked with his father and was listed at Hallfield in 1842, and as a merchant of Bradford married Jane Orr of Underwood at Paisley on 15 December 1847. The marriage had a financial motive and secured links with the prominent local firm of Orr & Co. [7]

The Addisons were yarn merchants at 14 Causeyside in 1851-52, near to Underwood Mill, but then traded solely in Bradford. In fact George resided at Chestnut Cottage, Daisy Hill near to Manningham Farm, and had two sons namely George William (1849) and Charles (1851).

He then moved to Bolton House, Calverley in 1854 and had several more children; whilst his father died at 8 Clifton Villas, Manningham in 1861 and had a deed for £10,000 with Charles Brook of Healey House and William Leigh Brook of Meltham Hall (in his will).

---

[7] Paisley was a centre for textiles and cottons, and famous for patterned shawls, whereas a wool-stapler graded the wool and sold it to the manufacturer.

The Orr family owned Underwood Cotton Mill and son John Orr was a partner. He was betrothed to Janet the daughter of his uncle William, and during a strike was shot at by four employees, but married two days later at Paisley Church and the conspirators were transported. The firm were cotton spinners - shawl makers, whilst the couple had a daughter Jane born in 1824.

The company ceased trading in 1865 and Elizabeth and her son William Brook Addison then resided at Clifton, whereas George and his family lived at 1 Catherine Place, Bath - which was a three-storey classical house at the corner of an elegant square (Goodwyn lived at No. 14).

However, George Addison a gentleman died at 2 Atlantic Terrace (West) in Weston-Super-Mare in 1874, and the family then resided at 1 Madeira Villas, Atlantic Road, overlooking the extensive bay, until 1916. This may have been "Madeira Mansions" situated at 20 Atlantic Road.

George William Addison attended Cheltenham College in 1863-66 and was in Boyne House with Renny-Tailyour, being in the school football XI. He then went to the R.M.A., Woolwich and was a lieutenant in the Royal Engineers, and was posted to the S.M.E., Chatham in 1869-71.

He was a staunch member of the Engineers football team and played as a back with Marindin, whilst he was stationed at Brighton and Newhaven in early 1872. He then played in the first Cup Final but returned to the S.M.E., Chatham the next year and joined Marindin, Merriman, and Renny-Tailyour in the 1874 Cup Final team (lost 2-0 to Oxford).

George W. Addison a lieutenant R.E. of Queen's Gate Terrace married Caroline Augusta Stevenson of Cromwell House, Cromwell Road at St. Stephen's, Kensington on 30 June 1875. This attractive church with its miniature chapter house and school-style entrance was at the southern end of Gloucester Road. [8]

He was then sent briefly to Portsmouth but joined the Torpedo Service, Malta in November, and a son George Henry was born in Valletta on 13 May 1876, and baptized at St. Paul's Anglican pro-Cathedral. The father may have lived near to Triq or Sqaq L-Inġinieri (Sappers) in the northwest corner of the city beside the Ponsonby memorial.

Afterwards he was at the P.O. Telegraph Service in Bristol and Aldershot from 1877-80, and was aide-de-camp to Major General T. Gallwey Insp. General of Fortifications at the War Office, Whitehall in late 1880.

He lived at 20 Elm Park Gardens, Fulham Road, Chelsea the next year with his wife, her parents, and their children, an austere four-storey grey house with a bay window and roof cornice. He remained at the War Office for four years and was promoted to captain and secretary at Chatham, then was at the G.P.O. Telegraphs, New Cross in 1884-85.

---

[8] George Robert Stevenson (1815) lived at Starcross, Devon and at Hawkhurst, Kent, but should not to be confused with the railway family. His children included Anna Harriet (1845) who married Henry Arthur Brassey of "Preston Hall" (see Betts), and also Caroline Augusta (1850).

However, he was assistant private secretary to the Right Hon W.H. Smith, Secretary of State for War, in 1885-86 - the latter being the founder of the famous stationers. He also had three children baptized at St. Peter's, Cranley Gardens, but returned to the G.P.O. Telegraphs, London in 1886-88 then was briefly in Weymouth and Portsmouth.

As a major he was made commander of the Telegraph Battalion, London in 1889-94, and lived at 54 Courtfield Gardens, Kensington, a white stucco house with porch opposite to St. Jude's Church. He was then a lieutenant colonel and an Inspector of Railways at the Board of Trade on 1 July 1894, his main concerns being telegraphic and electric development.

Edward Cecil Guinness, 1st Lord Iveagh contacted him when he retired in 1899, and invited him to be his personal assistant in England. He duly accepted the honour and became a director of Guinness with his old school friend and colleague Renny-Tailyour that same year.

He then worked for the company in London and no doubt contacted Lord Iveagh at Elverden Hall, although he was a non-executive consultant and had few dealings in Dublin. He stayed with them after Lord Iveagh's death in 1927, and resided at 16 Ashburn Place, Kensington (from 1901) where he died on 8 November 1937. Indeed, his obituary in the *Times* noted:

"He was a well-known and popular officer of the Corps, distinguished for his personal charm, professional ability, and skill at games. He chose to retire early and follow a civil career…. W.F.H. Stafford and C.V. Wingfield-Stratford (who won the Cup) are still living."

His funeral was at St. Jude's and those attending included the Addisons, Sir Leonard Brassey, the Earl of Iveagh, members of the Guinness Trust, Miss May Marindin, and Mrs. Pelham G. von Donop, whereas a large cross memorial was erected at Kensington Cemetery, Gunnersbury. [9]

ALFRED GEORGE GOODWYN

The Goodwyns also played a major role in British colonial development, but their original background was in the commercial world.

Indeed, Henry Goodwyn emanated from Great Massingham, Norfolk and married Frances Young in 1744, but moved to London and a daughter was baptized at St. John's Smith Square. However, it was in Deptford and the East End that the family made their considerable fortune.

---

[9] Pelham G. von Donop R.E. played for England in 1873/75 and in the 1875 Cup Final. George Henry Addison R.E. went to Wellington College and served in the Boer and the First Wars. He became a member of the I.M.E. in 1924 and was also the Engineer-in-Chief for India from 1932-36.

His son Henry Goodwyn (1745) married Elizabeth Gray at Deptford on 29 September 1766, whereas the father became a partner in the Red Lion Brewery at Lower East Smithfield on 8 November that year. [10]

Goodwyn then learned his trade in a long established concern and had his own malt-house by 1784, but soon realised the need to modernise. Boulton and Watt invented the reciprocating engine which was suitable for grinding malt, thus he visited the Soho Works and ordered an engine that could do the work of four horses. Indeed, he then wrote an important letter:

"The house must be ready by midsummer and the engine compleated [sic] for working by the end of July, therefore I entreat you Gentlemen not to lose one moment either in adjusting or prosecuting this business to a conclusion.... We flatter ourselves you will be duly sensible of the great trust and confidence we place in you respecting this business."

Boulton and Watt prepared the plans in May 1784 and the coppersmiths at the brewery were involved in the engine's construction. The season, in general, finished in June and started in August, hence the engine had to be installed in the summer and there was considerable urgency. In fact, Whitbread had also placed an order thus Goodwyn stated:

"It will be a great disappointment to me if this engine is not fixed by you before any other Brewing Trade, should it not, I acknowledge my pride and vanity will be much hurt."

The engine was running by 9 August 1784 and plans were drawn up for many other London breweries including: Whitbread (1784), Calvert (1785), Thrale (1786), and Gyfford otherwise Combe, Delafield (1787).

However, the King visited Whitbread's engine which was ten-horsepower and this was no doubt a blow to Goodwyn's "pride and vanity," whilst the problems of machinery were compounded when a serious fire devastated the works in 1788, and for a time they had to share premises.

Henry Goodwyn junior took over and worked with his partners William Skinner and Thomas Thornton at 21 Lower East Smithfield in the 1790s, by which time all of the operations had become mechanical.

His father of Maze Hill, Greenwich died in 1804 leaving an ample estate and the firm became Henry Goodwyn & Co., with Henry Hoare (banker) as a new partner. A large family were also baptized at St. Botolph's, Aldgate and they formed several significant associations.

---

[10] The Red Lion Brewery opened near to the Tower in 1492, the owners being Robert the Earl of Leicester and Sir John Parsons. His son Humphrey succeeded him and both were Lord Mayors, but they sold the brewery to Sir John Hynde Cotton of St. James's and Madingley in 1745. The latter died in 1752 and his son Sir John owned it with Marshe Dickinson (of Dunstable) also a Lord Mayor.

In particular, Mary (1767) married Samuel Enderby junior of the whaling firm, Harriet (1780) married William Barnard who built warships and East Indiamen in Deptford, and Thomas Wildman (1788) married Elizabeth Flower of a prominent family on 17 August 1809. [11]

Her father Charles was a cheesemonger and merchant at the Minories, and lived at Finsbury Square, being Lord Mayor in 1808-09; whilst her brother James became a partner in Combe & Co. in 1818 (see Bonsor). Sir Charles Flower died at Russell Square in 1834, and left large bequests including an estate at Mill Hill to his son - who then sat in Parliament.

Thomas and Elizabeth Goodwyn had six sons and a daughter baptized at St. Botolph's in 1810-26, although Alfred George was born at Mill Hill and Arthur John Bowdler at Eltham. Indeed, the Bowdler family campaigned for reform and expurgated *The Family Shakespeare*.

Henry Goodwyn & Co. operated at 21 Lower East Smithfield in 1806-24, but the father died at the latter date and his sons adopted new trades, thus a sixty-year connection with the firm was ended. [12]

Thomas ran Goodwyn & Bullock hard/soft soap-makers at Goodman's Yard in 1829-31 and resided at Bernard Street, Russell Square, Bloomsbury, but died soon after and left his wife with a young family. Charles Samuel was a starch manufacturer in Lambeth, and Elizabeth Goodwyn widow of Henry resided at Vansittart Terrace in Greenwich High Road.

Clearly the next generation were left in very good circumstances, with an inheritance from the Red Lion Brewery and £20,000 (£1 million) from Sir Charles Flower, yet they spent much of their time in India.

Of the sons, Thomas Wildman was a judge in Madras who left important papers, Henry William was a major of Milford, Hampshire, Arthur John B. worked in the Audit Office, and Julius Edmund was a general and 'Colonel of the Welsh Regiment' of Norton, Isle of Wight.

---

[11] Samuel Enderby (1720-97) of Greenwich founded a whaling firm; and his son Samuel opened up the Southern Oceans, beyond the Cape, in 1789 (after Cook), then wrote to Sir Joseph Banks and helped to establish Botany Bay. A grandson Charles operated at St. Paul's Wharf and Greenwich from 1829, and founded a colony in the Auckland Islands in 1849-53 - which led to the company's demise. Despite this they were immortalised in Hermann Melville's *Moby Dick*.

Henry William Gordon of the R.A. married Elizabeth Goodwyn Enderby at St. Alphage, Greenwich in 1817, and had three army sons including General Charles George Gordon of Khartoum, the second cousin of A.G. Goodwyn.

[12] Hoare & Co. owned the Red Lion Brewery at Lower East Smithfield for many years and the business was worth £1.6 million in July 1894. Charrington & Co. Ltd. took them over in 1933 however the company was liquidated by 1938.

Alfred George Goodwyn (1819) joined the Royal (Bengal) Engineers as a 2nd lieutenant in 1837 and was involved in the 1st Afghan War in 1839-42, including a disastrous retreat from Kabul. He then married Maria Anne daughter of Andrew Ross who resided at Meerut and Nussur.

In fact, his career was illustrious and he was at the Battle of Ferozeshah near to Ferozepore and the Sutlej River in December 1845. This was part of the 1st Sikh War (Sutlej) and for his part he received a medal, whilst he had two children and moved to Lansdowne near to Roorkee.

He also fought in the two major battles of the 2nd Sikh War (Punjab) in 1848-49. A large force engaged the Sikhs at Chillianwallah north of Lahore on 13 January 1849, but the weather was poor and the terrain incredibly difficult. Consequently the Engineers were sent ahead, under protection, to ensure that all the roads and bridges were passable.

There was intense fighting and both sides claimed victory, but the British had a more decisive win at Gujerat on 21 February 1849, and the E.I.C. secured their position in India. For his part he received a medal with two clasps and was promoted to major, while four more children were born in Roorkee in 1850-54 and he then went on leave to Ilfracombe.

Meanwhile, the Sepoy Rebellion began in Meerut in May 1857, and Delhi was taken, whilst the rebels laid siege to Lucknow thus the Europeans and native troops took shelter in the Commissioner's Residence.

Sir Henry Havelock a veteran of the Sikh Wars broke through, but also became trapped, thus Sir Colin Campbell (Lord Clyde) who had fought in many conflicts was sent from England with 5,000 troops.

He advanced from Calcutta on 9 November, while Thomas H. Kavanagh a clerk and Irish postal-worker volunteered to escape from the garrison to contact him. The latter, 6-foot tall with red-gold hair and brilliant blue eyes, risked almost certain death but reached Campbell and led the troops to the Lucknow garrison. He was one of only five civilians to receive the V.C. and has a memorial at North Front Cemetery, Gibraltar.

Major Goodwyn also received a medal with clasp for his part in the Indian Mutiny campaign - and the relief of Lucknow, and was then a lieutenant colonel stationed at Larding and Calcutta, but retired from the army as a major general in 1863. Initially, he lived at St. Stephen's Square, Bayswater near a church and garden (of that name), and made his will there in 1866, but had moved to Bath by 1869.

The family then resided at 27 Park Street not far from the Royal Crescent and the father died at Brislington House, Somerset on 11 April 1873. This asylum "for members of the nobility" was established in 1806 and had once been visited by Edward Wakefield the hospital reformer.

Alfred George Goodwyn junior was born at Roorkee on 13 March 1850 and was possibly educated in England. He attended the R.M.A., Woolwich and was a lieutenant in the Royal Engineers on 2 August 1871, then went to the S.M.E., Chatham in October of that year.

Clearly he was a good football player and appeared as a half-back in the first Cup Final, then played as a back for England at the Oval on 8 March 1873. He went to Bengal in early 1874 but died after a fall from his horse at Roorkee on 14 March, having served just 2 years 225 days.

The first cables were being laid to India and news was received at home, thus his mother administered his effects of £1,000 in December that year. His brother Henry fought in the Afghan, Egypt, and Burma Wars in the 1880s, whilst his mother and sisters moved to 14 Catherine Place in 1902-28 and the family have memorials at Locksbrook Cemetery.

WILLIAM MERRIMAN

During the 1872 Cup Final the reverse suffered would have been far more serious, "but for the extremely efficient goalkeeping of Captain Merriman." Indeed, his family have an illustrious history and are traced to Newbury, Berkshire in the early 17th century.

John Merriman was a captain in Cromwell's army, and his family were brewers at both Marlborough and Mildenhall. A great grandson Benjamin (1722) had scientific interests, whilst his brother Samuel (1731) graduated with an M.D. from Edinburgh in 1753.

He opened a practice at Queen Street, Mayfair and had fourteen children including a son William who worked with him. Indeed, he specialised as a midwife attending thousands of births, and his nephew Samuel (the son of Benjamin) also joined the practice and resided at Brook Street.

Nathaniel Merriman (1735) worked as a cheese-factor in Marlborough and had six children from 1768-80, several of them bankers and mayors in the town. One of his sons was in the E.I.C., whilst another was the Canon of Cape Town, and their descendants included John Xavier last P.M. of Cape Colony and Sir Frank Boyd who married Olive Maclaren Carver.

Meanwhile, the son John Merriman (1774) trained in London and was a member of the Royal College of Surgeons. He married Jane Hardwick at St. Mary Abbots, Kensington on 2 April 1800, the witnesses her uncle Thomas Hardwick (a physician) and James Merriman (H.E.I.C.S.).

The couple resided at Kensington Square and the practice was next to the house in Young Street, whilst Kensington Palace was nearby and Victoria grew up there with her mother the Duchess of Kent.

Indeed, John Merriman became general medical attendant to the duchess and her daughters Victoria and Sophia from 1827, whereas his sons John and James Nathaniel also trained as surgeons. Several weddings then took place at St. Mary Abbots with most of the large family in attendance.

John Merriman junior (1801) married Caroline Jones from Ross, Hereford and occupied premises with his brother on the Square and at 11-13 Young Street, whilst their father was apothecary extraordinary to Queen Victoria when she ascended to the throne in 1837.

He died in June 1839 and left all his property, gardens, and surgery to his wife, whereas his sons were also apothecaries to the queen. John Merriman junior lived at 45 Kensington Square, a two-storey town-house with cupola entrance, and the surgery was just next door at 18 Young Street.

In fact, W.M. Thackeray lived with his daughters at No. 16 from 1847 and completed *Vanity Fair* the next year. He became friends with the family, in particular with the son John Jones Merriman who was also his doctor, and in this way they were introduced to a large social circle. [13]

John Merriman retired to Bridgeman House, Teddington although he died at West Lodge, Putney in 1881, his effects £30,000. Of his sons Thomas H. Merriman (1828) a solicitor resided at the Manor House, Upper Richmond Road, Barnes, and had chambers at 3 King's Bench Walk.

Charles James Merriman (1831) had a notable army career and paved the way for his younger brother. He attended the H.E.I.C. Military College or Seminary, Addiscombe and joined the Royal Engineers at Chatham in 1850 transferring to the Bombay Engineers two years later. [14]

He served in Persia and saw action at Reshire, Bushire, and Koosh-Ab in 1856-57 and was engineer in Aden and India, then a major general in 1882. Indeed, he was also the chief engineer in Bombay sitting on the Legislative Council, and retired as a general in 1893.

The younger brother, William Merriman was born at 13 Young Street on 2 April 1838 and educated at Kensington School (a founder of the F.A.), then followed his sibling to Addiscombe College in 1854-56.

---

[13] Thackeray was acquainted with the Prinseps, Pre-Raphaelites, G.F. Watts, Julia M. Cameron, and Tennyson, whilst Leslie Stephen the publisher was married to his daughter Harriet Marian. Indeed, there was a strong connection to Freshwater on the Isle of Wight, since Ann Thackeray lived on the bay and corresponded with her friend John J. Merriman from the 1870s.

[14] Addiscombe Place, Croydon was built in 1500, but was home to the E.I.C. in 1808-63. It was replaced by Victorian villas, whilst "Ashleigh" and "India" 137-39 Addiscombe Road and a gymnasium on Havelock Road still remain.

He joined the Royal (Bombay) Engineers as a lieutenant in 1856 and was a captain by 1868, being assistant instructor in field works at the S.M.E. on 1 April 1871. Fitzroy Molyneux Henry Somerset was in charge of military discipline there, and emanated from a prestigious family. [15]

Indeed, William Merriman captain R.E. of Old Brompton was married to Emily Jane Anna Elizabeth (20) daughter of Col. Fitzroy M.H. Somerset at St. Stephen's, Kensington on 15 February 1872 (see Addison).

Boscawen T.G.H. Somerset rector of Mitchel Troy near to Raglan Castle performed the ceremony, whereas the bride was a great granddaughter of the 5th Duke of Beaufort with links to both Marindin and Kinnaird.

Captain Merriman played in the first Cup Final just a month after his marriage, then was a major on 13 March 1874 and played in the Cup Final the next day. The team included Marindin, Addison, and Renny-Tailyour but as stated they lost 2-0 to Oxford University.

Marindin became F.A. president in 1874 and Merriman followed him and was a member of the F.A. committee in 1874-77. He took charge of the soccer team and made a good challenge beating Marlow 3-0, Cambridge 5-0, Clapham Rovers 3-2, and Oxford University 1-0 in a replay.

He then captained the side in the final at the Oval on 13 March 1875 with Renny-Tailyour, Wingfield-Stratford, von Donop, and Stafford, whereas their opponents the Etonians included Bonsor, Kenyon-Slaney, Kinnaird, E. Lubbock, and C.M. Thompson and there was a 1-1 draw.

However, the replay on 16 March saw their opponents arrive late with a weakened team, thus the Engineers were generally in attack and won 2-0 to take the Cup for the only time in their history.

Merriman left the S.M.E. later that month and moved to Colchester, where his father-in-law was appointed commanding officer. He then served in the 1st Boer (Basuto) War during 1880-81, becoming a lieutenant colonel, and was made executive engineer 1st grade on the Bombay defences from 1882 (his brother Charles being the chief engineer).

---

[15] The family descended from John of Gaunt son of Edward III and had links to the Stuarts. Henry Somerset was 1st Duke of Beaufort in 1682 and the 5th Duke married Elizabeth Boscawen. His daughter Elizabeth married the V. Rev. Charles Talbot in 1796 and was grandfather of Frank E.G. Talbot (see Creswell).

His sons included Henry C. 6th Duke, Robert E.H. aide-de-camp to the King in the Peninsular, William G.H. father of Fitzroy M.H. of Chatham 1866-70 and Colchester 1876-79, Fitzroy J.H. aide-de-camp to Wellesley (Wellington) in the Peninsular and at Waterloo who married Emily Harriet Wellesley-Pole daughter of the 3rd Earl of Mornington. He was Wellington's secretary, and as Baron Raglan commanded in the Crimea and ordered the Charge of the Light Brigade.

Indeed, he remained in Bombay for a protracted time and was at the Staff H.Q. and superintending engineer for the 'West of India' defences during 1889-91. He also received the C.I.E. for his work in Bombay, Karachi, and Aden whilst he became a fellow of Bombay University.

During his time abroad he enjoyed cricket, football, hunting, shooting, rowing, and golf and was a member of the East India United Service and Byculla Clubs in Bombay. He retired in 1893 and went to live at Creffield, Colchester with his family where he died on 11 May 1917.

CHAPTER 10

F.A. Scandals

The tabloid press have made much of events at the F.A. in the modern era, in particular the antics of managers and players, both on and off the pitch. Transfer market bungs and other irregularities hit the headlines for a day or two, but are soon forgotten as the next 'important' story breaks.

In fact, two cases occurred in the early days of soccer, which out-stripped the worst of modern scenarios. However, they were not as prominent in the news, since the F.A. did not have centre stage and those concerned had left when the infamous deeds took place. Meanwhile, some later events partially redeemed each of these two situations.

JOHN FORSTER ALCOCK

The elder of the Alcock brothers was a founder of the F.A. and sat on the committee until 1866, but then departed and entered into a tumultuous marriage where the solicitors embarked on a field day.

Charles Rowse emanated from Ottery St. Mary and married Ann Saville then was a coffeehouse-keeper at 85 Crawford Street, Marylebone near to Bryanston Square. Their daughter Catherine Ruth was born in 1847, but they then removed to No. 55 and had eight lodgers, five of whom were in fact policeman (and were soon going to be needed).

Meanwhile, the family had greater aspirations and moved to Pimlico, while their daughter made a match over a cup of coffee! Indeed, John F. Alcock ship-agent of Chingford married Catherine (aged 20) of 5 Sutherland Place, by licence, at St. Gabriel's, Pimlico, on 27 August 1867. There were no family witnesses and it is likely that neither side approved.

Initially, the couple lived with her parents at 5 Sutherland Place however they had established their own residence at 2 Albert Villas, Amyand Park Road, Twickenham, by October 1868.

The road from Richmond wound into town along Church Street, passing between Lancaster Lodge and York House (see Welch), whilst Oak Lane was situated on the right and led down to 2 Albert Villas. The property was one of four semi-detached houses on the corner of Beauchamp Road, and was of grey-yellow brick with an arched doorway and two main floors, whereas a coal depot was situated to the rear. The arrangement appeared to be sound but there were severe difficulties from the start.

Catherine had apparently led an immoral life and reformed upon their marriage, but this did not last long. Indeed, the whole matter was destined for the divorce courts with several claims and counter-claims.

Initially, the wife was the aggrieved party, and she listed several incidents which occurred at 2 Albert Villas. In the first place she was assaulted and called a prostitute on 18 October 1868, whilst the couple lived there with a young domestic Kate Corbett (14) from Ireland in 1871.

Further to this Alcock assaulted his wife and knocked her down in 1872, and then again in the back kitchen and bashed her head on the ground in early 1873. There were also several humiliating incidents which took place around Twickenham, Richmond, and Kingston in 1871-73.

On one occasion he threw a dustpan and cut his cheek and he also hit her with a poker and threw bricks. He broke down the door into her bedroom and was often absent in 1871-72, including a period of three months. In fact he slept alone, blocked access to the bedroom, did not talk or provide her with conjugal rights, and finally deserted her on 10 May 1873.

Catherine then received a letter from him stating he would not return with an allowance, thus she filed a petition on 22 November claiming cruelty and desertion and asked the court for restoration of conjugal rights. However, this was in essence only the start of the matter.

Alcock employed an auctioneer on 28-29 December and sent 7 or 8 men to 2 Albert Villas and they removed all the furniture, including the bedding. Indeed, she claimed the men assaulted her, grossly insulted her, and called her "a divorced wife," then left her without fire or candle, and she was forced to procure some sheets and blankets from the neighbours.

Meanwhile, Alcock filed a petition for divorce on 18 February 1874 which was a cross suit, his main claim being a charge of adultery at Bloomsbury Street, six days earlier. In his petition he noted that she had taken to drink, was violent towards him, and sold all of the furniture after he left, then returned to her old life of prostitution in London.

Clearly the two stories were conflicting in the extreme, whereas Catherine lived at 69 New Compton Street, Soho in March 1874 and alimony was set at £3 per week in June. However, matters soon became worse and Alcock petitioned for his wife's insanity, and her mother Ann was appointed her guardian on 12 November that year.

A further affidavit was sworn on 6 February 1875 stating she should be brought to an asylum in London, her mother and solicitor to have access. Alcock was ordered to pay £3 per week to the Peckham House Asylum on 21 July, whilst the money was to be given to Catherine but at the discretion of the superintendent.

The records stated that she claimed both cruelty and connivance, but due to her intemperance was afflicted with mental disorder and placed in the asylum. In fact, her stay was only brief and she was discharged as cured, however after her release "she relapsed into her old vicious ways."

Catherine was residing with Mr. and Mrs. Wynne at No. 7 Nassau Street, Marylebone next to Middlesex Hospital, by the August, but there was an element of conspiracy in the matter. Indeed, J.F. Alcock and Ellen Wynne lodged an affidavit on 9 October 1875, to the effect that Catherine had engaged in adultery there.

This was followed by a petition on 18 October stating the details of the matter, namely that she committed adultery with two men (unknown) at her rooms in Nassau Street. In fact, the petition was served on her in the most humiliating of fashions as she walked along Cannon Street.

A High Court divorce case took place at Westminster on 27 November 1875, with an all male jury before the Right Hon. Sir James Hannen. The verdict was that adultery had taken place and there was no connivance or cruelty, thus the decree absolute was to be in six months.

Alcock had no wish to leave his wife destitute and paid 10 shillings a week for her support, whilst a report on Alcock v Alcock appeared in the *Times*. There was a bond with her brother Henry S. Rowse on 9 February 1876 which ended the matter after nine years, although the emotional scars no doubt lasted considerably longer.

It was during this period that his brother started the F.A. Cup, whereas John continued to work with his father as a shipbroker at 98 Bishopsgate Street (within), and resided at 20 Tyndale Place, Islington, situated at the north end of Upper Street, in 1881.

He lived there with his "wife" Alice (aged 25) who was born in Dalston and three servants, but he was not in fact married and was probably in no hurry to marry again - indeed divorce was quite rare during the 19th century with only 150-200 cases per year.

However, Catherine was far less fortunate and was a patient at Banstead County Lunatic Asylum at this time, being listed as C.R.A. (33) married, occupation none - and was in fact one of the many forgotten people who languished in Victorian institutions. [1]

Meanwhile, Alcock apparently had a penchant for young ladies and finally took the plunge again, although he was clearly determined not to make the same mistakes, and met someone from the higher echelons of society.

---

[1] Middlesex County had asylums at Banstead, Friern Barnet, and Wandsworth in the 19th century, whereas Ann Rowse a widow resided with her daughter Alice Haines at London Road, Hillingdon in 1881.

Indeed, John F. Alcock (45) a "bachelor" and merchant from Kensington married Augusta Lackland White (18) of Hampstead, by licence, at St. Stephen's in Hampstead on 21 April 1886. The church was on Havelock Hill and the bride was born at Middleton Cottages, Pelham Street by South Kensington Station - her mother being simply Sarah White.

In fact, the matter was not without complications, and her father's name Edward Lackland was erased on the birth certificate, and the reputed father was Edward Augustus Lamb, a barrister from Hammersmith. [2]

A son Frank Alcock was born in London in c.1886 but there is no record of the birth (under Alcock) and he was possibly illegitimate, perhaps Frank White - indeed it is unclear if John was actually the father.

The couple then had a respectable position residing at Egerton Terrace, High Street, Berkhamsted, and daughter Augusta Theodora was born there in 1888. The family had three servants, and John and his brother Arthur were brokers and ship owners at 21 Great St. Helen's in London.

There was a great contrast with his unfortunate first wife and Catherine Ruth wife of 'Alcock' (rank, profession, and address unknown) died of heart disease and bronchitis at Middlesex Co. Lunatic Asylum, Wandsworth, on 28 March 1891, aged 43, which was a sad end to the whole affair.

Meanwhile, the family moved a short distance to "Exhims," High Road, Northchurch later that year, which was an historic property situated just opposite to the local parish church of St. Mary's. [3]

J.F. Alcock & Co. were shipbrokers at 21 Great St. Helen's until 1894, and many other brokers, agents, owners, and merchants were in the building. However, the company then went in a new direction, and by the next year were "ice merchants" trading from the same address.

Alcock no doubt had shipping contacts and purchased Skjørsvik near to Kragerø, Norway from Thorsdals Iskompani, whilst the ice was shipped to England for large houses in Belgravia &c. and also country estates.

---

[2] Rev. George Augustus Lamb was the rector of Iden in Kent and married Julia Louisa Bancroft at St. Marylebone on 25 June 1806 - their son Edward was born at Iden in 1813. Her father Edward Bancroft came from Massachusetts and was a doctor and member of the Royal Society, but worked for Benjamin Franklin as an agent in London and Paris in the 1770s. He also operated under William Eden (Lord Auckland) since he paid more money.

[3] Thomas Exham owned the property in 1616 which was by the main road next to Darr's Lane. It was a two-storey red brick building with five windows across the front and a central doorway. There was a coach-house and stables to the rear, and a conservatory was built on the south side in the 19th century.

The Kragerø archipelago (with its 495 islands) was 90-miles southwest of Oslo and included the Sannidal district to the west, the town of Kragerø, and the coastal area of Skåtøy (Skaatø). It rose to prominence in the 19th century and became the sixth largest sailing-ship port in Norway, with the main industries being the export of ice and timber.

Skåtøy Island was at the centre of the archipelago, whilst Jomfruland a terminal moraine five miles long gave shelter to the area. Ships reached Kragerø along a channel between Skåtøy and the district of Løvdalen, while the latter estate had two outlying farms at Bjelkevik and Skjørsvik.

The second was built in 1650 and was above a sheltered bay where ships could moor for safety. J.C. Barth a ship owner and postmaster of Kragerø purchased Skjørsvik Farm in 1792, and added a large extension to the old farmhouse, but it was a subsistence unit during the 19th century.

This changed after Thorsdals Iskompani purchased the farm and land in the 1890s, and built stone dams to create two large lakes. The main one was called Blåbær-Tjenna (or blueberry little lake) and in winter this froze to a considerable depth, whilst a small dam also flooded a nearby field.

Local men would cut the ice blocks which were moved to the shore on wooden tracks and ramps, whilst the blocks were insulated using sawdust and transported by ship down to England.

Meanwhile, Alcock put his turbulent past behind him and a son John F. was born at "Exhims" in March 1896. The father then entered fully into local affairs and joined the parish council at its inception in 1898, being the chairman for ten years, and helped the aged poor of the parish and assisted both the church and local school.

The family had a comfortable life and went to Skjørsvik in the summer, which was an attractive coastal region with pine-covered islands and granite rock outcrops. Indeed, there are stories of an Englishman who came there, and Augusta was owner of Skjørsvik on a tax return in 1905. The family held both the farm-building and fields above, whilst Thorsdals Iskompani operated the Skjørsvik isforetn (or ice business).

Alcock supported Berkhamsted School and contested council elections in 1907, and despite losing felt no bitterness thus he proposed the winner on another occasion. Indeed, the most enduring image portrays him growing orchids in his conservatory (for which he was noted).

He died at "Exhims" on 13 March 1910 and his estate was then valued at £11,509, whilst Skjørsvik was sold soon after to Nicolay Wiborg and then to Erik Pedersen (alias Løvdalen) by 1911, whose descendants own it today. Meanwhile, Kragerø 'the pearl of coastal resorts' was popular with artists and writers, and Augusta died at Worthing in 1956.

THE BONSOR FAMILY

The second case of scandal was certainly no less dramatic and probably had more serious consequences. Indeed, A.G. Bonsor outshone his predecessor Alcock in terms of both football and philandering.

However, his family were extremely rich and influential and are traced to John Bonsor who married Eleanor Pinder at Clarborough, Nottinghamshire in 1754 and had seven children. Their son Joseph was born in 1768 and entered the profitable stationery trade in London, whilst he married Jane Hartshorne (of East Retford) at St. Martin in the Fields in 1796.

The family business was at 132 Salisbury Square behind St. Bride's and south of Fleet Street, a centre for publishing. Indeed, Dr. Samuel Johnson (1710-84) of dictionary fame lived just to the north in Gough Square.

Salisbury Square was a small oasis among narrow streets leading down to the Thames, and had unusual numbering viz. 1-19, 46-49, and 132-140. The reason for this oddity remains uncertain, whilst Bonsor's home was on the east side next to St. Bride's Passage. In fact, the business was more than lucrative and he soon purchased a small home in the country. [4]

Polesden Lacey at Great Bookham in Surrey was an estate of 341 acres, and was owned by R.B. Sheridan in the early 19th century. The latter had severe financial difficulties and pursued the politician Samuel Whitbread for £12,000. He believed he was owed the money from Drury Lane Theatre which was being rebuilt after a fire, whereas S. Whitbread, D. Kinnaird, and Lord Byron sat on the committee.

Sheridan was unsuccessful in his claim and ended up in debtors' prison and died soon after in 1816. His son Charles then put Polesden on the market, although it was generally described as "being in decay."

Bonsor purchased both the house and land at auction for £10,000 and demolished the remains of Sheridan's abode, then employed Thomas Cubitt to build a Regency home for £7,600. Large amounts were also spent on the wallpaper, furniture, and china and it was finally ready in 1824.

There was an Ionic colonnade and pediment to the south facing towards Ranmore, whereas an entrance portico of four Doric columns lay on the east side. Nearby was a walled garden and 20,000 trees were added during 1824-25, whilst further money was spent on the estate and land purchases, and the total expenditure eventually reached £47,000.

---

[4] Salisbury Square was mostly rebuilt, but No. 1 an historic town house remains. The site of No. 132 has an old white-fronted property, and a red-brick building with two wings - the latter probably being part of Bonsor's abode.

Royal Engineers Team (1872) - Back: Merriman, Ord, Marindin, Addison, Mitchell
Front: Hoskyns, Renny-Tailyour, Creswell, Goodwyn, Barker, Rich

Dubton House, Montrose
Home of the Renny-Tailyour family

Royal Engineers Memorial, Gibraltar
The Soldiers Artificers formed 1772

Gibraltar - The Creswells arrived in 1822 and ran the postal service for 90 years

Above: Bruce Castle
Near to Tottenham

Below: Brackenbury's
A military academy at Wimbledon

Edmund W. Creswell attended both in the 1860s

6 Douro Place, Kensington and Cloister Ramp, Gibraltar "Old Town"

Hugh Mitchell (1849-1937) left the army and worked as a solicitor

Valletta, Malta - John Cotter was stationed at Fort St. Elmo from 1851-55, and
E.W. Cotter was born in the city in 1852 - G.W. Addison R.E. was also sent there
and his son was baptized at St. Paul's Cathedral (in the foreground)

The Engineers Quarter - Near to the Ponsonby Memorial in northwest Valletta

"Druries" at Harrow
John and Charles Alcock
were pupils in 1855-59

"Exhims," Northchurch
The home of J.F. Alcock , with
conservatory to the left

Skjørsvik Farm (and below) - The Alcocks owned the property from 1895

Blåber Tjenna
Thorsdals Iskompani
worked on the lake

**A view towards
Kragerø** - Ice was
shipped to London
from the quayside

Polesden Lacey, Surrey - Birthplace of Alexander G. Bonsor in 1851

6 Hill Street, Berkeley Square - Home of the Bonsors in 1853-68

Sir Francis A. Marindin (1838-1900) F.A. president from 1874-90, and nine times Cup Final referee

"Craigflower," Scotland - The Colvile's residence built in the 19th century

22 Sussex Villas, Kensington
Marindin's home from 1882-96

William McGregor (1846-1911)
Founder of the League in 1888

Lord Arthur Fitzgerald Kinnaird (1847-1923)

He won five Cup Finals, and was F.A. president from 1890

Left: 35 Hyde Park Gardens - His birthplace (built by Crake)

Right: 10 St. James's Square - The residence of three P.M.s, and his home from 1892

Meanwhile, his brother-in-law Musgrave Lamb had a sailcloth factory in Reading and it was said, "They produced so much sailcloth for the Royal Navy that the Battle of Trafalgar was won in Katesgrove." Indeed, his sons Henry and Thomas worked with their uncle Joseph in London, and the family later occupied the property at Salisbury Square.

Joseph Bonsor junior was born at No. 132 on 15 August 1807, and was educated at Eton, then went to Exeter College, Oxford in 1825-29. He initially worked in the law whilst his sister Jane married Malcolm Orme in 1829, the latter being a proctor of Doctors' Commons.

The father died in 1835 and has a large memorial at St. Nicholas, Great Bookham, whereas his son Joseph married Eliza Denne Orme (17) at St. Pancras Church on 14 June 1836. Indeed, there was a large settlement of £34,760 8s 10d upon their marriage. [5]

The couple had a family of ten children and resided at 'Polsden Mansion' in 1841, whilst the father was a stationer at Salisbury Square. The house was generally rented out in 1836-47, but they then took up residence and had sons Henry Cosmo Orme (1850) and Alexander George (1851).

By this time the estate covered 670 acres, and in addition to their eight servants they employed 28 labourers. Indeed, the father was no idle country gentleman and there were soon some major changes. Firstly, he sold the business at Salisbury Square to his cousin Henry Lamb in 1852, and then sold Polesden Lacey (presumably for a large sum) in 1853. [6]

As a result the family took up residence at 6 Hill Street just to the west of Berkeley Square, which was a tall red-brick property in the Mayfair district. Meanwhile, the father invested his money into Combe, Delafield & Co. a long established brewers at Covent Garden in the heart of London.

The brewery was established at Wood Yard near to Castle Street (renamed Shelton Street) in the mid-17th century, and William Gyfford took over in 1739. He was then joined by Peter Hamond and they traded in a similar form as Gyfford & Co. until 1787.

---

[5] Alexander Orme (1760) of the E.I.C.S. was married to Hannah Mary Fortnom at Berhampur in 1789. They had three children in India but returned in 1803, and lived at 35/39 Fitzroy Square, St. Pancras designed by Robert Adam.

[6] Henry Lamb & Co. wholesale stationers traded at 132 Salisbury Square in 1852-1902, then went to 20 Tudor Street, but were part of Venables, Tyler by 1911.

Walter R. Farquhar purchased Polesden and erected a new entrance, the old one being removed to the long walk. The Greville's came in 1906 and made major changes, thus Edward VII was entertained and it was the honeymoon retreat of George VI and Queen Elizabeth. It was bequeathed to the N.T. in 1942.

Joseph Delafield had seen the advantages of steam power whilst working at Whitbread's, and with Harvey Christian Combe (M.P. and Lord Mayor), he became a partner in the newly formed Combe, Delafield & Co. that year. They immediately installed one of Watt's engines and were the sixth firm in London to take up this innovative invention.

There were several equity changes but the most significant were when Sir Charles Flower and his son James joined in 1818, and Abraham Wilday Robarts of the banking firm arrived in 1838. Indeed, the latter coincided with an enlargement of the premises across Langley Street.

Joseph Bonsor invested £80,000 into a business that was worth £400,000 and thereby owned a 16/80th share, whilst the other partners were Harvey Combe (30), William Delafield (14), John William Spicer of Esher Place (14), and John Samuel Tanqueray of Hendon (6).

Meanwhile, Hill Street bustled with life and the father (a magistrate and brewer) lived there in 1861 with his wife, ten children, and eleven servants. The next year he agreed to pay £2,200 into the joint stock per annum until 1866, and helped transform the business into a major player.

All of his sons were educated at Eton and the family moved to 10 Hill Street in 1869-71, and to 1 Belgrave Square in 1872-74. The latter property on the northeast corner, a grand stucco residence of classical proportions, was designed by George Basevi and built by Thomas Cubitt.

Joseph Bonsor died in 1873 whilst his sons Henry and Alexander were his executors. He stated that he was a partner in Combe & Co. at Castle Street, Long Acre and had a 9/37 share in the capital of £370,000 by the articles of 1866. He had given his son Henry a 1/37 share and now left him a further 6/37 to pay an annuity to his mother, whilst Alexander had the other 3/37. The entire estate was then valued at nearly £300,000.

His family were well provided for and his widow Eliza lived comfortably at 51 Eaton Place in 1876-88, and at 11 Upper Belgrave Street in 1889-1909. Indeed, she lived there with just three daughters and twelve servants (!), and they provided the model for "Upstairs Downstairs." [7]

The four sons, however, displayed a great dichotomy with regard to their future inclinations, which were polarised in the extreme.

Henry Cosmo Bonsor (1848) resided at 38/40 Belgrave Square and was a partner in Combe, Delafield from 1873. He was the main force behind the company's growth and became a director of Watney's at Pimlico, whilst he was also a director of the Bank of England in 1885 and a Conservative M.P. for Wimbledon from 1885-1900.

---

[7] Malcolm and Jane Orme lived at 7 Upper Belgrave Street; whilst Alfred Lord Tennyson resided at No. 9 (in 1881).

He purchased "Kingswood Warren," Epsom and enjoyed horse racing, whilst the partners of Combe, Delafield were: Combe (five members), John Spicer, Henry Bonsor, and Alexander Bonsor. The balance sheet of 1892 showed 12,000 shares of £100 and 80,000 5% preference shares of £10, making a total value of £2 million with £1.9 million debtors.

Indeed, it was a very healthy position and they invested £300,000 in the colonies and ten railways, mostly in England, whereas Henry negotiated a merger to form Watney, Combe & Reid in 1898. The new company was initially at Pimlico, Castle Street, and Mortlake, however Combe & Co. was liquidated in 1899 and Wood Yard was closed down in 1905. [8]

Cosmo Bonsor ran the newly formed brewery and was chairman of the S.E. Railway in 1898-1923, although his son Malcolm died whilst serving in Palestine in 1918. He was made a baronet in 1925 but died at Nice, France in 1929 and his estate was worth £717,528. Today Warren Drive, Warren Lodge, The Warren, and Bonsor Drive are situated in Tadworth.

Of his brothers, William J. Bonsor (1853) went to Eton and Christchurch, Oxford then married Annie (Daisy) Brown the daughter of a merchant. He resided in Mayfair and was a wholesale clothier and warehouseman but died in 1904 - indeed his effects were just £10,576.

The youngest brother Herbert Webb Bonsor (1855) had a chequered story and married Evelyn Sarah Moon the daughter of a rector (and baronet) at Fetcham, Surrey in 1878. He was also a maltster and moved to Worcester Park, but his wife filed a court petition against him in 1889.

She stated they lived at several locations and had three children, but that he committed adultery with a woman Harcourt and lived with her as man and wife at 4 Sisters Avenue and 31 Lavendar Sweep, Clapham Junction.

A request was made for judicial separation and custody, whilst the papers went to Mrs. Bonsor at 11 Upper Belgrave Street, but the case was struck out by 1890. Evelyn then lived at "Chessington Cottage," Cuddington with her children and servants, but there were soon further developments.

She filed a petition of abandonment in 1895, and stated her husband lived as Mr. and Mrs. Harry Brett at Helena, Montana. The cause was undefended in England and Derland E. Swinehart and Charles W. Wiley gave evidence of the adultery. The marriage was dissolved by Hon. Sir John Gorell Barnes in 1896, whereas Evelyn continued to live in Cuddington. [9]

---

[8] Some warehouses and hoists remain at Old Brewer's Yard near to Seven Dials and Covent Garden - between Neal, Shelton, Earlham, and Langley Streets.

[9] Helena was a gold town in 1864, capital in 1875, and the Northern Pacific came in 1883. Severe fires burnt the town in 1894, and it then relied on agriculture.

ALEXANDER GEORGE BONSOR

The fourth brother had an even more dramatic story, and was born at Polesden Lacey on 7 October 1851 and educated at Eton in 1865-68, then took part in four Cup Finals with his contemporaries.

He appeared for the Wanderers in the first final in 1872 and for England against Scotland at the Oval on 8 March 1873. During the game Kenyon-Slaney scored the first international goal after one minute, and Bonsor the second on ten minutes - the eventual score being 4-2 to England. [10]

The Wanderers reached the second final without playing a game on 29 March 1873, and the side included five players from the previous victory viz. A.G. Bonsor, E.E. Bowen, A.C. Thompson, R.C. Welch, and C.H.R. Wollaston. In addition, they fielded Kenyon-Slaney and Kinnaird and were a strong side thus they defeated Oxford 2-0. The game was played at Lillie Bridge, Fulham, so they could see the Boat Race in the afternoon.

Bonsor inherited shares in Combe, Delafield & Co. valued at £30,000 when his father died, but he did not play a major role in the company and enjoyed the leisurely life of a Victorian gentleman.

He played for England again at the Oval on 6 March 1875 with both C. Alcock and Wollaston, whilst the referee was Major Marindin (2-2). One week later he returned there and played for the Old Etonians against the Royal Engineers in the Cup Final on 13 March 1875.

Most of his former team-mates also appeared for the old boys and they included Kenyon-Slaney, Kinnaird, Lubbock, and C.M. Thompson, whereas the referee was Charles Alcock. During the game Bonsor scored a goal to secure a 1-1 draw, although his team lost 2-0 during the replay.

His last appearance was for the Old Etonians v the Wanderers in the final on 11 March 1876, with Kenyon-Slaney, Kinnaird, and C.M. Thompson. Again they secured a 1-1 draw although lost the replay 3-0, whereas he then departed the sports arena and took part in a far greater drama.

Bonsor lived with his family at 51 Eaton Place from 1876 and proved the will of his uncle Malcolm Orme in May 1878, but also spent some of his time abroad. As a result he met Maria Charlotte (a Belgian citizen who was born in Antwerp in 1857), and together they resided at the Grand Hotel, Charing Cross in 1881.

---

[10] William Slaney Kenyon-Slaney (1847-1908) was born in Bombay and went to Eton then joined the Grenadier Guards. He played in Cup Finals in 1873, 75, 76 and for the M.C.C., then married Mabel Selina Bridgeman and lived at Belgravia and at the family home "Hatton Grange," Shifnal, Shropshire.

He was described as a brewer whilst Maria was his "wife" (although they were never married), and with them was a lady's maid from Chichester. In fact, just six doors away were Frederick and Isabella Carver who have been discussed regarding the Creswells.

His role in the company is unclear and although he was a partner in 1888, he had retired from Combe & Delafield by 1892 and then lived off the resulting funds. Indeed, he married Jeanne Marie (24) daughter of Maurice David (of France) at the Register Office, St. George's Hanover Square, on 24 June 1893. The couple initially lived at 14 Davies Street near Berkeley Square and then at a grand property 1 The Boltons. [11]

However, there was trouble from the start, and his wife put in a petition for divorce in 1895 stating that he was continually drunk at both houses. In addition, they stayed at the Hotel Brighton, Paris in March-April 1895 and he was out all night, returned drunk and violent at 5-6 in the morning, and once grabbed her hair and pulled her out of bed.

There were more problems at 1 The Boltons in 1895 when he swore and threw various items including some spirits and a chicken. He threw water over her in bed, tore her nightdress, and pushed her against a washstand.

Further to this, he pushed her to the ground and she had to seek refuge with the servants, and when she was in bed ill he broke the door panel. He also committed adultery with Mrs. Hamilton at 1 Serpentine Road, Regent's Park, and with Mrs. D'Este at 41 Michael's Grove, Middlesex, on divers occasions during that year.

His wife then went to the Hotel Continental, Paris and corresponded via the vice-consul. She gave further evidence, whilst Bonsor's solicitors failed to lodge a response and he was ordered to pay alimony in 1896. There was a hearing before Sir John Gorell Barnes, who found in favour of his wife and the marriage was dissolved (at the same time as his brother's).

Bonsor already had a relationship with Claire (Clara) Marie Silvie Kint who was born at Ostende in 1872. Her parents had recently died and she was possibly a servant at The Boltons. Indeed, soon after the hearing they went to Vilvoorde, north of Brussels, and registered there on 14 April 1896.

Once the decree was received they married in Vilvoorde Town Hall on 27 January 1897, in front of her brother-in-law François Claredenes merchant of Brussels, two police commissioners, and the chief clerk.

---

[11] The Boltons just south of Brompton Road was a farm and market gardens until the mid-19th century. St. Mary's was built by George Godwin (the architect of St. Jude's, Courtfield Gardens) in 1850. 1 The Boltons, a semi-detached three-storey white stucco mansion with cornice and columns, was on the northeast side near to Bolton Place and Brompton Road.

Several requests came from London regarding outstanding maintenance, and they moved to Villa Digue de Mer at the corner of Lippenslaan and Sea Promenade in Knocke in April 1897. He then made his last will in London and left all of his estate solely to his second wife.

Meanwhile, Joseph Ignatius Bonomi (40) a gentleman of 35 Duke Street, St. James's married Jeanne Marie Bonsor née David (28), divorced, of 10 Bedford Avenue, St. Giles, at Westminster Register Office on 12 June 1897. Indeed, the Bonomis had considerable artistic credentials. [12]

Bonsor then moved to Dudzele (Bruges) in December of that year and was briefly at Ostende, but made a final move to 56 Rue Locquenghien in the northwest of Brussels in 1899. He died there on 17 August 1907 and was a resident whose 'domicile' was 11 Upper Belgrave Street, London.

His widow proved his will, but it was a formality since his gross estate in Britain was just £5. So what happened to the Bonsor fortune? There is no evidence in Belgium since such information is unavailable, and his widow Claire moved to Saint-Gilles near to Brussels on 31 August 1908.

THE FIRST CUP FINAL

The Engineers had a more defensive side than the Wanderers, playing with three backs as oppose to two, and were led by Marindin who later played in goal for the Old Etonians. They were favourites due to a strong run, whilst the match took place at the Oval on 16 March 1872 and was reported on in the *Sportsman Newspaper* as follows:

On Saturday the last of the matches which have taken place in the competition for the possession of the Challenge Cup, presented by the committee of the Football Association, took place at Kennington Oval. The two clubs left in to contend for the honour of holding the trophy for that year were the Wanderers and the Royal Engineers, and as the rivals on this occasion were certainly the two most powerful organisations supporting Association Rules, the excitement, not only among the partisans of the respective sides, but among the lovers of football generally, was intense.

---

[12] Joseph Bonomi of Italy came to London and had two sons. Ignatius (1787-1870) worked as an architect in Durham, and built a railway bridge for the Stockton & Darlington in 1825. Joseph (1796-1878) studied in Rome and went on expeditions to Egypt and worked with James Hali-Burton (son of builder James), exhibiting at the British Museum. He also designed the Egyptian Court at the Crystal Palace in 1853, and was curator of the Sir John Soane Museum at Lincoln's Inn in 1861. His son Joseph I. (1857-1930) was a lieutenant in the infantry.

It may here be as well to state that during the earlier heats the Royal Engineers had defeated the Hitchin Club, the Hampstead Heathens, and the Crystal Palace, all without difficulty; while on the other hand the Wanderers had only defeated the Clapham Rovers by one goal, having drawn with the Crystal Palace, and enjoyed a walk over in their tie with the Harrow Chequers. Mainly a consequence of their easy triumph over the Crystal Palace Club on the previous Saturday, the Engineers were great favourites with the public, and that the estimation in which they were held was not unjustifiable may be gathered from the fact that for a period of two years they had never been vanquished.

Moreover, the clever and effective manner in which they have always played, and still play, together, tended to produce a belief that they would be able, by better organisation and concentration, to defeat their opponents, despite the acknowledged superiority of the latter in point of individual excellence and skill. No pains, however, were spared by the Wanderers to collect their best representative eleven, and in this they succeeded admirably, as without doubt they mustered on this occasion the very best forces at their disposal, having both weight and speed forward, and certainly the two best backs in England to support the efforts of the ups.

Within a few minutes of three o'clock the ball was set in motion by the Engineers, the assemblage of spectators being very fashionable, though the numbers were hardly so large as might have been expected, owing, possibly, in some measure to an advance in the price charged for admission.

The captain of the Wanderers won the toss, and thus at the outset his side gained not only the aid of the wind, but a considerable advantage in addition in having a very powerful sun at their backs.

At once the Wanderers set to work with the greatest determination, and at the outset their play forward displayed more co-operation than is their custom, the backing-up being vastly superior to anything they have shown during the present season. By this means, and with the aid of faultless kicking on the part of their backs, they were able during the first quarter of an hour to besiege the Sappers closely, to the surprise of many of the spectators. Thus consistently they maintained the attack, till at length, after some judicious "middling" by R.W.S. Vidal, the goal of the Engineers fell to a well directed kick by A.H. Chequer.

Ends were now changed, but any expectations of an alteration in the state of affairs were unfulfilled, as without any diminution of energy the Wanderers, although now faced by wind and sun, continued to besiege the lines of the Engineers without allowing any opportunities to the forwards on the later side of effecting the rushes for which they are noted.

Not long after the above goal the ball was again driven through the posts of the military goal by C.W. Alcock, but owing to a previous breach of the handling rule by another Wanderer, the claim was rightly disallowed.

Still the game was maintained with the most remarkable animation on both sides, Renny-Tailyour, Mitchell, and Rich striving hard to pass the backs of the enemy. Once Muirhead, by an excellent run, did succeed in guiding the ball into the vicinity of the Wanderers' fortress, but A.C. Thompson interposed at the right moment, and the leather was safely removed. After this, one or two chances were offered to the Wanderers, but none were realised, although more than one would doubtless have been successful but for the extremely efficient goal-keeping of Capt. Merriman.

On one occasion a protracted bully raged on the very edge of the Engineers' lines, and once during its course the ball was absolutely driven against one of the posts; but here, too, the Wanderers failed to score. During the latter part of the game it was generally imagined that the Engineers would outstay their opponents, but until the finish the play was continued as fast as ever, and soon after half-past four o'clock time was called, the Wanderers thus gaining the privilege of holding the cup for a year by one goal. It was generally admitted that the play all round was superior to anything that has been seen at the Oval.

The Wanderers unquestionably surprised the spectators by the effectiveness of their play collectively, and certainly they have never shown to such advantage as in this contest. The Engineers played hard and well throughout, but they were outmatched in this instance, as they only on two occasions endangered the enemy's goal. It was in some measure the superiority of the backs on the side of the Wanderers that tended to produce the defeat of the Sappers, as the certainty of kicking displayed by Lubbock and Thompson throughout enabled the forwards of the victors to attack without fear.

In extenuation of the reverse suffered by the Engineers, it should be stated that one of their best players, Lieutenant Creswell, broke his collar-bone about ten minutes after the start, and too much praise cannot be accorded to him for the pluck he showed in maintaining his post, although completely disabled and in severe pain, until the finish.

Thus ended one of the most pleasant contests in which the Wanderers have ever been engaged; the posts of umpires and referee being absolutely sinecures. On behalf of the Wanderers, though all played up throughout in fine form, R.W.S. Vidal and T.C. Hooman attracted notice by their skilful dribbling.

Wanderers: C. Alcock, Bowen, Bonsor, A.H. Chequer (or Betts), Crake, Hooman, Vidal, and Wollaston (the forwards), Thompson (half-back), E. Lubbock (back), and Welch (in goal).

Engineers: Bogle, Cotter, Creswell, Mitchell, Muirhead, Renny-Tailyour, and Rich (the forwards), Goodwyn (half-back), Addison and Marindin (as backs), and Merriman (in goal).

The Wanderers had won the first Cup contest, but there were no steps to climb and it was a most gentlemanly affair. Indeed, Charles Alcock must have felt somewhat humble since he won the competition he introduced. Meanwhile, the Cup was presented at the Wanderers' annual dinner at the Pall Mall Restaurant in Charing Cross some four weeks later.

The Engineers were strong throughout the 1870s, and played 86 games from 1871-75 including 74 wins and 3 defeats, with 244 goals for and 21 against. In fact, they reached the final four times and were undefeated in the season when they won the F.A. Cup (before a crowd of 3,000), the referee being Charles Alcock.

Their last appearance was against the Wanderers in 1878 and they lost 3-1, whilst they won the Amateur Cup in 1908. Indeed, the club supported the amateur game and their captain was one of its leading advocates, thus he is discussed in detail in the following chapter.

CHAPTER 11

The Amateur Game

Pember and Morley were presidents of the F.A. during the formative years but it was Major Marindin who took over the role in 1874. He stood firm against changes to the amateur game and was a noted player and referee, who watched over and promoted the growth of the F.A. Cup.

COLVILE AND CRAIGFLOWER

It is some surprise to discover that the third F.A. president had his origins on the Continent and that one Pierre Marindin was residing at Congeveaux, Vallage de Movat, Switzerland in c.1590. His son Pierre was the governor and his grandson moved to Vevey beside Lake Geneva in 1662.

A great grandson Pierre Marindin (1701) was town councillor at the latter and with his wife Esther had four sons, however the third son Jean Philippe (1742) moved to England and anglicised his name. He lived at Hallow near to Worcester, but traded as a Birmingham merchant and married Elizabeth Rann, whilst two sons were baptized at St. Phillip's Cathedral.

Samuel Peter Marindin (1774) married Catherine Louisa the co-heiress of Samuel Webbe of Henbury, Bristol in 1805, and then resided at Edgbaston. The couple had four children there and at Henbury, but the mother died and he was then married to Elizabeth (Eliza) Iddins of Bromsgrove.

Samuel was likewise a merchant and traded at 2 Great Charles Street, near the cathedral west of Snow Hill, in 1815-23, while Mrs. Marindin resided at No. 141. He was also a partner with Mr. Abick in 1821 and had premises at Perry Barr until 1823, thus amassing a considerable fortune.

Due to such successes they moved to Worfield, Shropshire and daughter Catherine L. married William Sharington Davenport on 22 December 1835, the latter inheriting the nearby "Davenport House" in 1842. [1]

---

[1] The Sharingtons acquired Lacock at the dissolution and John Talbot a relative of the Earls of Shrewsbury married Olive Sharington. Henry Davenport of Worfield married Elizabeth daughter of Sharington Talbot in 1665, and son Henry married Mary Lucy Chardin and Barbara Ivory (a granddaughter of Sir John Talbot).

"Davenport House" passed to the descendants of his first wife, whilst "Lacock" was inherited by William Davenport (grandson of Barbara) in 1778. He changed his name to Talbot and his son William H. Fox Talbot (1800-77) was a pioneer of photography there.

Samuel Peter Marindin died at the High Street, Bridgnorth in 1839, and left his property at Chesterton near Worfield to his wife, his farming stock and crops to his son Samuel, his house at Great Charles Street to his son Henry Richard, and his Worcester Canal shares and some family pictures to his daughter Catherine Louisa Davenport.

The Marindins had a long association with Chesterton and his widow Eliza was a landed proprietor there in 1851 (she died at Leamington in 1859), whilst his son Henry joined the 1st or Royal Regiment of Foot in 1833 and retired as a major when his step-mother died. In addition, the Davenports lived just nearby and had no less than sixteen servants.

Samuel Marindin (1807) attended Shrewsbury School in 1821-25 and was likewise destined for the army. He was a cornet and sub-lieutenant in the 2nd Regiment of Life Guards (under the King) in 1831-34, but then took a new direction which was to pay substantial dividends.

He married Isabella Colvile of Beckenham, Kent on 13 March 1834 whose family had a notable double-barrelled Scottish ancestry, whilst the liaison saw the start of several associations with Jamaica and slavery. Indeed, she was descended from the Wedderburns of Inveresk. [2]

To understand the association it is necessary to consider her background. Her father Andrew was a partner in Webster, Wedderburn & Co. in 1798 and married his cousin Elizabeth, but she died at Inveresk, while he made a significant match to Louisa Mary Eden at Bromley, Kent in 1806.

Due to her father's diplomatic work the latter was born in Spain, but then resided at "Eden Farm," Beckenham, which was a classical mansion and meeting place for reformers such as Wilberforce. [3]

---

[2] John Wedderburn, 5th Baronet fought at Culloden and forfeited the baronetcy; thus his son John (1729) moved to Jamaica, and a grandson David retrieved the title. A brother James (1730) a doctor on the plantations bought Inveresk Lodge, Edinburgh in 1773 and married Isabella daughter of Andrew Blackburn and great-great niece of Robert, 3rd and last Lord Colvile of Ochiltree, Ayrshire, in 1774. The Colviles also owned Craigflower at Crombie, Fife near to Dunfermline.

A cousin John (1743) owned Spring Garden plantation then formed Webster, Wedderburn & Co. a West India House at 35 Leadenhall Street, London and lived at Clapham. James and Isabella had four sons at Inveresk: John (1776) died in Jamaica, Andrew (1779), Peter (1781) Wedderburn-Ogilvy whose grandson was a baronet, and James (1782) Wedderburn. Indeed, Isabella inherited Craigflower in 1799 and the family took the name of Wedderburn-Colvile.

[3] Her uncle Robert Eden was Governor of Maryland, whilst her father William Eden, 1st Lord Auckland, operated intelligence during the American War and was an Ambassador to Spain and the Netherlands.

As a result the couple moved to "Langley Farm," Beckenham part of the Langley Park Estate and had thirteen children, many of them baptized in the local church. Indeed, Isabella was born in 1812, whilst her father took the name Colvile in lieu of Wedderburn by Royal Licence in 1814.

There were then further changes and Andrew became senior partner in Wedderburn, Colvile & Co. when John of Clapham died in 1820, and he inherited the Craigflower estate from his mother the next year. However, there was a family secret poised to upset the whole sugar barrel!

Stories of promiscuity between master and slave in the West Indies are well-known, and James Wedderburn (1730) formed two alliances. The first was with his housekeeper Rosanna by whom he had three sons, however she was sold to Lady Douglas with all of her offspring.

Her youngest son Robert Wedderburn (1762) grew up on the lady's estate, but claimed that his father made him and his brother James 'free at birth.' Meanwhile, he saw both his mother and grandmother whipped. Indeed, he had plenty of reason to challenge his family in Britain and as a sailor came there in 1779, but shortly afterwards converted to Christianity.

Wedderburn, "the black preacher," had a chapel at Hopkins Street, Soho and campaigned against slavery, believing there was a conspiracy against the poor. He was associated with Thomas Spence and his later movement thus he was at the Spa Fields Riot in 1816. He spoke out against the "Peterloo Massacre" three years later and was sent to Newgate for libel, and after the Cato Street Conspiracy was placed in Dorchester Gaol in 1820-22.

Wilberforce visited him at this time and confirmed he had some "white blood," whereas he wrote to *Bell's Life* about slavery in 1824. In the letter he claimed he was the son of James Wedderburn of Inveresk, but Andrew his reputed brother retorted with a strong denial. The matter then blew over and after the Reform Act little more was heard of him.

Andrew Colvile of Beckenham and Craigflower made his last will in 1834 and left the estate to son James William, then to son Eden, and thereafter to his other children the co-heirs (which was a significant fact), while George Eden the 2nd Lord Auckland was one of the executors.

Meanwhile, Samuel and Isabella Marindin began married life at Worfield and had sons Henry Colvile (1834) and Eden (1836) *infant*. The father then entered the church and was rector of Buckhorn Weston, Dorset from 1837 adding the nearby parish of Penselwood, Somerset in 1845.

The family lived at Shanks House, Cucklington although their son Francis Arthur was born at Melcombe Regis near Weymouth on 1 May 1838. They then had sons Philip Samuel and George Eden, whereas Emily Colvile and six servants also resided at the property.

Rev. Marindin made his will in 1842 with his wife, Andrew Colvile, and James William Colvile of Ochiltree and Crombie as executors, whilst he had three daughters and a son Charles Randal in 1851. Indeed, four of his sons attended Eton and joined the Army and the Civil Service, thus helping to form the strong backbone of the British Empire.

However, Samuel died at Cucklington in 1852, and his wife Isabella had inherited the property at Chesterton by 1859. The latter became the family home for several decades, with many relatives sojourning there, and after Isabella died in 1896 it passed down to her three daughters. Meanwhile, the rest of the family spent much of their time in the colonies.

Henry Colvile Marindin (1834) a barrister of Lincoln's Inn and Temple practiced in Calcutta, but died in 1872. His son Arthur had an army career and resided at Fordel north of Glenfarg, Perth, whilst his granddaughter Barbara Eunice married Charles Keith Adam of Blair Adam - a relative of the architectural family which included Robert Adam.

Philip Samuel Marindin (1839) joined the Royal Engineers and worked on the Ganges Canal, but died at Euston in 1876, whilst his brother George Eden Marindin (1841) was a classics teacher at Eton from 1865-87 and then resided at Frensham, Surrey until 1939. Charles Randal Marindin (1851) was a magistrate and commander in the I.C.S. and died in 1929. [4]

---

[4] The Craigflower estate was near to Torryburn port by Torre Bay, on the north banks of the River Forth. The house was separated from cottages by a stone wall and a causeway led to the pier and bay. A track ran along the coast to Crombie Old Church, which fell into decay after the parishes were combined (1622).

Andrew Colvile was the largest landowner in the district and was also a governor of the Hudson's Bay Co. and a director of the Puget Sound Agricultural Co., thus "Craigflower Farm" was built at Maple Point on Vancouver Island in 1854.

He died in London in 1856 and was buried at Holy Trinity, Brompton, whilst his son James William Colvile a judge of the Bengal Court employed David Bryce who re-modelled Craigflower in the Scottish baronial style with towers, crenellations, gables, the family arms, and a grey-slate roof, in 1862.

Sir James William Colvile died at 8 Rutland Gate, Knightsbridge in 1880 and the estate passed to Eden Colvile who died in 1893. Alison Cunningham was born at Craigflower (1822) and nursed Robert L. Stevenson (1850-94), whilst she read him the Bible and Scottish history inspiring his writing. Her parents have a memorial at Crombie, and inside are ones to Sir James William Colvile, Eden Colvile &c.

FRANCIS ARTHUR MARINDIN

The second son took a similar course and grew up at Cucklington then was a boarder at 15th House, Keats Lane, Eton, from 1851-53. He attended the R.M.A., Woolwich and was a 2nd lieutenant in the Royal Engineers in 1854 when aged sixteen, but was promoted to 1st lieutenant and was at Chatham, Portsmouth, and Woolwich the next year.

He soon saw some "action" and was sent to Scutari in the Crimea at the height of the conflict in September 1855, and remained for nearly a year. He was then stationed at Aldershot, Chatham, and Pembroke until June 1858; however he then had a posting that would change his life.

The records show that he was stationed in Mauritius with special duties in Madagascar from 1858-64, whilst he was A.D.C. and private secretary to Sir William Stevenson, the Governor of Mauritius, in the years 1860-63. It is unclear exactly how he secured the position but there may have been some connection to the Colviles, or perhaps to the writer (R.L. Stevenson) whose family were lighthouse builders and owned a West India house.

Indeed, the Lawrence family settled in Jamaica in 1675 and had plantations at Ironshore and Running Gut (or Profitable Valley) at St. James Parish, in the northwest of the island. The brothers John and Benjamin Lawrence owned in total 10,000 acres, whilst James (1709) built Charles Square in Montego Bay and married Mary James in 1738.

The latter couple had seven children and Richard Lawrence (1745) and his descendants lived at Liverpool and Salisbury, whilst Mary Lawrence (1749) married John Robert James and had a daughter Mary Lawrence James. In addition, James Lawrence (1751) was the father of Emily who married Dr. Frederick Burt Zincke, of a local family, in 1811.

William James Stevenson was born in Jamaica in 1764 and married Mary Lawrence James at Trelawny Parish in 1795. The couple had at least seven children at Hanover, St. James, and Kingston and resided in the capital by 1814, whereas the father noted that he provided for his family by investing small sums of money and "the gift of a few Negroes." He died at Hanover Street, Kingston on 16 April 1830 and Mary Lawrence Stevenson a widow proved his will in London (then lived at Cheltenham).

Their son William Stevenson (1804) married Mary Charlotte Allwood at St. Catherine's Parish near Kingston in 1839, and had two children: Kathleen Mary (1840) and William Lawrence (1844). The father was a barrister-at-law and a judge of the Supreme Court on the prison circuit in Jamaica, but his wife Mary Charlotte died soon after their son's birth.

There was then some match-making back in England, therefore William Stevenson married Caroline Octavia daughter of Joseph Seymour Biscoe at Barnwood, Gloucester in 1852. The two returned to Jamaica and a son was born but died in infancy, while the father was made Governor of Mauritius in 1857. The island was noted for its sugar production and the capital Port Louis was a supply station for ships going to Australia.

Shortly before his arrival there was a serious outbreak of cholera, and one of his first actions was to reform quarantine and health laws. He was also moved by the plight of the indigenous poor and established an orphanage and provided some improved local schools.

The exact sequence of events is unclear but Lieutenant Marindin married Kathleen Mary Stevenson, the daughter of the governor, on 18 July 1860. Indeed, he was his secretary for the next three years, and no doubt helped implement some of these exigent reforms.

However, William Stevenson was in poor health and made a will in 1862 leaving £8,000 to his wife and £2,000 to his daughter, in addition to a settlement of a similar amount. He also left money to his son, but noted there were no children from his present marriage and made his wife, Rev. Foster B. Zincke of Wherstead, and F.A. Marindin his executors.

During that year he became a baronet and also added a codicil to his will. By then his wife was expecting a child, and the latter was to share with his other two children in the estate, whilst he made provision for his wife to return to England as soon as possible after his decease.

Indeed, Francis Seymour Stevenson was born at Moka, Mauritius in 1862, whilst the father died there on 9 January 1863 and has a memorial in the courtyard of Government House, Port Louis (just behind one to Queen Victoria). This was the end of the family's sojourn overseas, and the main players then returned to England.

In fact, Rev. Foster B. Zincke married Caroline Stevenson at St. Mary's, Bryanston Square in 1865, the witnesses W. Lawrence and F.A. Marindin. It was 'a marriage of convenience' since they lived apart and Rev. Zincke was the vicar of Wherstead, Suffolk from 1847-93, and chaplain-in-ordinary to Victoria in 1858. He was a writer who travelled to Switzerland, whilst Lady Stevenson lived at Cromwell/Ennismore Gardens, Knightsbridge, and her son owned Playford Mount - an estate near to Ipswich.

Marindin was promoted to captain in 1861 and stayed in Mauritius after his father-in-laws death, but was posted to Aldershot in 1864 and his only child Kathleen Mary Isabel was born there the next year. He was then the adjutant at Chatham from 1866, and spent a brief time at Devonport, but was brigade major at the S.M.E., Brompton Barracks from 1869-74.

He formed a bond with his fellow officers, and the discipline and team spirit used in their work was soon transferred to the sports field. Indeed, he ran the Engineers' soccer team with Merriman, and they were extremely proficient in the game and also quite competent at cricket.

Marindin resided with his wife, daughter, and three servants at Brompton Barracks in 1871, and joined the F.A. committee that year, being present when the Cup contest was initiated at the Sportsman Office.

He captained the Royal Engineers in their two Cup Final defeats in 1872 and 1874, whilst he received a promotion at the F.A. and became president at the latter date, a post which he held for sixteen years. He was then less active on the pitch, although as the president of the Old Etonians he played for them in goal and also became an important referee.

Regarding his career he spent a number of weeks at Pembroke Docks and Colchester, and was appointed to the Eastern District at Harwich in 1875. He ran the line in the fourth international England v Scotland at the Oval on 6 March 1875, but apparently declined to play in the final between the Engineers and Old Etonians on 13 March.

In general it was thought there was a conflict of interest, but he may have simply been busy with his work in Harwich. In fact, he missed the team's greatest moment as the Engineers won the Cup 2-0 in a replay.

His army role was soon reduced and he was seconded as an Inspector of Railways at the Board of Trade, like both Addison and Rich, in 1877-79. In fact, he retired with a pension of £2,000 after 24-years service, and gave an address 5 New Street, Spring Gardens (now Admiralty Arch).

He continued at the Board of Trade, namely: "To examine the permanent way, bridges, stations, and signals of *many* new railways and branch lines, and *subsequently* to hold inquiries on a number of accidents."

Major Marindin then led the F.A. through some difficult times, with the emergence of professionalism, and was held in high regard being described as, "One of the very few referees who really know all the rules."

The first northern clubs played in the Cup in 1878, but Marindin and the F.A. wanted to retain amateur status, fearing money would compromise the ideals of the founders and cause a decline in the ethics of play.

The most significant encounter was a quarter final between Darwen and the Old Etonians the next year. The Lancashire club attracted Jimmy Love and Fergie Suter from Scotland with financial incentives, and the contest was a lengthy struggle settled over three meetings at the Oval.

The inhabitants of Darwen were gripped by 'Cup Fever' and undeterred by the costs made collections to fund the trips. In fact, the expense of sending a team to London was huge, and Darwen exhausted by all the travelling lost the final encounter 6-2 (after 5-5, 2-2). The victors defeated Nottingham Forest and Clapham Rovers to win the Cup, however Darwen were accused of playing a professional game and trouble was in the air.

Marindin then refereed the final between Clapham Rovers and Oxford University in 1880; however Forest and Darwen reached the semi-final two years running and other Scottish players came to the northern clubs. The F.A. then formed a sub-committee to look into the problem in 1882.

The president himself was residing at 22 Sussex Villas, Kensington, from 1882-96, a semi-detached stucco property between Victoria Grove and Cornwall Gardens. It was in fact the last house and was built in the 1840s, whilst it had a grand entrance, large dome, and adequate gardens. [5]

Meanwhile, there was mounting pressure and Blackburn Rovers finished as runners-up to the Old Etonians by 1-0 in 1882 (the last amateur victory), but they were found guilty of paying their players. The next year Blackburn Olympic a team of plumbers and weavers won the Cup, but Accrington were expelled for a similar indiscretion.

Indeed, Preston North End were also banned after a game against Upton Park, and their manager "Major" Sudell openly defied the F.A., saying he had to pay his players to maintain the club's status.

Marindin then refereed a final between Blackburn Rovers and Queen's Park in 1884, and 'reputedly' cost the latter a famous victory by disallowing two goals for offside. In fact, Blackburn Rovers won the Cup three times from 1884-86 and the amateur days were basically over.

Amateur sides could no longer compete with such pecuniary outfits and the F.A. had to concede, thus the professional game was finally approved at Anderton's Hotel, Fleet Street in London on 20 July 1885.

Despite such changes Marindin became a prominent referee and was the official in nine Cup Final games, including those at the Oval from 1885-90 and a replay at the Racecourse Ground, Derby in 1886.

As a result he was present when Preston achieved the "double" in 1889, and the next year when Blackburn Rovers defeated Wednesday 6-1 at the Oval, in front of 20,000 spectators. However, he was an ardent supporter of the amateur game and ultimately could not adjust to professionalism, thus he resigned as president of the F.A. in 1890.

He then adopted a more serious role as Inspector of Railways, assisting the Egyptian State Railway; whilst he discovered that many employees worked long hours and submitted a report to the House of Commons leading to some essential improvements.

---

[5] Sussex Villas became Launceston Place in 1905, and the properties were later Grade II listed buildings in the *De Vere Conservation Area*.

Despite these efforts there was a serious collision at Thirsk in 1892. The signalman had worked 24 hours, and Marindin stated that companies must use technology to make such accidents impossible, unless the driver passed through fixed signals. He also advocated the use of relief signalmen and the provision of more convenient local housing.

He implemented several railway reforms and made all companies aware that: "The office at 8 Richmond Terrace, Whitehall was not likely to allow irregularities to remain long unnoticed." He also had a contact address at Craigflower in 1892, and inherited the estate from his mother Isabella (a co-heir of Andrew Colvile) in 1896.

In his work he established an electric lighting system in London, and was on the Engineer and Railway Voluntary Staff Corps from 1897, composed entirely of high officials in the railways. He was also an honorary colonel and was knighted during the Diamond Jubilee celebrations.

Sir Francis Arthur Marindin resided at 3 Hans Crescent, Knightsbridge (Exeter and New Streets) from 1897, which was an opulent city mansion behind Harrods and now an embassy. He died there on 21 April 1900 and his funeral was at Crombie with a service at Holy Trinity in Sloane Square; indeed a broken memorial can be found at the old church.

Lady Marindin then resided at 3 Sloane Court (East) near to the Royal Hospital, Chelsea, a building consisting of eleven flats, and was there until her death in 1939. Her daughter remained unmarried and significantly was described as "of Craigflower."

The house was possibly rented out and Thomas D. Boyd was resident in 1914, whilst F.G. Wailes founded Craigflower Prep School there in 1923. It became a charitable trust and the school made an appeal for funds, but was forced to close in 1979. Soon afterwards the building was listed, and more recently it was restored and converted to luxury flats.

CHAPTER 12

The Professional Era

The Football League came into existence mainly due to the efforts of one man in 1888, and was a separate organisation from the very start. Indeed, he had connections with Aston Villa and saw football as a speculative venture, like many others who were to follow him.

WILLIAM MCGREGOR

Gregor McGregor a tailor married Jean McNicol at Muthill, Perth in 1825 and a son William (the youngest of nine) was born on 27 January 1846. He promptly took up his father's profession and with his brother Peter opened a tailors and linen drapers in the city of Birmingham.

William McGregor of Albert Road, Aston married Jessie Scrimgeour of Moneydie, Perth at St. Peter & St. Paul's on 13 January 1876. The church was situated right beside the Aston Lower Grounds, a pleasure park where a number of sports and amusements took place.

Indeed, McGregor was soon drawn to football and in particular to a team called the Quilters who played on the Meadow, at the western end of the complex. Aston Villa had just been formed and also played games there, but they removed to Wellington Road, Perry Barr, and he then joined their committee and helped to promote the sport.

He worked as an umpire, district organiser, and charity worker, being "A bearded Scotsman of liberal beliefs with considerable energy and humour." He also supported the F.A. Cup but was not a player like his counterparts in the south, and stated, "'I've never taken part in active football. I tried it once when young and had to take to bed for a week!'"

William McGregor lived with his wife and two children at 301 Summer Lane, Birmingham in 1881, and was a tailor with five assistants at 306-07 Summer Lane and 131 Gooch Street. Indeed, it was from this background that he promoted the formation of a Football League.

He believed a contest was needed similar to that operating for cricket (there was an unofficial county championship from 1873), and took further inspiration from the American Baseball League. It was only under such conditions that the game could develop and prosper, thus he sent letters to Aston Villa, Blackburn Rovers, Bolton Wanderers, Preston North End, and West Bromwich Albion on 2 March 1888.

This significant epistle stated: "I beg to tender the following suggestion; that ten or twelve of the most prominent clubs in England combine to arrange home and away fixtures each season...."

A meeting of interested parties was arranged at Anderton's Hotel, Fleet Street on 23 March 1888, whilst Preston North End and West Bromwich Albion contested the Cup Final the next day. There was an initial suggestion to call the competition "The Association Football Union" however this was later changed to "The Football League."

No southern clubs expressed any interest, therefore the next meeting was at the Royal Hotel, Piccadilly, Manchester, on 17 April 1888. After studying Cup fixtures and the like it was found there were twenty-two free days in the season, and 12 out of the 15 applicants were admitted viz. Accrington, Aston V., Blackburn R., Bolton W., Burnley, Derby Co., Everton, Notts Co., Preston N.E., Stoke, West Bromwich, and Wolverhampton.

Major Sudell of Preston gave the clubs the grand encomium, "Founder Members of the Football League," however there was not room for all the applicants and Halliwell, Nottingham Forest, and the Wednesday were the unlucky teams. Meanwhile, the League was started under such guidelines on 8 September 1888 and was soon a great success.

There was much excitement on the first Saturday, as ten clubs laced up their boots, while Jack Gordon or Frank Dewhurst scored the first goal for Preston v Burnley at Deepdale. This had the highest attendance of 6,000, whereas Derby overcame a 3-0 reverse against Bolton to win 6-3.

Indeed, this gave new impetus to the Cup and the final of 1889 had the first attendance of over 20,000. McGregor may have felt disappointed since the "Old Invincibles" of Preston won the "double," however his own team Aston Villa were champions six times by 1910.

The southern clubs continued to play on amateur principles, whilst the Royal Arsenal turned professional in 1891 followed by Millwall (1893) and Southampton (1894). This led to the formation of the Southern League in 1894, whose teams were later the basis of the Third Division (South).

McGregor lived at Summer Lane, Birmingham in 1904 and was made a 'Life Member' of the Football League, but died in 1911 aged 65. He was then a retired draper of 8 Salisbury Road, Birchfields near Handsworth and lived with his daughter Jessie and her husband Ernest Hinchley.

Meanwhile, the F.A. baton of office was passed over to a gentleman from the highest levels of society, whose family also came from Perth in Scotland. Indeed, Lord Kinnaird was a great character in the game, and a player of considerable ability on the pitch.

THE KINNAIRD FAMILY

The family's origins are traced to the Carse of Gowrie in the 12th century, and they owned Inchture by 1396. This was an area of fertile lowland north of the River Dee and they lived at Moncur Castle in the 16th century, with the motto "Qui Patitur Vincit" or "He conquers who endures."

George Patrick Kinnaird was a Royalist in the Civil War, and met General Monck the commander of the Republics army in Scotland. He represented Perth and his country, and put forward their concerns, whilst the general helped restore Charles II and Kinnaird was made a peer in 1682.

George Kinnaird (1752-1805), the 7th Lord, attended Pembroke College, Cambridge, and was a banker in London with important links to the Whig persuasion. He married Elizabeth Ransom at St. George's Hanover Square on 22 July 1777, whereas her father Griffin Ransom was a banker of New Palace Yard beside the Houses of Parliament.

The couple had six sons and moved to the more modern Drimmie House north of Inchture, and George became a representative peer from 1787-90. With William Morland he founded the Dundee New Bank in 1802, whose London agents were in fact Ransom & Morland.

Charles Kinnaird (1780-1826) attended Eton, Edinburgh, Glasgow, and Trinity, Cambridge then entered Lincoln's Inn in 1799. However, he had refined tastes and using his father's connections was a Whig for Leominster from 1802-05. He abandoned this role when he became the 8th Lord, and married Lady Olivia Letitia Catherine Fitzgerald in 1806.

Drimmie House became unfashionable at the start of the 19th century and he started a new home up the hillside away from the main road. The village of Rossie was situated near to the development (on the estate) and being in an inconvenient position was demolished, and the residents were moved to Baledgarno to the west. Only the village cross and church then remained, and the latter became a private family chapel.

The new house Rossie Priory was begun in 1807, and was a long building of red stone with a chapel at the centre. It had a commanding position on the hillside above the river, and Charles secured many Continental works during the Napoleonic Wars and had a large picture gallery there.

His brother Douglas James Kinnaird (1788-1830) was a student at Eton, Göttingen, and Trinity, Cambridge and also entered Lincoln's Inn in 1807. He travelled on the Continent and was at the battle of Culm in 1813, but returned home from Paris in 1814, and then worked in the Ransom & Morland Bank who traded at Pall Mall.

He had significant literary connections and Lord Byron called him, "My trusty and trustworthy trustee and banker and crown and sheet anchor." In addition, he joined the committee to rebuild Drury Lane Theatre with the former, G. Lamb, and S. Whitbread and was also a friend of Sheridan. On one occasion he listened to a piece by Coleridge, but was not impressed, thus he offered up a two-piece act of his own instead!

He represented Bishop's Castle, Salop in 1819-20 and his maiden speech supported Lord Althorp's motion for a select committee on *The State of the Nation*! The partnership with Sir F.B. Morland was then dissolved, and he became the chief manager of Ransom & Co. based at 34 Pall Mall in 1819, and at 1 Pall Mall East by 1829.

His nephew George William Fox Kinnaird (1807-78) was born at Drimmie House and educated at Eton then briefly entered the army. He became the 9th Lord and Baron Rossie on the recommendation of Earl Grey in 1831. This was in recognition of the service given by his father and grandfather to the Whigs, but was exchanged for Baron Kinnaird of Rossie (in 1860).

Initially, George spent much of his youth in Italy and conducted some important excavations near to Rome, bringing back Roman antiquities to Rossie Priory, which were added to his father's collection of art.

Indeed, the family's party connections paid dividends and George W.F. Kinnaird married Frances Anna Georgiana Ponsonby at Inchture on 14 December 1837. This was a significant match with noteworthy links to the Spencers and also to the Dukes of Devonshire. [1]

---

[1] John Spencer (1734-83) owned Althorp and married the ambitious Margaret G. Poyntz in 1755. He was a Whig M.P. for Warwick in 1756-61 and 1st Earl Spencer and Viscount Althorp in 1765. His son George was an M.P. and Home Secretary whilst grandson John Charles was Chancellor of the Exchequer.

Of his two daughters, Georgiana married the 5th Duke of Devonshire in 1774. Their home Devonshire House (Berkeley and Stratton Street) on Piccadilly was a centre for Whig politics, and Charles Fox and others made it a base for political intrigue, gambling, and even secret liaisons.

Henrietta Frances married Frederick Ponsonby (3rd Earl Bessborough) in 1780 and daughter Caroline was raised by her aunt Georgiana at Devonshire House. She married William Lamb M.P. for Leominster in 1805, and had an affair with Lord Byron, whilst her husband became Lord Melbourne and P.M. in 1834-41.

Of the sons, Frederick Cavendish Ponsonby fought in the Peninsular War and Waterloo and became Governor of Malta in 1826-35. The remains of a column to his memory are found near to Hastings Gardens and Sappers Street in Valletta. William Francis Spencer Ponsonby married Barbara Ashley-Cooper in 1814, and their daughter Frances Anna Georgiana was born at Roehampton in 1817; whilst the father became the 1st Baron de Mauley in 1838.

The family had addresses 5 'Mansion House' Albany, Piccadilly in 1830 and 1 Pall Mall East in 1841, whilst George was a Whig in the Lords with much influence. He was a great reformer establishing industrial schools, and was friends with Cobden and Bright of the "Anti Corn Law League."

Indeed, he presided over a large meeting of the League at Covent Garden, since it was believed the Laws kept prices high, restricted competition, and caused other social ills - consequently they were repealed in 1845.

He also spent considerable time with Mr. Fox Talbot (see Marindin) and aided in the development of photography. In fact, D. Brewster sent a letter regarding the "Talbotype" in 1847 and talked of his visit to Rossie and the bountiful help of Lord Kinnaird and his wife.

In addition, he had a large geological connection under the guidance of Sir Charles Lyell, instigated agricultural reform in the Carse of Gowrie, built local schools, and promoted the East of Scotland Railway from Perth to Dundee whilst supervising the construction over his land.

The family maintained addresses at Grosvenor Square and Street as well as at Rossie Priory, whilst his three children all died before him and the title eventually passed down to his younger brother.

Arthur Fitzgerald Kinnaird (1814-87) was born at Rossie and was baptized with the middle name of Wellesley, with regard to the Duke of Wellington who was his godfather. However, there was a major falling out over some political dispute, and it was promptly changed to Fitzgerald.

He attended Eton College in 1829 and then went to the Foreign Office, thus he was attached to the British Embassy at St. Petersburg in 1835-37, and was private secretary to the Earl of Durham, the Ambassador. However, he returned to Britain and succeeded his uncle at Ransom & Co., Pall Mall East, and eventually became leader of the banking firm.

He was a Whig-Liberal and represented Perth in the House of Commons in 1837-39, whilst he had an address at 5 Albany, Piccadilly. Through his banking connections he married Mary Jane Hoare at Hornsey on 28 June 1843, which was a suitable match since his wife was not only aristocratic, but like him was imbued with the philanthropic spirit.

The couple initially resided at 35 Hyde Park Gardens, Paddington opposite to Victoria Gate, a property built by the Crake family. This was comprised of two white stucco terraces, the first (1-24) being parallel to Bayswater Road and the second (25-38) located at an inclined angle.

The family remained there until c.1860 and had seven children baptized at nearby St. James's, Paddington, whilst they had nine servants. The father was elected M.P. for Perth from 1852-78, whilst his wife edited "Servants Prayers" and with Lady Canning sent nurses and aid to the Crimea.

He sat under Palmerston, Russell, and Gladstone, spoke frequently on Indian matters, promoted many working class concerns, and championed emancipation. Indeed, like his brother he was a tireless philanthropist and had special links to both missionary societies and homes, whilst he ranked in zeal with Lord Shaftesbury (Ashley-Cooper), always being present at Exeter Hall (in the Strand) and the May meetings.

The family then moved to 2 Pall Mall East by Trafalgar Square and a new firm Ransom, Bouverie & Co. operated next door by 1862. Their home was a centre for philanthropic and religious meetings, whilst his wife founded a number of charitable organisations - including the British Ladies Female Emigration Society and the Y.W.C.A.

Outside of London they had properties at West Farm, East Barnet and Pickhurst Manor, Hayes but the main one was a palatial mansion Plaistow Lodge, Bromley from c.1874. This was near to a small hamlet of the same name, and had extensive grounds with a long sweeping drive.

The main building was of white stone and brown brick, with a portico entrance and several columns adorning the façade. There were classical pediments and scrolls at the roofline, whereas the two sides had a wing and conservatory with some elegant niche statues.

Arthur Kinnaird was the 10th Lord in 1878 whilst the Barony of Rossie became extinct. He then owned Rossie Priory as well as the properties in London and lived with his wife, his daughters, and some fourteen servants at Nos. 1-2 Pall Mall East. He died on 26 April 1887 and A.F. Kinnaird of 50 South Audley Street and Roland Yorke Bevan (son-in-law) of 9 Rutland Gate were granted probate, his personal estate in the U.K. £257,235. The estate and title then passed to his only son. [2]

---

[2] Gerard Noel Edwards married Diana Middleton, Baroness Barham in 1780 and inherited Exton Park, Rutland changing his name to Noel in 1798. Charles Noel (1781) married Arabella Williams in 1820 and was 3rd Baron Barham of Barham Court and Teston, Kent. He was 1st Earl of Gainsborough in 1841 and daughter Mary Arabella Louisa married Sir Andrew Agnew of Lochnaw, Wigtown - Mary Alma Victoria their daughter was born at Exton in 1854 (see later)

Louisa Elizabeth Noel (1784) married William Henry Hoare a member of the banking family at Teston in 1807. They had four children including Mary Jane at Blatherwyke in Northampton in 1816, however her mother died soon afterwards and William then resided at The Grove, Mitcham.

She grew up with her uncle Rev. Baptist Wriothesley Noel (1798) of Hornsey, then helped form the St. John's Training School for Domestic Servants in 1841, with a branch in Brighton. Her cousin Rev. Arthur Malortie Hoare was related to the Badeley and Pember families.

ARTHUR FITZGERALD KINNAIRD

This pioneer of soccer was born at 35 Hyde Park Gardens on 16 February 1847, and baptized at St. James's, Paddington, being educated at Cheam Preparatory School in the 1850s.

His parents then moved to Pall Mall East, and he was a fifth-former at Eton in 1862, however unlike his family he found a fresh outlet in sport. He won the 350-yards race there in 1864 and played soccer on the school fields with the likes of Bonsor, Lubbock, and Thompson.

He was admitted to Trinity, Cambridge in June 1864 and matriculated the next year, whilst he formed the Old Etonians as an undergraduate in 1867. Indeed, he excelled in all he touched and whilst at Cambridge won the 50-yards, 100-yards, half-mile swim, fives, and lawn tennis v Oxford.

Kinnaird obtained his B.A. in 1869 (and M.A. in 1873) and then worked with his father at Ransom & Co., but he remained keen on sport, thus he joined the F.A. committee and captained Scotland against England during the unofficial match at the Oval in 1870.

He did not play in the first Cup Final but made his mark the next year, and eventually appeared in nine such games. Indeed, Charles Alcock wrote of him in an annual in 1873: "He is without exception the best player of the day, capable of taking any place in the field, is very fast and never loses sight of the ball, an excellent captain."

He appeared for Scotland at the Oval on 8 March 1873, losing 4-2, and for the Wanderers in the Cup Final at Lillie Bridge on 29 March 1873. The team included five players from the first final, whilst Kinnaird scored the second goal clinching a 2-0 victory over Oxford University.

Kinnaird was single at this time and resided with his parents at 2 Pall Mall East, whilst he captained the Old Etonians in the final on 13 March 1875 although they lost to the Engineers during a replay.

He then married his second cousin Mary Alma Victoria Agnew at Leswalt, north of Stranraer, on 19 August 1875, and in fact her brother Sir Andrew Noel Agnew also attended Trinity. The couple initially took up residence at 50 South Audley Street, Mayfair (now gone), on the corner of Grosvenor Square, and he captained the Old Etonians in the final at the Oval on 11 March 1876, although they lost 3-0 to the Wanderers.

He remained on the F.A. committee from 1869-77 and was the treasurer in 1878-87, whilst he became a partner in Ransom, Bouverie & Co. in 1877. The family stayed at 50 South Audley Street and had seven children (two of whom died young), whilst they also had eleven servants.

Meanwhile, he returned to the winning side and won the F.A. Cup with the Wanderers in 1877 and 1878. He was the goalkeeper in the first tie but scored an own goal, and was a half-back in the second when he scored at the correct end. He also won the Cup with the Old Etonians in 1879, after an epic quarter final against Darwen.

Kinnaird then witnessed the arrival of professional clubs from the north and his next victory was especially sweet. He captained the Old Etonians against Blackburn Rovers at the Oval on 25 March 1882, in front of 6,500 spectators, and his team won by just a single goal.

He was so overcome by events that he stood on his head in front of the Oval pavilion, and no doubt caused considerable amusement. In fact, the celebrations needed to be enjoyed as this was the last amateur victory.

His last final was for the Old Etonians against Blackburn Olympic at the Oval in 1883. There was a crowd of 8,000 and the amateurs took the lead, but Kinnaird had a goal disallowed which went in (directly) from a free kick. The game was levelled and Kinnaird agreed to extra time even though one man was off injured and another lame. His team might have won in a replay but they lost 2-1. Indeed, it was a most honourable decision, and he was a gentleman who always turned out in white flannel trousers.

He became the 11th Lord Kinnaird in 1887, and inherited all the family estates including Rossie Priory, Plaistow Lodge, and 1 to 2 Pall Mall East. As a result he resigned as F.A. treasurer, but a new vacancy arose with the departure of Marindin and he became the president from 1890.

Meanwhile, in terms of business Barclay, Tritton & Bevan of 54 Lombard Street merged with Ransom, Bouverie by 1892 and Lord Kinnaird was later a director of Barclay & Co. He also removed to 10 St. James's Square, Piccadilly which was previously occupied by Mr. Gladstone. [3]

Kinnaird played football until 1893 long after most of his contemporaries had given up, and was also a keen amateur cricketer. Meanwhile, he became an honorary colonel of the Tay Division of the sub-marine miners (a coast Battalion near Dundee), part of the Royal Engineers, that same year.

He initially worked with Charles Alcock at the F.A., but under Frederick Wall the new secretary there were further developments. The Oval was no longer suitable as a venue for the final, and after games at Fallowfield and Goodison it was moved to the Crystal Palace in 1895.

---

[3] St. James's was laid out in the 17th century, and this was a notable red-brick building on the north side - next to Duke of York Street. The property Chatham House has an L.C.C. blue plaque: "Here lived three Prime Ministers, William Pitt Earl of Chatham 1708-1778, Edward Geoffrey Stanley Earl of Derby 1799-1869, William Ewart Gladstone 1809-1898."

Kinnaird then worked with Wall to establish this purpose built arena, and games took place over several years with crowds in excess of 100,000.

He sold Plaistow Lodge in 1896 and was responsible for the break-up of the estate for housing, whilst he resided at 10 St. James's Square in 1901 and lived there with his wife, three children, and eleven servants. [4]

He supported evangelic religion like his parents and sisters (Louisa and Emily) and once travelled to India, speaking on behalf of missionaries. He was also a J.P. in London and Perth, the president of the Y.M.C.A., and helped to establish homes for poor and destitute boys.

Indeed, he was Lord High Commissioner of the Church of Scotland in 1907-09, but football was never far from his mind and he stated, "I believe that all right-minded people have good reason to thank God for the great progress of this popular national game."

Lord Kinnaird continued to be a character and there were high jinx at New Cross in 1910. He was cordially invited to open The Den but arrived (in error) at the Ilderton Road End. As a result he was hauled and pushed over the wall, then rushed across the arena, where he performed a brief ceremony and led the teams out onto the pitch.

He was greatly admired in the game and was presented with the second F.A. Cup trophy in 1911, having won the Cup on five occasions. However, he lost his sons Arthur and Douglas of the Scots Guards in the war; and although he maintained 11,900 acres at Rossie, the property at Pall Mall East was replaced by "Kinnaird House" in 1922.

He was quite old at the time when Wembley was being built, and missed the first final there. Indeed, Lord Kinnaird died at 10 St. James's Square soon after his wife on 30 January 1923 - the other headlines at the time including the first photographs of Tutankhamen's tomb.

There was a service at St. Martin in the Fields, whilst his funeral was at Rossie Church and a memorial was erected, his land and property being valued at £250,000. His son Kenneth was 12th Lord and also became Lord High Commissioner of the Church in 1936-37, whilst Patrick was a director of Barclays. The peerage became dormant-extinct in 1997 and Rossie Priory was then an exclusive hotel for corporate customers.

---

[4] Quernmore School occupied Plaistow Lodge for many years, whilst Kinnaird Avenue was nearby. More recently it housed the Parish Primary School.

CHAPTER 13

Balham F.C.

There was a vacuum at the F.A. after the departure of Charles Alcock in August 1895, but who could possibly fill his boots? Whether it was by luck or good judgement a worthy successor was found, and he proved to be a skilful administrator who negotiated through times of great change.

However, there was a degree of mystery and secrecy regarding the new secretary, since his origins proved to be humble in the extreme. No doubt he was judged solely on his merits, although he had to work with the likes of Lord Kinnaird and to some extent the truth was concealed.

WILLIAM WALL OF WORMLEY

John Wall was an agricultural labourer at Rainham, Essex and had seven children with his wife Ann from 1813-33. He resided there in 1841 with his wife, his children George (15) a labourer, Mary (12), and William (10), and two other families of similar occupation.

The brother George then married and lived at Upminster Road, Rainham, whereas William was soon to take a more lucrative path. Indeed, his father John Wall became a grocer and may have moved the family to London.

The most significant event to occur was when William a servant married Elizabeth Mansfield at St. Botolph's, Bishopsgate on 13 May 1850. The witnesses included her brother Joseph, whilst they lived at 12 Bishopsgate Street not far from the City near Bishopsgate Station, the terminus of the Great Eastern Railway (Liverpool Street was built in the 1860s).

However, the greatest point of interest was the origin of her antecedents. William Mansfield a shoemaker came from Wormley just north of Waltham Abbey, and with his wife Frances had eight children in 1811-31, including Elizabeth (1821) and Joseph (1823); then was a shoemaker with his son in the High Street in 1841/51.

Meanwhile, the Wall family moved to Stratford in east London and had two sons: William George (1852) and Arthur Alfred (1856), whereas their third son Frederick Joseph was born at 2 St. John's Road, Battersea on 14 April 1858. The house was near Clapham Junction and Lavendar Hill and the two youngest were baptized at St. Mary's, Battersea, while William Wall a coachman domestic lived there in 1861 with his wife, three sons, a niece Eleanor Wall, and also two lodgers.

Clearly the family circumstances remained limited however Frederick was educated at St. Mark's College, Chelsea and this greatly improved his career opportunities. Indeed, there is evidence the family were raised in the social scale and his father, a coachman, lived at 3 Shelgate Road off Northcote Road with his wife and sons, and a servant girl, in 1871. [1]

The Balham area developed as a separate parish in the 1850s, after the arrival of the London, Brighton & South Coast Railway, whilst the Clapham Park estate was just to the east. Despite such growth there were a number of fields, and Balham Cricket Ground was laid out on Bedford Hill Road, between the railway and Elmfield Road, in the early 1870s. Indeed, a gravel pit in the southwest corner was cleared in readiness.

Frederick no doubt played soccer at school and was a founder of Rangers F.C. at the cricket ground in 1875, although they made little real progress (unlike their Scottish counterparts). He usually played in defence and was described as a stout halfback and also a notable goalkeeper.

He continued to reside with his family just to the north and they were at "Clifton House," 3 Shelgate Road in 1878, but had moved to a newly-built property called "Clifton Villa," 118 Northcote Road by 1880. Indeed, the road only went as far as Belleville Road (at this time). [2]

Meanwhile, there was further evidence that the family had crossed the social divide, and Frederick a solicitor's articled clerk married Marie Louise the daughter of Charles White, a gentleman of Clapham, at St. Mary's, Battersea on 2 September 1880. In fact, the marriage was cosmopolitan and the bride was born at Passy near to Paris in 1859.

---

[1] The National Society founded teachers' colleges and purchased Stanley House, Little Chelsea in 1839, once the home of Sir Robert Stanley the Earl of Derby's second son. It became St. Mark's Training College for schoolmasters and Principal Rev. Derwent Coleridge (son of the poet) added a school for 260 pupils.

This was an eight-sided octagon beside the college chapel on Fulham Road, but merged with St. John's Battersea in 1923 and moved to Plymouth. King's College then used the site until the 1980s, whereas the octagon became a private junior school. The college buildings and chapel were recently refurbished as part of the "Kings Chelsea" development near to Stamford Bridge.

[2] 108-118 Northcote Road was a terrace between Wakehurst and Belleville Road, near a Baptist church. All the houses had grey brick, an ornate band of plaster, and flower detail (at both floors), and a moulded plaster entrance with columns, but behind was a normal red brick terrace. 118 Northcote Road had an additional rear extension along Belleville Road - with a back door at ground level and three sets of windows. These houses are still present today and are impressive, but 118 had a desirable corner location thus it became an estate agents.

This was certainly a dramatic change of circumstances, but his father William Wall, a coachman domestic, still resided at "Clifton Villa" in 1881 with his wife Elizabeth and 'Alfred' a shorthand solicitor's clerk.

His brother William married and had two children being a mercantile clerk in the tobacco trade. He had a number of addresses including Lancroft Terrace, East Dulwich and "Gothic Villa," 4 St. John's Road, although the latter was demolished for shops in 1889, and then 33 St. John's Hill Grove just to the north. Arthur was also married and entered the church, whilst he resided nearby at 29 Beechcroft Road, Wandsworth.

The façade of their home indicated some success, but there were hidden problems and Elizabeth Wall died of chronic alcoholism (three years) and related ailments at 118 Northcote Road on 22 March 1890. Such problems were little understood and the family had to deal with this on their own.

Meanwhile, the father a cab proprietor and employer lived there with his groom, housekeeper, and one servant. In fact, such progress continued and William Wall "of independent means" died at 5 Harbert Road, Battersea on 10 January 1901 - near to St. John's Hill Grove. There is a flat grey marble memorial at Wandsworth Cemetery just beyond the chapels.

FREDERICK JOSEPH WALL

The youngest son had clearly made a most propitious match, and began married life at 19 Temperley Road, Balham. Indeed, he continued to play for Rangers F.C., half a mile away, and then took part in the F.A. Cup in 1880-81. After receiving a bye in the first two rounds, his team lost to the Royal Engineers 6-0 at home (and this was their only Cup game).

His property was in fact a short walk from Northcote Road, and a son Frederick Mansfield Hastings was born in 1881. The father was described as a solicitor's clerk but had no servants, while his mother-in-law Mary Ann White was a widow and dressmaker living in Paddington.

Frederick soon rose up the ranks of football's administrative pyramid and was honorary secretary of Rangers F.C., then was elected to the council of the London F.A. in 1881. He also kept goal for the latter, whilst his own team were drawn in the Cup against "Romford" but withdrew.

Indeed, he maintained a number of interests outside of football being a colour sergeant in the 7th Surrey Rifle Volunteers, a pioneer cyclist, a keen cricketer, and spent his leisure time rowing on the river.

His family continued to live at 19 Temperley Road which was just a small terraced property, and three children were born: Arthur (1883) *infant*, Ethel Marie (1887), and Herbert William (1889).

Meanwhile, there were plans afoot to build housing on Balham Cricket Ground, and Rangers F.C. were forced to close down in 1888 - Frederick remained a member of the club throughout its short history. [3]

He then had more time on his hands and was elected to the council of the Middlesex Co. Association that year, and was their honorary secretary and treasurer in 1890, eventually becoming their vice-president.

In addition, he moved to a house just around the corner and was described as a solicitor's managing clerk at 148 Ramsden Road in 1891 with his wife, three children, and one servant. This was a larger terraced property, with an elaborate entrance, some columns, and moulded plaster lintels.

Indeed, he was on the way up and represented Middlesex on the F.A. council from 1891, and was vice-president of the London F.A in 1892. He also became secretary of the Amateur Cup when it was started at the latter date, and his last child May was born during that year.

By this time he had accrued considerable credentials, consequently he was appointed F.A. secretary in place of Alcock in August 1895, despite any questions about his forebears. His predecessor shared his time with both cricket and journalism, but the position was now far more demanding (and paid since 1887) thus Wall was employed full time. Some records had him down as a lawyer, but he was in fact a company secretary and a fellow of the Chartered Institute of Secretaries (F.C.I.S.).

His family also moved to 15 Cavendish Villas (No. 54), St. Julian's Farm Road, West Norwood that year, which was one of twenty semi-detached cottages on the south side with moulded windows and mosaic paths.

However, this was still quite modest and he relocated down the road to "Casewick House," 1 Casewick Road, by 1901 and lived there some twenty years. This was a large semi-detached property on the corner of St. Julian's Farm Road, with a double frontage and fine architectural detail.

His occupation was recorded as "secretary to the F.A." and he lived there with his wife Marie, his son Frederick an electrical engineer, three children, his mother-in-law Mary Ann Churchman, and one servant.

He was also instrumental in securing the rights of referees and was the first president of the Society of Referees in 1902, whilst he worked for the F.A. at 104 High Holborn in 1902-10. Indeed, the Cup Final venue at the Crystal Palace was less than a mile from his home, and he always attended games in a top hat and frock coat. In fact, his tenure coincided with the first finals there, with large crowds averaging 75,000.

---

[3] Larch Road covered the site and the plots occupied the field; whilst Larch Close has replaced the Victorian housing and the old field boundary can still be seen. It is of interest that the Royal Engineers once played there.

Meanwhile, he was a co-founder of the British Olympic Association at the House of Commons in 1905, and as a result helped to host the Olympics in London three years later.

He was a well-known sporting figure in bowler hat and moustache, who showed infinite patience, wisdom, and courtesy as his duties increased. In fact, he constantly travelled to committee meetings and inquiries around the country, and attended representative and international matches, as well as being a regular at games on a Saturday afternoon.

However, his wife Marie Louise Wall died of influenza and pneumonia at "Casewick House" on 15 February 1913, and his son Herbert was an army captain from 1914-17 - being awarded the Military Cross and O.B.E.

The F.A. moved to 42 Russell Square, Bloomsbury near to the British Museum, but he probably had little work to do since the Cup and League were suspended for four years in 1915-19. Meanwhile, there were dramatic changes in both the class structure and social fabric after the war, and there were also considerable adjustments for the F.A. secretary.

There was soon a wedding, and Frederick Joseph Wall (60) a limited co. secretary of "Casewick House" married Agnes Frances Hall (32) of 26 Janson Road, Stratford at West Ham Register Office on 12 June 1918. The names may have caused some confusion, although the registrar was Alfred Hall, and her father was Alfred Henry Hall an engineer.

There was a fine line to be drawn regarding his elevated position at the F.A., and on the marriage certificate he described his father William Wall as a "farmer," although there was still a degree of intrigue to follow. Football recommenced after the war, but there was soon some sad news received since his daughter Ethel died at Winnipeg in 1920.

Meanwhile, the F.A. was confronted with a very serious problem - where should they play the Cup Final? The Crystal Palace was upgraded in 1905 but had financial problems, and was an army depot in the war, thus Old Trafford was used in 1915 and Stamford Bridge in 1920-22.

Frederick Wall then took part in important negotiations and helped to secure the site at Wembley, and took the F.A. Cup there for many decades to come. As a result the game was played on a superior stage.

It seems likely he moved to Russell Square in 1921 since there is no other record of his address, and his wife Agnes was a hostess at the F.A. over the next seventeen years; whereas the decade witnessed several internationals against Belgium, France, Sweden, Luxembourg, and Spain.

Wall received a presentation cheque of £1,000 from Sir Charles Clegg in 1928, and a national presentation the next year, the Prince of Wales and Lord Mayor being patrons. However, there was still more work to do.

The F.A. moved to new offices at 22 Lancaster Gate, a former private hotel, in 1929. This was a terrace building near to Lancaster Square (in white stucco) with a columned porch, pilasters, and window pediments. It was also recorded as the home address of Mr. and Mrs. Wall. [4]

Indeed, it was a substantial property and Frederick and his wife entertained guests there in style, being F.A. ambassadors at home and abroad, while he received a knighthood for his services to football on 6 March 1930. During these later years he was an associate of Sir Charles Clegg, John McKenna, and William Pickford and attended some major internationals abroad.

England played Germany at the Deutches Stadion, Berlin-Grunewald on 10 May 1930 (3-3), and Italy at the Stadio Nazionale del Partito Nazionale Fascista, Roma on 13 May 1933 (1-1). On each occasion the crowd was around 50,000 and the couple met both Hitler and Mussolini.

Sir Frederick Wall retired in 1934 since he felt that at 76 years, he was too old to rule the game of soccer. Indeed, he had witnessed great changes as the secretary and 1,000 members had risen to 750,000 by the time he left. He received a large cheque of £10,000 from the F.A., which may have been a payment in lieu of the residence at Lancaster Gate, whilst he became a director of Arsenal F.C. upon his retirement.

He initially resided at "Kinsale," 37 Langley Park Road, Sutton, a large Victorian red-brick house in 1935, but had moved to No. 35 (otherwise "Weetwood") the next year. His daughter May died at Bulawayo, Southern Rhodesia at that time, and he then spent his retirement in Sutton being a familiar character regarded with both affection and respect. [5]

Indeed, he was keen to share his sporting experiences and published *Fifty Years of Football* in 1935, whereas his wife was involved in local women's organisations and also the Conservative party.

Sir Frederick became ill in c.1940 and his wife then nursed him, whilst in his will he stated, "I bequeath to my said son Frederick Mansfield Hastings Wall all my presentation cups and vases and medals."

There was then a twist to the story and an interesting entry appeared in Kelly's titled, landed, and official classes in 1943, as follows, "Sir Frederick Wall son of the late 'William Wall of Wormley' and secretary of the Football Association 1895-1934." Indeed, his father was raised up to the aristocracy, although he had never actually lived in Wormley at all!

---

[4] The F.A. moved to 16/17 Lancaster Gate in 1972, but sold it for £7.25 million and moved to 25 Soho Square in October 2000.

[5] The former is now a hotel (No. 57), and the latter "Rotorua" has been rebuilt. H.G. Wells resided in a terraced property at No. 25 from 1893-94.

Sir Frederick J. Wall died at "Weetwood," 35 Langley Park Road on 25 March 1944, and the headline declared, "Football World loses Grand Old Man." Mr. H.J. Huband and S.F. Rous represented the F.A. at his funeral, whilst there is a marble memorial at Wandsworth Cemetery.

Lady Agnes remained at 35 Langley Park Road and many ex-servicemen stayed there in 1945-47, but she then dropped out of sight. Indeed, this was the end of an era for soccer, but he left the lasting legacy of Wembley and laid a foundation for the "glory days" of the 1950s.

The F.A. Secretaries

1863-66	Ebenezer Cobb Morley
1866-68	Robert Watson Willis
1868-70	Robert George Graham
1870-95	Charles William Alcock
1895-1934	Sir Frederick Joseph Wall
1934-62	Sir Stanley Rous
1962-73	Sir Dennis Follows
1973-89	Edgar Alfred Croker
1989-	Chief Executive position (Initially Graham Kelly)

CHAPTER 14

Sheffield 'Rules'

The last F.A. official to consider came in the eleventh hour, and was made president as a reward for years of dedicated service to soccer. Indeed, like Sir Frederick Wall his family had humble origins, and his antecedents were connected to the metalwork industry in Sheffield.

WILLIAM JOHNSON CLEGG

Thomas Clegg married Betty Buxton at St. Peter and St. Paul's, Sheffield in 1754 and had several children including Charles (1765-1842) and possibly John (1770-1816). The former was a cutler and married Mary Ann Johnson, whilst his son Charles was a trumpeter, music professor, and gentleman at Cheney Row beside the town hall. [1]

There was an agreement between the burgesses and Mary Johnson (widow of George) in 1814, referring to a plot of land in Little Sheffield near Button Lane and a parcel at the back of Carver Street. A deed of exchange of 1817 showed that the parties included, "Charles Clegg and his wife Mary (née Johnson) - child of George Johnson."

Meanwhile, John Clegg married Ann (Hannah) Johnson at St. Peter and St. Paul's on 14 August 1795 and had four children baptized at the church: William Johnson (1797), Elizabeth (1799), Harriet (1803), and Charles (1804). The father being a labourer, tool maker, and file smith.

His son Charles Clegg married another Mary Johnson at Rotherham on 7 August 1825, the bride being born nearby at Attercliffe. Initially, he was a victualler at the Mermaid in Orchard Street, but entered the profession of cutler and became quite successful in the early 19th Century.

In fact, he had just one child William Johnson Clegg who was born on 23 September 1826, and baptized at the cathedral. The family then resided just south of the town at Sylvester Street near to Bramall Lane in 1841, and the son William was recorded there as a clerk. [2]

---

[1] St. Peter and St. Paul's Church was situated in the old town amongst alleys, streets, and courtyards. It became Sheffield Cathedral in 1913.

[2] Charles Clegg (1830) son of William and Sarah lived at *Wisewood* near Wadsley Bridge in 1861, and owned Hague, Clegg & Barton at the Æmilian Works, Sylvester Lane, but he was not related.

His father's business was nearby at 115 Porter Street and Earl Street in 1849-56, and he was described as a master cutler employing 12 men and a spring knife manufacturer. He had a residence at 54 Hermitage Street near to London Road, but his wife Mary died there on 29 January 1858 and was buried at St. Mary's, Bramall Lane.

Despite this there was little time to grieve and he married Sarah Jeyes (née Morgan) at St. Mary's on 9 November that year. Both of the parties resided in Hermitage Street and William Johnson Clegg was a witness. [3]

However, soon after the marriage the couple travelled eighty-miles south, and Charles Clegg a cutler lived at 53 Silver Street, Northampton in 1861 with his wife Sarah and daughters-in-law Sarah and Jane Jeyes - all of them shoe-closers. He was then variously listed as a shopkeeper, leather cutler, and hardware dealer in Silver and Crispin Streets.

He continued to work into his seventies and made a will in 1877, leaving his estate to his wife and son, whilst the witnesses were John C. and Mary E. Clegg in Sheffield. He died at 53 Silver Street in 1881, but he was not wealthy and his estate was valued at £85 16s 9d - indeed, there was no state pension and his wife continued to trade but she died in 1890.

Meanwhile, his son William embarked on a more lucrative path and was an attorney's clerk at Paradise Square. He married Mary Sykes at Sheffield Church on 3 November 1847, her father John being a cutler at Jessop Street (near to Sylvester) and a coffeehouse keeper at Coalpit (Pit) Lane. [4]

Clegg continued to improve his situation and was a solicitor's managing clerk and highway rate collector, living at 53 Broom Spring Lane and 127-9 Cemetery Road west of the city. He had seven children including John C. (1850), William E. (1852), and Mary E. (1856), and also employed a servant Sarah Sykes; however four died as infants and their mother in 1860, and there is a memorial beside the tower of St. Mary's.

----

[3] Sarah Morgan (1804) daughter of John and Elizabeth a rope maker was born in Northampton, a centre for shoe making and allied trades. She married James Jeyes a mason and had seven children including Sarah (1836) and Jane (1839). They lived at Silver Street with its alleys in 1841/51 and three daughters were shoe-binders, whilst James Jeyes died there in 1856.

[4] Paradise Square with its Georgian housing and steep cobbled streets, near the cathedral, was popular with solicitors, doctors, and portrait painters. It was the pulpit of John Wesley on 15 July 1779: "I preached in Paradise Square in Sheffield to the largest congregation I ever saw on a weekday." Today, no houses remain in Sylvester Street, but there are signs of old industry such as "Sylvester Buildings" which is a warehouse.

William Clegg, highway rate collector, lived with his three children and a housekeeper at Cemetery Road in 1861, but married Asenath Harrop at Sheffield later that year. Indeed, he was also an agent for the *Temperance and General Provident Institution* and supported the temperance movement.

His wife was the daughter of Samuel and Mary Harrop of Hathersage, and their children born from 1825-36 had some intriguing names viz. Alfred, Absalom, Asenath, Abner, Amanda, and Aramenta. Indeed, the first son married Eliza Holland and played a part in the later story.

Meanwhile, William had three more children with his new wife namely Asenath Harrop (1864), Sara Amanda (1865), and Leonard Johnson (1867), and left his former 'unpopular' profession to be a student of law.

At this time, his brother-in-law Alfred owed him £922 13s 10d, and an agreement was drawn up to cover this amount plus further sums up to £1,200. The mortgage was secured on some premises and four houses in Orange Street, with the boilers and steam-engines thereon - the works being located next to West Street and not far from the cathedral.

Clegg was then admitted to the Law Society as a country solicitor on 25 September 1868, while the leasehold regarding Orange Street went missing and he took possession of the premises when Alfred died in 1870.

Indeed, the family had improved circumstances and William J. Clegg a solicitor lived at "Alliance Villa," 22 Victoria Road, Broomhall Park in 1871 with his wife, six children - Charles and William solicitor's articled clerks, and two servants. The house was on Ecclesall Road near to *Collegiate Hall* beyond the confines of the old town (and remains today).

W.J. Clegg & Sons (solicitors) were initially at 27 and 57 Bank Street near the cathedral in the early 1870s, but then moved to "Victoria Chambers," 14 Figtree Lane in 1878 (and remained there until at least 1937).

The new chambers were just around the corner and the lane ran downhill from Hartshead towards Bank Street. The west side had several shops or chambers (7-25), and the east side three (6, 10, 14), these being the offices of accountants, solicitors, and landscape & portrait painters. [5]

The family remained at 22 Victoria Road and Amanda Harrop was their housekeeper, whilst her nephew Arthur was an articled clerk with the firm. The Cleggs also owned a property at Bradwell near to Hathersage and were agents for the *UK Temperance Institution* in 1884, then commissioners for oaths and official receivers in bankruptcy in the late 1880s.

---

[5] 14 Figtree Lane is a building of brown sandstone, white-stucco front, columned porch, and pediments, and is little changed being a solicitors and commissioners for oaths, whilst the street is both narrow and cobbled. *Sheffield Hospital for Women* was there from 1864-78 but then removed to Jessop House.

Concurrent with this new status, William J. Clegg a magistrate lived with his wife and two servants at "Cliff Tower," 10 Whitworth Road, Ranmoor, high in the hills above the city, in 1891. The property was a two-storey, double-fronted palatial house of yellow brick, plaster detailing, and tower entrance with extensive gardens (and is still present today).

Indeed, it was just above Upper Hallam, and not far away was Sandygate football ground which was the home of Hallam F.C. - established in 1860. A dry-stone wall surrounded the cricket pitch with the dales just beyond, whilst it became the oldest football ground in the world.

William Johnson Clegg left his solicitor's business to his three sons and his leasehold property at 22 Victoria Road and £8,000 to his wife, the residual estate in trust for his six children. He died at "Cliff Tower" on 15 June 1895 and his estate was valued at £31,677.

The Orange Street works were assigned to Messrs. Blyde & Middleton for a sum of £750 in December 1896, whilst Asenath Clegg died in Sheffield in 1907, and there is a fine family memorial at Christchurch, Fulwood on the western outskirts near to Ranmoor. Indeed, it is of monumental scale with scrolls, marble columns, carvings, and multiple bases.

JOHN CHARLES CLEGG

The fifth F.A. president was born at 53 Broom Spring Lane on 15 June 1850, and was then educated at a private school in the city. Indeed, he lived in a metropolis that was a hotbed of soccer and early sport.

The significant factor was a half day on Wednesdays allowing for leisure time, thus racing and various sporting contests became common. Bramall Lane was established in 1854 and there were other venues nearby, whilst a number of early clubs were formed such as Sheffield (1857), Hallam (1860), and Wednesday (1867) - the Sheffield Rules soon followed.

Indeed, the Sheffield Association played a significant role in the evolution of the game, and the first contest against London took place at Battersea on 31 March 1866, which then became an annual fixture.

Clegg was greatly involved in these sporting activities and was an athlete from 1867-74 who won 120 prizes - he held the 600-yard record and could run 100 yards in 10 seconds. Indeed, running was a most serious business and the Lillie Bridge 'Riot' is discussed in detail in the next chapter.

He never trained but kept fit through ordinary exercise and temperance, whilst he was a fast and strong forward for Broomhall, Sheffield, Albion, and Wednesday. His brother was also involved and they played for Sheffield against London in c.1870 and thus came to the attention of the F.A.

His busiest year came in 1872, and as a law student he married Mary Sayles at St. John's, Manchester on 2 September; then was admitted to the Law Society and became a partner in the family firm two weeks later.

In addition, he played in the first Sheffield v Glasgow contest and for England at the West of Scotland Cricket Ground on 30 November. Like many Victorians he had his hand in several pies and was an administrator, businessman, and a leader of Sheffield society.

The couple had three children namely Charles W. (1873), Colin (1877), and Edith Margaret (1879), whilst they had a residence at "Mackenzie Place," 4 Wharncliffe Road, Broomhall Park quite near to his father.

In local terms he was a town councillor and a member of the Sheffield & Hallamshire F.A., whilst he became known as a clever and popular referee. Indeed, Clegg was the main official at the Cup Final on 25 March 1882 when the Old Etonians beat Blackburn Rovers.

Meanwhile, he was an affiliated representative for Sheffield at the F.A. in 1885-87, and was elected to the F.A. committee in 1886, then became the first permanent chairman in 1890 - a post which he held until his death.

He resided at 1 Collegiate Court (Crescent), Broomhall in 1891 with his wife, daughter, and two servants. This was an affluent area with merchants, manufacturers, ministers, the chief constable, and persons living on their own means nearby; whilst he was a commissioner of oaths and a 'deputy' official receiver in bankruptcy at Figtree Lane.

Regarding soccer he refereed the last Cup Final at the Oval between West Bromwich and Aston Villa in 1892, and had to keep his nerve since the crowd was 32,810. His father William died on his 45th birthday and he then became both senior partner and official receiver, while his cousin Arthur Harrop was at "Harold Chambers," 19 Figtree Lane.

The family's business success was quite apparent and he had moved to a grand property "Clifton House," 32 Cavendish Road, high on the hill above Ecclesall Road, by 1901. This was a two-storey yellow brick building in a tree lined avenue at the corner of Chelsea Road, and had large bay windows, extensive gables, a copious leafy garden, substantial coach-house to the rear, and a dry-stone wall around the perimeter. His son Charles was a solicitor, although Colin was a civil engineer in Battersea.

His progress continued and he was a president of both the Sheffield clubs, sat on the League appeals committee, and was vice-president of the F.A. in 1904. Indeed, he was a formidable administrator of high principles, stating, "Nobody gets lost on a straight road." He was also a chairman of the local employment committee, a J.P., a supporter of the Band of Hope Union, and a president of the British Temperance League.

On the death of Lord Kinnaird he was appointed president of the F.A. and was a representative at the first Wembley final in 1923. He then worked with Frederick Wall and guided the F.A. between the wars, including the provision of several tours abroad.

In fact, he was involved in soccer for nearly seventy years and watched it develop from its small origins to some memorable finals at Wembley. He received a knighthood in 1927, but this was for services to the Board of Trade and Ministry of Labour rather than any sporting contribution.

His son Charles died that year and he became ill, thus he was unable to attend the Cup Final between Cardiff and Arsenal, and had a telegram from King George V regarding his health. He then lost his other son Colin and his wife, thus he left his estate in trust to his daughter and her family.

He died at Cavendish Road on 26 June 1937 and had tributes from Mr. S.F. Rous and Sir Frederick Wall, whilst a Football Council telegram stated, "For more than half a century he has been the outstanding personality in our game and has won the affection of all of us." His estate was valued at £24,834 and his name appears on the family memorial at Fulwood. [6]

The job of running the F.A. passed to a new generation, and W. Pickford was briefly president, whilst Sir Stanley Rous became long-term secretary. England then played games against Germany in Berlin and Italy in Milan in 1938-39, but these were overshadowed by the politics of war.

---

[6] William E. Clegg played for Sheffield, Albion, and for England on 8 March 1873 then married Viola daughter of Henry Gilles Carr at Camberwell and joined the Law Society. He played for England in the first game against Wales on 18 March 1879 and was the Lord Mayor of Sheffield in 1898-99, then lived at Loxley House (Wadsley) and Anston and was knighted for public service in 1906.

CHAPTER 15

Up for the Cup

The most important action taken by the F.A. was to start the Cup, and the interest this created led to a proliferation of teams, whilst many of them started leagues and remain prominent in the game today. Indeed, the F.A. provided the blueprint for similar organisations around the world, and the Scottish F.A. was formed in 1873 (and the Welsh in 1876).

The Scottish Cup started the following year and sixteen clubs entered the first contest, whilst Queen's Park won the first three without conceding a goal, and went on to form the basis of the national team.

THE OVAL, KENNINGTON

This was indeed the home of early soccer and hosted twenty Cup Finals but only a handful of amateur teams played there i.e. the Wanderers, Oxford University, Royal Engineers, the Old Etonians, Clapham Rovers, the Old Carthusians (Charterhouse), and Queen's Park of Scotland. [1]

The Wanderers won the first Cup Final (as discussed), and the contest went to Lillie Bridge the next year, however it then became a permanent fixture at the Oval under the guidance of Charles Alcock.

Oxford University and the Royal Engineers had their only successes in 1874/75, whilst there were some unfamiliar entrants such as Brondesbury, Farningham, Uxbridge, the Swifts, and also Sheffield F.C.

The Wanderers won three times from 1876-78 and were presented with the Cup, but being gentlemen returned it to the F.A. Indeed, amongst their players was A.G. Guillemard one of the founders of the Rugby Union.

The rules of the F.A. combined with the northern game in 1877, and this hastened the arrival of professional clubs in the contest. In fact, Darwen, Notts County, Nottingham Forest, and Reading took part in 1878-79, and Kinnaird and the Old Etonians won the competition - but only after an epic struggle against Darwen and their 'professional' players.

---

[1] Charterhouse School was established on the site of a Carthusian monastery. The team beat Darwen 4-1 in the semi-final and the Old Etonians 3-0 in the final of 1881, and won the Amateur Cup in 1894/97. They had four international players and Charles Wreford Brown born Clifton (1867) played for England in 1889, and was credited with the invention of the word soccer.

The big guns Aston Villa, Blackburn Rovers, and an early Birmingham side appeared the next year, although amateur sides Clapham Rovers and the Old Carthusians managed to win in 1880 and 1881 respectively.

The Old Etonians had the last amateur victory a year later, and the first northern success went to Blackburn Olympic; while Blackburn Rovers won three times in 1884-86, twice against Queen's Park and then against West Bromwich in a replay at the Racecourse Ground, Derby.

Indeed, the next six finals were won by northern clubs who were founder members of the League. The attendance was 14,000 for the first game between Blackburn and Queen's Park in 1884, whilst it had reached 22,000 when Preston beat Wolves to take the Cup and League in 1889. In fact, the problems of such a venue were apparent, and the last final between West Bromwich and Aston Villa in 1892 had an attendance of 32,810.

LILLIE BRIDGE, FULHAM

The F.A. arranged two test matches in this area of London, one at Beaufort House in 1867 (played at Battersea), and the other at Lillie Bridge Athletic Ground or the West London Running Grounds in 1868.

The venue was just beside West Brompton Station and the West London Extension Railway, whilst nearby were some fields and orchards. Indeed, the area remained undeveloped and to the west was Beaufort House, the latter also having a path or track and a rifle range adjacent.

Clearly the venue was familiar to the F.A., thus it was chosen for the final on 29 March 1873. In fact, the kick-off took place in the morning, so that the teams could watch the Boat Race in the afternoon.

The Wanderers had a bye all the way to the final, whereas Oxford beat Crystal Palace 3-2, Clapham Rovers 3-0, Royal Engineers 1-0, Maidenhead 4-0, and had a walk over against Queen's Park. Other competitors were 1st Surrey Rifles, South Norwood, and Windsor Home Park.

A small crowd of 3,000 assembled for the final but Oxford were exhausted by all their efforts and the Wanderers won the Cup (2-0). Indeed, it was a bad day for the university since Cambridge also won the Boat Race by three lengths in a good time - being one of five consecutive victories.

This was the only time that the venue hosted an F.A. Cup Final however this significant game was not to be the end of the story.

Despite new competition from Stamford Bridge Athletic Club, established just to the south in 1877, it remained an important arena with some major meetings. In fact, the whole history of sport in the area could have been different but for some dramatic events on 19 September 1887.

A running contest was arranged between Henry Gent of Darlington who had won the Sheffield handicap at Easter, and Henry Hutchens who was a noted champion short-distance runner. The latter had just returned from competing in Australia and normally trained in Leicester.

The event was a great topic of conversation and the runners were touted like derby favourites. Gent wanted a four-yard start on the 120-yard race, but fair terms were agreed and £100 stake was placed. The race was to take place on the Monday at 5.00 p.m. and a large crowd was expected.

Indeed, 1,000 persons were in place at 4.30 and this figure had doubled by 5.00, with many people still arriving. The spectators had come from all parts of the country (especially from Sheffield) and paid good money, whilst most were in the low-priced areas by the road, and the remainder in the main stand with its veranda and dressing rooms.

However, there was a large amount of betting involved and the scene soon turned rather ugly. Gent had favourable odds of 3-1, but this fell to 10-1, and some wagers were made that the race would not be run.

Hutchens came out and circled the ground with his trainer, followed by Gent who seemed in good condition. However, Gent's people were sure their man would lose and decided to forfeit their stake, thereby saving the money previously betted. A fight between the two parties was narrowly averted, but an agreement was reached and they retired.

The runners left the arena and most spectators were unaware of events until 6.30. Once it became known, the crowd of 3,000 demanded their entrance money back, but it was already removed for safe-keeping.

Initially, some of the men and lads broke down the railings before the pavilion, pulled down the flagpole, and smashed chairs. Indeed, only three or four officers were on duty and once the mob realised this they took more drastic action. One group attacked the refreshment and dressing-rooms on the Seagrove Road side, a second tackled the railings by the railway, and a third threw missiles at the pavilion.

Many not involved in the fracas attempted to escape, but were blocked by those looking for money at the turnstiles. Consequently they tried another route on the embankment, but were stopped by railway employees and in the ensuing dispute a rail-worker died of a heart attack.

The rioters set fire to the buildings and some were only saved due to a brick-wall, whereas those parts not burnt were ransacked for money and compensation. Indeed, the private lockers of club members were all torn open and a dozen bicycles (normally used there) were smashed up. Both the police and firemen were pelted with stones, and several large fires blazed around the ground - with flames 30-40 feet high in the air.

One report stated that some 10,000 people were involved and many were bruised or crushed, while several policemen were badly injured. The riot was quelled once reinforcements arrived and the fire brigade extinguished the flames by 10.30, and handed the arena over to the police.

The Lillie Bridge Ground with grandstand, refreshment room, dressing-rooms, and gymnasium was in fact basically destroyed and never recovered. Indeed, there was already some terraced housing to the west, and due to the costs of rebuilding the venue was sold to the railways by 1895.

Lillie Bridge Coal Depot was developed on the site, whilst Lillie Road and Lillie Yard are found on present day maps. The demise of the venue paved the way for the growth of Stamford Bridge in 1905, and without the riot there might have been a completely different story.

FALLOWFIELD & GOODISON

The 1893 Cup Final took place at Manchester University Athletic Ground, just behind Owens Park in the Fallowfield district south of the city centre. In fact, this was the only time it was played in Manchester itself, as Old Trafford was situated outside the city boundaries.

Wolves beat Everton 1-0 in front of a record crowd of some 45,000, and Fallowfield Terrace and Wanderers Avenue were built near their old ground at Dudley Road, with stone replicas of the Cup outside the houses.

Meanwhile, Everton played at Anfield Road in 1884-92 but their backer John Houlding was unhappy with the arrangement. When they joined the League he raised the rent from £100 to £250, and the club refused to pay this, therefore they transferred to the other side of Stanley Park.

Goodison Park was the country's first major ground and had tall covered stands on three sides, and a large bank on the other - the touchline was a distance from the stands avoiding the cramped situation at Anfield. Lord Kinnaird and Frederick Wall were at the opening ceremony which included an athletics meeting, concert, and fireworks on 24 August 1892.

Houlding was most unhappy and tried to start another Everton F.C., but the F.A. would not allow it. However, he had support from John McKenna (the club chairman and League president), thus Liverpool F.C. were formed at Anfield with an initial ground capacity of about 20,000.

The venue for the 1894 Cup Final was then an easy choice. Notts County beat Bolton 4-1 in front of 37,000 at Goodison Park, and became the first Second Division club to win the Cup, while James Logan scored the second hat trick in a final (William Townley of Blackburn scored the first in 1890). In fact, an international was played there the next year.

THE CRYSTAL PALACE

Despite such indecision after leaving the Oval, the F.A. wanted to find a more permanent venue in London, thus the Cup Final was taken to Anerley and remained there for a further twenty years.

The Great Exhibition was staged in the Crystal Palace, Hyde Park, which was designed by Joseph Paxton in 1851. The glass building was 1,500 feet long and covered 26 acres, whereas in six months there were 6 million visitors. The profits helped to fund the new museums at South Kensington, whilst the Crystal Palace was moved to Anerley Hill and re-opened as part of the Victorian pleasure grounds in 1856.

Indeed, with such a prominent profile, the amateur team Crystal Palace F.C. were formed there in 1861. They soon joined the F.A. and took part in the first Cup contest, whilst their players were members of the committee; however the club had faded by the end of the century.

Meanwhile, the Crystal Palace was the hub of the area and attracted many thousands of people annually, bringing great prosperity to local shops. The transport network converged in all directions on the concourse with two rail routes, buses, and trams, whilst there were large circular towers at each end and below were terraced gardens and lakes (with prehistoric models).

A grand central walk ran through the site and at the lower end were two gigantic fountains, each of them a staggering 800 feet wide. However, these were uneconomic from the start and the cascades were removed in 1880, and the fountains filled-in by 1894. The site was then a sports arena with an athletic ground to the north and a football ground to the south.

Clearly there was huge potential with a national landmark, good transport infrastructure, catering facilities, and a site that could accommodate 100,000 spectators - thus a managing company was formed to develop the site.

John Aird & Sons were involved in the construction at Hyde Park and undertook the work. The pitch was at the centre of an oval track and to the west was a pavilion with a forward-slanting roof. The latter was flanked by two stands, angled inwards towards each end of the pitch, and clearly the shape of the original fountain dictated this arrangement.

However, the stands were of frugal construction and only had seats for 3,000, whilst the majority of spectators stood on a low curving-bank with some meagre wooden terraces and poor sight lines.

The ground then staged some exceptional contests and Aston Villa beat West Bromwich Albion 1-0 in the first final in 1895, in front of Charles Alcock, Lord Kinnaird, and a limited crowd of 42,560.

Indeed, some new teams were soon to make their mark and Millwall and Southampton of the Southern League played a semi-final there in 1900. The score was 0-0 in front of 34,760, and Southampton won the replay at Elm Park to become the first non-league team to reach the final. However, they lost the latter contest to Bury by a 4-0 score line.

Non-league Tottenham beat four First Division clubs on the way to the final in 1901 and met Sheffield United with a record crowd of 114,815 (2-2). Yet, the replay at Burnden Park, Bolton attracted only 20,470, as the local railway company refused to provide cheap-day tickets.

In the replay Spurs were 1-0 behind at half time but came back to win 3-1, and were the only non-league winners in the 20th century. The game was a commercial disaster for Bolton with severe over-catering and thus became known colloquially as "Pie Saturday." Who ate all the pies?

Bury played Derby County in the final of 1903 and won by a record 6-0 score line in front of 63,102 spectators; which was something of a shock as Derby had conceded only one goal on the way to the final, although Bury had let in none at all during the whole competition.

Indeed, the venue was a great success and the F.A. negotiated a new five-year deal (for the Cup Final) with the Crystal Palace Co. in 1905. The three sides of terracing were then improved and two multi-gabled stands were erected around the pavilion, thus raising the number of seats to 5,000. The extensive banking gave the ground a huge potential capacity.

Aston Villa beat Newcastle United 2-0 in front of another six-figure crowd of 101,117 in 1905, and the latter team did not enjoy their visits south as they lost three finals in 1906, 1908, and 1911 (after a replay). In fact, they also drew the final in 1910, but were determined to win the replay by any means and in an unattractive match beat "Battling" Barnsley 2-0 (the latter won the Cup two years later after playing ten games).

The venue experienced financial problems by 1911 and was beginning to show its age, thus it was offered up for sale but there were no takers. Indeed the F.A. declined to purchase the venue for the nation in 1913.

Despite this the ground achieved its apex that year when Aston Villa beat Sunderland 1-0 in front of a world record crowd of 121,919. George V attended the following year and cheering crowds lined the route all the way from Buckingham Palace to Sydenham. There was clearly an excitable and patriotic atmosphere and Burnley (the Royalites) beat Liverpool 1-0 in front of a slightly smaller crowd of 72,778.

The modern Crystal Palace F.C. played there in 1905-15, but moved to Selhurst, and in the war the ground was an army depot. However it became home to the Corinthians a famous amateur club from 1922-36.

The team were successful at the time and played some epic games there, including a Cup encounter against Millwall with 32,500 in 1930 (which went to three games). Britain's first speedway track was laid around the pitch and a crowd of 9,834 watched the initial meeting in 1928, but the sport moved to New Cross in 1933 and the Crystal Palace burnt down in 1936.

This hastened the departure of the Corinthians who then joined with the Casuals and played at the Oval in 1950-63, whilst all that remains is some old banking just beside the modern athletics stadium.

OLD TRAFFORD & STAMFORD BRIDGE

The F.A. then had a familiar problem regarding the Cup Final, and with war looming put any major decisions on ice, and decided to use club grounds yet again. Despite the outbreak of war the 1914-15 season continued to its conclusion, however as the casualties mounted, many questioned whether these games should have been played at all.

Old Trafford was inaugurated in 1910 and like Goodison was the most advanced stadium of its time, thus it was the obvious choice for the final in 1915. Sheffield United defeated Chelsea by a 3-0 margin in front of 49,557, but the atmosphere was subdued and it was dubbed the "Khaki Cup Final" due to the large number of soldiers in the crowd.

The Football League restarted in 1919 and the F.A. chose Stamford Bridge for the next three finals. A running track was laid out there in 1877, and it was home to the London Athletic Club, whilst a large arena was developed as a speculative venture in 1905 and Chelsea were formed that year.

There was a main stand on the east side, a large terrace, and a running and cycle track around the pitch. At first the attendances were small, but there were 67,000 for a visit of Manchester United in 1906, and a Cup-tie against Swindon attracted 77,952 in 1911. However, there was almost a problem in 1920 when Chelsea reached the semi-final, but fortunately they lost 3-1 to Aston Villa. The three games were then as follows:

1920	Aston Villa 1 Huddersfield Town 0	(50,018)
1921	Tottenham Hotspur 1 Wolves 0	(72,805)
1922	Huddersfield Town 1 Preston 0	(53,000)

The low scores at these games were a result of the pitch, which suffered when it was used for other events such as athletics and baseball; whereas the low attendance was due to the use of a club ground and high prices. In fact, these were deliberately raised to keep the numbers down.

WEMBLEY STADIUM

However, the F.A. council was not idle during the years at Chelsea, and they soon opened a stadium far grander than any that went before.

Watkin's Tower or Folly was built at Wembley Park in 1894 and was to emulate the Eiffel Tower in Paris, but hardly got off the ground and was removed in 1907. In fact, this was the site chosen for the new stadium.

The initial development was as part of the British Empire Exhibition and Robert McAlpine (contractors) carried out the work in a remarkable 300 days - at a cost of just £750,000. An 'army' of workers and soldiers tested the safety of the ground by marching up and down upon the terraces, whilst it was ready just in time for the Cup Final in April 1923.

It was originally designated as the Empire Stadium and later received the encomium the Venue of Legends, while for many years playing at Wembley was the ultimate goal of clubs and their players.

Indeed, it was undoubtedly the largest and finest stadium in the world with its two distinctive towers linked by a balcony. Inside was a dazzling white interior, whilst terraces curved around the pitch and were reached through arched entrances. Two sides were seated and covered, and the Cup was presented from the Royal Box at the top of the famous stairs.

Bolton Wanderers played West Ham United in the first final, although it was nearly abandoned when an estimated 250,000 spectators descended on the ground. The official attendance was much lower at 127,000 however the arena was completely over-crowded.

The huge crowd spilled onto the pitch before the kick-off and a single policeman rode forth to settle them down, thus it was dubbed "The White Horse Final." However, during the game the ball bounced off the wall of spectators, and as a result remained in play. Yet, the game was completed and Bolton won 2-0 to receive the Cup from King George V.

Due to such problems all future finals were made all ticket and the crowds were initially 93,000. Indeed, after the Empire Exhibition there were doubts over its future, but the first international was against Scotland in 1924 (1-1), and the F.A. Cup went to Cardiff in 1927. Meanwhile, any questions were settled when Wembley Arena was built in 1934, and the complex was then further developed raising the capacity to 100,000.

There were no matches in 1940-45 however Wembley staged the Olympic Games in 1948, and was the venue for the Matthew's Final in 1953 when Blackpool came back to defeat Bolton 4-3. This was followed by Spurs victory over Leicester in 1961 to secure the first modern "double."

There were few later developments although the terraces were covered in 1963 and Wembley Way replaced the former Olympic Way. No doubt the most iconic event was the 1966 World Cup Finals when England beat West Germany 4-2 to take the Jules Rimet Trophy. A number of great contests took place, with many highs and lows, and none more remarkable than Arsenal's Cup victory in 1979 and Wimbledon's in 1988.

The venue was converted to an all seated stadium in 1990 with an Olympic Gallery, reducing the capacity to 79,000, and a new walkway was erected leading up to the entrance. This prepared the ground for the European Football Championships in 1996 when England came so close to emulating their success of thirty years earlier.

There was a brief sojourn to Cardiff in 2001-06, however the game had grown way beyond any dreams of the founders, and there was a return to Wembley under the arch at a cost of nearly £800 million in 2007.

F.A. Cup Final Venues

1872	**The Oval**
1873	**Lillie Bridge**
1874-92	**The Oval**
Replays	1875, 1876 The Oval
	1886 The Racecourse Ground, Derby
1893	**Fallowfield**
1894	**Goodison Park**
1895-1914	**Crystal Palace**
Replays	1901 Burnden Park
	1902 Crystal Palace
	1910 Goodison Park
	1911 Old Trafford
	1912 Bramall Lane
1915	**Old Trafford**
1920-22	**Stamford Bridge**
1923-2000	**Wembley**
Replays	1970 Old Trafford
	1981, 1982, 1983, 1990, 1993 Wembley
2001-06	**Millennium Stadium**
2007-	**'New' Wembley**

CHAPTER 16

Archibald Leitch

Regarding the design of football grounds there is one cognomen which stands out above all the others. Indeed, Archibald Leitch occupies a place in many club histories, and with respect to the current fashion might well be considered, "The Father of Football Grounds."

The great period of ground building began at the end of the 19th century, since the emerging clubs played at a number of unsatisfactory venues, and naturally wanted a more permanent home. Indeed, the locations which they moved to became deeply etched within football folklore.

Further to this, there was a stringent desire to provide expansive room for the paying supporter, and many clubs looked to build improved stands with permanent terraces. However, there was no A-Z of ground builders in the local yellow pages, and clubs increasingly turned to one man.

In fact, Archibald Leitch was ultimately responsible for all of the major grounds in Glasgow and some 25% of those in England, including nearly all of the premier clubs. Yet, he was not the obvious choice for such work, and initially had a background in Scottish engineering.

ARGYLL AND GLASGOW

The Argyll peninsula, eighty miles long and ten miles wide, was situated fifty miles west of Glasgow between two sounds, with several islands including Arran nearby. In general, it was an area of heath and moorland, whilst the main development was the Crinan Canal built by John Rennie in 1794. This linked the Sound of Jura and Loch Crinan to Ardrishaig, thereby saving a one hundred and twenty mile round journey.

The Leitch clan lived in the northern districts of Glassary to the east, and North and South Knapdale to the west and south, which extended from the River Add down to Loch Tarbert. The total population was 7,500 in the 1830s, whilst 1,300 lived in the main township of Lochgilphead beside an inlet of Loch Fyne - with its daily steamboat links to Glasgow.

Knapdale, meanwhile, had a dispersed population with some small villages on Loch Sween, and the three localities included a number of churches, a total of six parishes, and several primary schools. Indeed, this rugged-land of Highland farming communities and sea lochs provided an unlikely source for industrial innovation.

Certain families were prominent in Argyll in the 18th century, and John Leitch married Margaret McLachlan at Glassary in 1789 then had four children. There was a strong clan system in the area and their second son Dugald (1792) married a relative Anne, daughter of Archibald McLachlan, at Knapdale on 11 December 1819.

The family were itinerant in both occupation and residence thus Dugald worked as a labourer, shepherd, and fisherman, and lived at Inverneil near Ardrishaig and at Lochgilphead in Glassary. He had three children during this period namely John, Colin, and Archibald in 1822-31, then moved to Dunoon on the Firth of Clyde and had Dugald and Flora.

The story continues with Archibald Leitch who was born at Lochgilphead on 15 June 1831; however he then moved to the city and was a blacksmith at 37 Stevenston Street, Calton, in the west of Glasgow. He married Agnes Flint Kent (1833) a domestic servant at Bothwell on 31 December 1855, and had six children within the metropolis from 1857-70.

Continuing to work as a blacksmith, he resided at 1 Comley Park Street just north of Bridgeton (near to Celtic Park), in an area now largely rebuilt; but moved around the corner to 631 Gallowgate and lived there with his wife and children Archibald, Agnes M., and Flora in 1881.

Meanwhile, his brother Colin lived at Inverkip just across the water from Dunoon, whilst his sister Flora married Robert Robertson son of a seaman and lived at Govan. Of his other children Dugald a mercantile clerk resided at Anderston, Robert Kent a calico-engraver was nearby at Bellfield Street, and his daughter Margaret McGregor was also at Govan.

The father remained at Gallowgate and lived there with his wife, daughters Margaret (factory worker), Agnes (dressmaker), Flora (shopkeeper), and niece Agnes Robertson a visitor in 1891. Indeed, his daughter advertised her services as a dressmaker and sons Dugald and Robert lived nearby.

His daughter Agnes McLachlan married James Barrie (not the author) at Bath Hotel, Blythswood in 1893, whilst her brother Archibald adopted a career of pecuniary benefit and helped his parents retire to the country.

They resided at 30 Wyndham Road, Rothesay on Bute in 1901 with their daughter Margaret a housekeeper and grandson Hendry, although Dugald lived in Govan and Robert at Partick - the father died at Daisy Cottage, Ardbeg in 1907 and his wife Agnes at Bothwell in 1911.

However, their son Archibald Leitch j. was born at 1 Comley Park Street on 27 April 1865 and was destined for greatness, being the most influential person in early ground design. Indeed, he grew up at Gallowgate in the west of Glasgow and learnt about his father's blacksmiths, giving him some basic knowledge of both metal work and design.

EARLY CAREER

The most significant factor in Leitch's progress was a good education, and initially he attended Hutcheson's Grammar School, just south of the river, at Crown Street and Rutherglen Road, from 1876-81. [1]

He then spent a year at the Andersonian College and took his first steps in his chosen profession by joining Duncan Stewart & Co. (London Road Iron Works) at 47 Summer Street, Glasgow, in 1882. The works were situated a short walk from Gallowgate just next to Bridgeton Station. [2]

The proprietor Duncan Stewart clearly saw some promise and gave him this opportunity, whilst the firm were listed as engineers, millwrights, and boilermakers. He stayed for five years and gained experience in the pattern shop, fitting shop, and drawing office, whilst in the last six months he had some further training as a draughtsman.

There was then a complete change of direction and he went to sea as an engineer in 1887-90, and thereby gained a Board of Trade certificate. Upon his return, he was superintendent draughtsman of the marine department at Duncan Stewart & Co. but stayed for just eight months. Indeed, this short tenure may have been related to his forthcoming marriage.

As an engineer's draughtsman of 631 Gallowgate he married Jessie Hardie Black of 17 Wesleyan Street at Albert Hall, Bridgeton (of the Free Church or Presbyterians) on 20 June 1890. She was the daughter of James Black a dairyman from Blackridge near to Torpichen in Linlithgowshire.

He then moved south of the river and made a significant choice when he entered the employ of Messrs. Mirrlees, Watson & Co. Ltd. at the Scotland Street Iron Works, 45 Scotland Street, in Tradeston. [3]

----

[1] David Hamilton designed the school in 1841 and the entrance on Crown Street had a classical tower with dome. The building was demolished to make way for the Hutcheson E scheme (in 1969), but some of the latter was also replaced.

[2] The iron works and all other buildings have gone, while the only remnants are cobbles in Olympia Street (Mile End Quarter) - with Celtic Park in the distance.

[3] The firm began in 1840 and William Tait and William Renny Watson took over. They traded as Mirrlees, Watson & Yaryan and W.R. Watson leased 7,000 acres at Kauai in 1889; then formed the Hawaiian Sugar Co. with Robinson & Gay who were the largest cane employers. He was knighted in 1892 and they made the third ever diesel engine in 1897, and worked for the Admiralty in the First War. They became Mirrlees, Blackstone & Co. part of Hawker Siddeley in 1969.

The company were engineers, iron and brass founders, boilermakers, and manufacturers of all kinds of machinery and apparatus for making and refining sugar, and Leitch was put in charge of the ordering department of their drawing office in late 1890.

At first, he had limited finances, and lived with eleven other families in a four-storey tenement at 20 McLellan Street, Plantation. The building with its austere façade was just south of Scotland Street, and a few streets from the first Ibrox (opened in 1887), whereas it faced a variety of engineering works, iron foundries, factories, and the nearby railway. [4]

His son Archibald Kent Leitch was born in April 1891, whilst he worked for Mirrlees, Watson for five years and became an experienced mechanical draughtsman. In addition, he lectured on machine design at the Glasgow School Board, the Christian Institute, and the Glasgow Athenaeum in St. George's Place during this time.

He then moved away from the city and a daughter Jean Black (*an infant*) was born at 8 South Dean Place, Mount Florida in 1894; however, he had greater ambitions and started his own business as a consulting engineer at 97 Buchanan Street, in the centre of Glasgow, in late 1895. [5]

Initially, he had several general engineering contracts and was consulting engineer for Lanarkshire C.C. (Middle Ward), whilst a daughter Jane Hilda Roberts (Jeanie) was born at 12 Clincart Road that year. The property was a middle class terrace just southeast of the "second" Hampden Park.

Leitch's marine experience secured him membership of the Institution of Engineers & Shipbuilders (Scotland), and with the future in mind he applied to the Institution of Mechanical Engineers, 19 Victoria Street, London.

Sir W. Renny Watson and Duncan Stewart his former employers proposed him, and he was granted associate membership of the I.M.E. on 25 March 1897. Further to this, the business went to 40 St. Enoch's Square, a five-storey classical building on the west side, and from that address he began his greatest work (The Electrical Engineers are at No. 14).

---

[4] A motorway now divides the road in half, whilst the Scotland Street Schools (built by C.M. Rennie in 1903-06) and Howden's Works (of 1910) remain.

[5] This upmarket street provides a glimpse of an opulent past with the Clydesdale Bank (1891) and impressive Argyll Arcade (see below). St. Enoch's Station opened to the south in 1896, but St. Mungo's Cathedral to the east was 13th century.

97 Buchanan Street had shops at the ground floor and was of grey stone with pediments. Today, it has a re-creation of the Willow Tea Rooms, Ingram Street designed by Charles Rennie Mackintosh in 1900 - Kate Cranston gave the latter his first commission and he also worked on her tea rooms at No. 91-93.

FOOTBALL GROUNDS

Meanwhile, Glasgow had three major football clubs, and by chance the Leitch family lived near all of them. Indeed, such proximity then provided a clear opportunity in terms of the engineer's future direction. [6]

Celtic F.C. were formed in 1887 and moved to Celtic Park or Parkhead in 1892. A large ground was developed and a reporter dubbed it "Paradise," whilst only Goodison Park compared, and the scale was revealed when 45,017 watched an international against England on 7 April 1894.

The club purchased the freehold and added a north stand and pavilion, to the oval track and substantial banking. As a result the ground hosted four more internationals with England up to 1904, and the attendance was never below 40,000, whilst the highest was 63,000 in 1900.

Leitch is credited with working on Celtic Park but was not responsible for the original design as he was not in business then. In fact, his company were involved in factory design for many years, and it was this adroit aptitude that attracted him to what was clearly related work.

Rangers F.C. were formed in 1872 and played at the first Ibrox from 1887, hosting one international with a crowd of 20,000 in 1892. Indeed, there was much competition for these pecuniary events and they went to the present Ibrox Park, with a 40,000 capacity, in 1899. It was of a similar design with a south stand, corner pavilion, oval track, and earth banking.

Leitch was more involved on this occasion and the layout may have been suggested by Celtic Park. Meanwhile, his company designed the west terrace with wooden planking and an iron framework the next year. The structure was passed as safe - however others were less sure due to its huge scale.

He was well located for such contemporary work and his daughter Jessie Hardie Leitch was born at 1110 Cathcart Road on 29 March 1901. The property was next to Bolton Drive and opposite to Somerville Road, which led down to the third Hampden Park - the latter was in fact being built by his company at the time (see below).

The house was an up-market tenement of red sandstone however Leitch a civil engineer and employer lived with his wife, children, a servant from New York, and a nurse at 1011 Cathcart Road with its five rooms in 1901. It seems possible that the numbers were transposed, however any error is unlikely since his neighbour was Henry Hunter the registrar.

---

[6] The city also had three other clubs: Clyde F.C. (1878) who played at Shawfield, Partick Thistle (1876) who played at Firhill Park, and Third Lanark who were founders of the Scottish League in 1890.

Ibrox Park was then severely tested when a vast crowd attended a Scotland v England game on 5 April 1902 (either 68,114 or 80,500). The wooden terraces were saturated with heavy rain the night before, thus there was a partial collapse leading to several deaths and many injuries.

The game was abandoned and declared void whilst a later enquiry found it hard to apportion blame, but suggested a number of possible reasons which included the design, workmanship, or most likely the stamp of approval. However, Leitch was apparently unaffected despite such controversy, and soon took on many more significant contracts.

Queen's Park F.C. were formed at Queen's Park Recreation Ground as early as 1867 and then established an impressive record. They played in the first F.A. Cup in 1872, and were the core of the international team, whilst they moved to an enclosed venue the first Hampden Park, near Hampden Terrace, in 1873. The latter was near to Cathcart and Clincart Roads.

The club hosted all of the internationals against England at the West of Scotland Cricket Ground in 1872, 74, 76, and at the first Hampden Park in 1878, 80, 82, whilst they were F.A. Cup finalists in 1884/85.

A new railway was extended to Mount Florida forcing them to move to Titwood Park (Clydesdale C.C.). Meanwhile, Scotland beat England 1-0 at Cathkin Park north of Prospecthill Road in the first British championships on 15 March 1884 - which was just east of their other ground.

Clearly this provided a new opportunity and the club then developed the site with brick pavilion, banking, two open stands, and a cinder-track as the second Hampden Park in October 1884. Internationals then took place in 1886, 88, 90 and the attendance at the last date was 26,379. However, there was much competition for these prestigious events, and they lost the game to Rangers in 1892 and then to Celtic from 1894.

As a result the club purchased 12.5 acres of land just south of Prospecthill Road on Somerville Drive, the aim being to attract internationals back to their ground. Queen's Park joined the Scottish League as amateurs in 1900 and the costs for such an outfit were prohibitive, however they contacted Leitch and the third Hampden Park was built from 1900-03.

In general, he was concerned with mechanical/structural aspects of design, but at Hampden he was the architect of a colossal ground. There was oval banking around the track and pitch, and a central pavilion on the south side flanked by two stands (each for 4,000), giving a capacity of 65,000.

It was similar to the Crystal Palace and as a result Glasgow had three of the largest grounds in the world. However, despite these investments Celtic Park was used again in 1904, thus the terracing at Hampden was increased in size and it attained a completely new magnitude.

There was then a game between Scotland and England at Hampden on 7 April 1906, and a crowd of 102,741 saw a 2-1 victory. Indeed, it became the permanent venue and Scotland remained undefeated against England there prior to the First War, with an attendance of 127,307 in 1912. [7]

Meanwhile, Leitch had considerable work and was a consulting mechanical engineer for Lanark and Renfrew C.C.s, Ayr County Hospital, Kroonstad Corporation, and an engineer for several principalities in India.

However, his firm's main occupation was factory design, and one of the largest contracts was for Alexander Hope Jun. & Co., a manufacturing chemist who moved from Port Dundas to Provanmill. Indeed, their new *Anchor Chemical Works* at Garngad Road cost them £25,000.

His other major work was for the Stirling Boiler Co. Ltd. water-tube boiler makers at 45 Hope Street, Glasgow at a cost of £20,000. Further to this he constructed new or part works for the Union Tube Works, Coatbridge (£12,000), Clydesdale Tube Works, Glasgow (£8,000), and Caledonian Tube Works, Coatbridge (£1,000). [8]

"TRACING GLASGOW"

Leitch's company were a good prospect and his designs had innovative detail, but most significantly a competitive price. In fact, knowledge of his acclaimed work soon spread south of the border to England.

Bramall Lane hosted the first official club soccer match in 1862, but was initially used mainly for cricket. In fact, some cricketing members formed Wednesday F.C. in 1867, who over twenty years hired it for major games; whereas it staged the first floodlit match with 20,000 in 1878, and had three early internationals in 1883, 87, and 97.

---

[7] A fire destroyed the pavilion at Hampden Park in 1914 (replaced), and extra land was purchased at the west end in 1923. A second pitch was built with pavilion and banked-terracing on three sides (still remains), but was only for reserve matches, and Queen's Park played in the national stadium. The terracing was increased by 25,000 places in 1927, making it a vast uncovered amphitheatre towering over the nearby houses. The record attendance was then 149,415 in 1937.

The second Hampden Park became home to Third Lanark and was renamed as New Cathkin Park in 1903. However, they folded up in 1967, and only the grass outline of the pitch then remained.

[8] Archibald Leitch was listed in trade directories as a consulting engineer, and also as a factory architect or inspecting engineer. Meanwhile, tube works manufactured the metal tubes used in the boilers of steam engines.

Wednesday also hired the Sheaf House Ground just to the south, and played at various venues on a regular basis, but moved permanently to the nearby Olive Grove arena in 1887.

This left a vacuum at Bramall Lane which had a short cover and stand on the John Street side, with terraces going past the football/cricket pitch to the pavilion. The ground committee formed Sheffield United in September 1889, and the club joined the new Division Two in 1892. Indeed, they were very successful and won the League in 1898 and Cup in 1899/1902.

The John Street stand was originally built in 1895 with 2,000 seats, and there was a cover at the Shoreham Street end, but a fire damaged the stand in November 1900 and the club approached Leitch for a new design. This appeared quite un-original at first glance and consisted of a basic structure with raised seating behind a terrace.

However, it was in fact rather innovative for its time, and had electric lighting, a running track under the seats, and a mock-Tudor gable at the centre. The latter became his hallmark and the design used at Sheffield was soon seen all around the country. The work was finished in 1902 at a cost of £12,000, and this can be compared to his more major work at Ibrox which cost the club almost double at £22,000. [9]

By then he was a consulting engineer for 6½ years, superintending large works with all their mechanical and structural details. As a result he applied for full membership of the I.M.E. at Storey's Gate in St. James's Park (now 1 Birdcage Walk). He noted that he employed thirty people at St. Enoch's Square and quoted several large tube works and the two football grounds in his application. Indeed, these were the credentials of a successful business and he was made a full member on 17 June 1902.

Meanwhile, his next contract was in Middlesbrough, whose football club played at Linthorpe Road on an enclosed pitch with grandstand next to the cricket ground. Some of their members formed Ironopolis in 1889-94, who spent two seasons in the League and played at the Paradise Ground, just to the south. As a result Boro gave up their professional status and won the Amateur Cup in 1895/98, but then entered the League in 1899.

They wanted to leave Linthorpe Road and after promotion to Division One in 1902, they received notice to quit. As a result they contacted Leitch and with little time available he designed a complete ground, which was to become Ayresome Park. It was a landmark in his career, since he supplied the required stand and terraces but at a reasonable price.

---

[9] The John Street stand was damaged in the war and was rebuilt without its gable in 1954. The last cricket match was in 1973, and the fourth side was developed. Leitch's stand was demolished in 1994 and replaced three years later.

There were 2,000 seats under a barrel-roof with a semi-circular gable, and the Linthorpe Road stand was erected on the south side to give an initial capacity of 33,000; whilst it was opened with a friendly against Celtic on 1 September 1903, although some work remained unfinished. [10]

Leitch made considerable profits from his factory and football work and moved to "The Tannoch," 27 Maxwell Drive, Pollockshields in 1903-08. This large detached villa was just south of McLellan Street across the railway and his last child Agnes MacGregor (Nancy) was born there in 1904, but this was in fact only the beginning of his attainments.

He soon worked on two significant contracts in the capital connected with some major players in the 'game.' Joseph Mears was a speculative builder at Queen Street, Hammersmith, and also had premises at Wyfold Road and Crab Tree Wharf in Fulham. Indeed, Mears & Co. built Craven Cottage on the site of an old Tudor house in 1896.

Meanwhile, Henry G. Norris was born in Lambeth in 1865 and started life as a solicitor's clerk, but progressed to be a property developer and also a director of Fulham F.C. by 1903. He soon became the main force behind the club who then played in Division One of the Southern League.

Some serious problems developed the next season when London County Council tried to close the main stand (The Rabbit Hutch) for safety reasons. This led to a court case in January 1905 and Fulham called a number of experts including Leitch. The club clearly needed to make improvements, thus Norris asked the engineer to design a new ground on the site, whilst there were some further developments nearby.

The London Athletic Club laid out Stamford Bridge in 1877, while Fred Parker a promoter was acquainted with Joe and Gus Mears who purchased the freehold in 1904. The three then formed a partnership and were the driving force behind the evolution of the ground. [11]

For a while the plans were almost abandoned and the site was nearly sold to the railway as a goods yard. However, the three travelled up to Glasgow and witnessed the scale of the grounds in that city, and were encouraged to go ahead as planned. As a result they employed Leitch to design a ground that would rival the Crystal Palace, so he set up a temporary office at 33 Victoria Street, Westminster, from 1905-07.

---

[10] A two-tier south stand for 9,000 was erected at Ayresome in 1936-37 (possibly by Leitch), and the record was 53,802 against Newcastle in 1949. The final game was against Luton to take the 'new' First Division title on 30 April 1995.

[11] Joseph Theophilus (1871) and Henry Augustus Mears (1873) were the sons of the builder, and became local entrepreneurs at a very young age.

In addition, he formed a partnership of many years, which made a great impact on football ground development. Indeed, Humphreys had an *Iron Building Works* at 199-205 Buckingham Palace Road by Ebury Bridge, and near the Grosvenor Canal with its wharves and barges (Victoria Station), whilst their offices were at 187-193 Knightsbridge.

The two then set to work at Stamford Bridge and laid out a major venue suitable for football, athletics, and cycling, with large banked terraces and a substantial main stand located on the east side.

Mears & Co. built up the terraces using excavations from the Kingsway tunnel and Piccadilly line (brought to Crab Tree Wharf), while Humphreys built the main stand with a central gable and criss-cross ironwork columns. Both of these were to become the Leitch hallmarks; however it remained basic in design with seating for just 5,000 spectators.

The Mears brothers then tried to attract Fulham to the ground, but this move was blocked by Norris who wanted to retain control. As a result they had to form a new team and considered Stamford Bridge, Kensington, or London F.C. but finally settled on the more prestigious Chelsea. In addition they attracted some top players, such as goalkeeper William Foulkes from Sheffield United, and were elected straight into Division Two.

Their first game was at the newly opened Edgeley Park in Stockport on 2 September 1905, and Foulkes let in the only goal, although the *West London Press* said the ground was no better than "a cabbage field."

Stamford Bridge opened with a friendly against Liverpool two days later in front of just 7,000, but the paper praised Mears and his new stadium, stating that the ground had a staggering potential capacity of 130,000! [12]

All of these developments took place parallel to those at Fulham, and Norris hoped his ground would compete with his rivals. Indeed, the three sides of terracing were extended, but the most important innovation was the new main stand and the adjacent corner pavilion.

Leitch provided the design and Humphreys the ironwork to produce a stand with raised seating above a narrow paddock, and a pitched roof with the club's name on a central gable. This was all fairly standard, but it was the frontage on Stevenage Road that was of most significance.

No expense was spared on the ornate brickwork with its five pediments, coursing, club motifs, and openings reminiscent of a London mews. Indeed it was far superior to Chelsea's, and the pavilion with wrought-iron balcony added a touch of gentility - being a feature copied from Scotland.

---

[12] Chelsea reached Division One in 1907 and the first England game was in 1913, whilst the record crowd was 82,905 for a League game v Arsenal in 1935. The main stand was replaced in 1972 and the terracing removed in 1997.

The first game at their "transformed ground" was against Portsmouth in the Southern League on 2 September 1905, being a goalless draw in front of 20,000. Indeed, Fulham entered the League in 1907, whilst Norris left for Arsenal three years later and received a knighthood. [13]

Meanwhile, the status of these grounds was confirmed when they were used for internationals soon afterwards: Bramall Lane in 1903, Ayresome Park in 1905 (and 1914), and Craven Cottage in 1907.

Leitch then moved to some prestigious offices at 34 Argyll Arcade, 30 Buchanan Street, in 1907-39. The Regency arcade was built in 1827 and a new façade and offices were added in Baroque style in 1904. His chambers were found just inside the door, up a marble staircase, and his intriguing telegram address was in fact "Tracing Glasgow."

ETRUSCAN DAYS

With such successes under his belt Leitch soon became most prolific, and worked on fifteen other grounds before the First War. However, there was little inherent deviation and he used the same tried and trusted formula.

In the first instance a new main stand was built on Nuttall Street at Ewood Park, Blackburn, for the aptly named chairman Laurence Cotton, in 1907. This was "in the style of Leitch," and had an oak-panelled boardroom, and was angled at the centre to accommodate the irregular site.

Indeed, he worked on both grounds in Liverpool which over time had fallen behind others. An international took place at Anfield in 1905 and the ground was found wanting, thus Leitch raised the pitch, and built a new main stand to the west with 3,000 seats and a mock gable. The principal innovation was the use of reinforced concrete to support the stand.

In addition, he raised a huge bank at the south end which became the famous "Kop," and the first game at the rebuilt ground was against Stoke in the First Division, in front of 32,000, on 1 September 1906. [14]

Meanwhile, Everton's ground had a stand on Bullens Road and a cover on Goodison Road in 1895. Leitch then built a large double-decker main stand with extensive terracing in front, and a smaller stand at the Park End of the

---

[13] The main stand at Fulham was listed and restored in 1999, and is one of the last surviving examples of Leitch's work.

[14] The name Spion Kop was first used at the Manor Ground, Plumstead in 1904, and referred to a battle in the Boer War - Ernest Edwards a journalist applied the name to Anfield. Joseph Watson Cabré designed a new roof in 1928 and the main stand gable was replaced in 1970, whilst the Kop was demolished in 1994.

ground, in 1907. One of the main innovations at Goodison was criss-cross ironwork in the balconies, and it then staged two internationals, whereas this was the start of a thirty year association with the club. [15]

Leitch then travelled eastwards to Bradford and worked at Park Avenue whose team were formed by the local rugby club that year. He developed a ground with end terraces, two narrow stands, and a corner pavilion backing onto a cricket pitch. The club played for one year in the Southern League but joined Division Two with Tottenham in 1908, whereas the ground was used for an international against Ireland with 28,000 in 1909.

Their rivals Bradford City were formed by Manningham Rugby Club at Valley Parade in 1903, and were accepted into the League before they even had a team! The ground staged an Amateur Cup Final in 1904 and there were talks of a merger, however Leitch soon developed the arena.

He faced a particular challenge due to a sloping site but built a main stand on the west side with double-pitch roof, and raised the size of the terracing at the Manningham end. On the Midland Road side he built a stand with reinforced concrete supports and three mock-Tudor gables, though it was not a success and was eventually left as terracing. The club were Division Two champions in 1908, and had a record attendance of 39,146 on the way to their Cup Final victory in 1911. [16]

Clearly most of Leitch's work was now in England so he shifted his focus south and lived at "Inverclyde," Nicholas Road, Blundellsands, not far from Liverpool, in 1909-14. Indeed, he also had offices at Prudential Assurance Buildings, 36 Dale Street in the centre of the city at this time. His telegram address was of course "Terracing" indicating his main line of work.

Tottenham Hotspur had moved to White Hart Lane in 1899 and won the Southern League and F.A. Cup the next two years, while they were elected to Division Two with Bradford in 1908 and their ground had a capacity of 40,000. Leitch then worked with Humphreys and built a stand on the west side - larger and grander than those seen at Chelsea and Fulham.

The new main stand had a pitched roof on columns, with seats for 5,300 and a paddock for 6,000, but the principal feature was a large mock-Tudor gable showing the club's name. It was completed in 1909, whereas Leitch went back there several times and the stand lasted until 1980.

---

[15] The main stand at Goodison was replaced in stages from 1969-70, and the Park End stand became obsolete and was demolished in 1994.

[16] Valley Parade was to be ill-fated and the Midland Road stand was dismantled in 1951, and the roof sold to Berwick Rangers, whilst there was a disastrous fire in the main stand in 1985.

However, his busiest year came in 1910, which was no surprise as eight clubs opened new grounds that year. In the first instance he developed a large new venue for Huddersfield Town, who had played at Leeds Road in the Midland League from 1908.

The club wanted to take a step up and asked Leitch to develop the ground to support their League application. Humphreys were the main contractors and turned the pitch by a full 90°, so it was end-on to Leeds Road. The main stand on the west side had 4,000 seats with a paddock and a pitched roof/gable, whilst banking was raised on the other sides with a cover at the Leeds Road end, resulting in a total capacity of 34,000.

The club were then elected to Division Two and the ground opened in September 1910, but crowds were under 10,000 and the pitch became a messy bog, hence they considered suing Leitch. However, most problems were resolved and they won the League three times from 1924-26, and the capacity was then raised to a colossal 67,000.

Another aspiring team were Millwall Athletic who started on the Isle of Dogs in 1885, but then became promoters of the Southern League. In fact, they reached the Cup semi-final in 1900/02, and decided to leave North Greenwich for New Cross in the hope of attracting greater support.

They obtained an idiosyncratic site between the railway lines next to Cold Blow Lane, and Leitch and Humphreys built The Den for just £10,000. There was a main stand with gable to the south surrounded by un-covered terraces, and it staged an international against Wales with 22,000 in 1911, whilst there was a record of 48,672 during a Cup run in 1937. [17]

Leitch then went to Manchester and worked with architects Brameld & Smith to design a ground superior to any that went before. Newton Heath played at North Road and Bank Street and joined the League in 1892, while a local businessman John H. Davies reformed them as Manchester United in 1902, and then purchased some land at Old Trafford in 1910.

The main stand on the south side had a multi-span roof (like a factory) with a central gable, cushioned seats, plunge baths, massage rooms, and a gymnasium, whilst the large curving terraces provided an 80,000 capacity and dictated the future shape of the venue.

It immediately hosted Cup semi-finals and the final of 1915, whereas the ground was gradually developed over the years, and the highest attendance was 76,962 for a Cup game between Wolves and Grimsby in 1939.

---

[17] The terraces at The Den were eventually roofed, but the north and main stand were both destroyed in 1943. In fact the ground was not rebuilt until 1962, whilst it was demolished in 1993, and the club moved to a site nearby which was called the New Den - again situated amongst the railway lines.

This was just one of several major grounds developed by Leitch, and he then turned his attentions to the North East. Sunderland played their games at Newcastle Road from 1886, and entered the League in 1890, whilst their manager Tom Watson (later Liverpool) assembled "the team of all talents" and they won the League in 1892, 1893, 1895, and 1902.

The first game at Roker Park was against Liverpool with 30,000 in 1898, and both grounds hosted internationals; whilst Alf Common was purchased from Sheffield United for £375 in 1902. He was then sold three years later to struggling Middlesbrough for the first £1,000 fee, and scored the winner at Bramall Lane for a much needed away win. This caused considerable consternation at the F.A. and to Charles Clegg the owner of Sheffield, thus they promptly introduced a transfer ceiling of £350. [18]

The Roker End terrace was originally of wood, however Leitch replaced this with reinforced concrete supports at a cost of £6,000 in 1911. Indeed, the club then won the League and were Cup runners-up in 1913.

Meanwhile, Fulham were less successful and remained in Division Two, thus Henry Norris purchased the ailing Woolwich Arsenal in 1910. Their Manor Ground was in a poor location and he suggested a move to Fulham, but this was rejected so he took them to Highbury in 1913, although there were objections from both Spurs and Clapton Orient.

He then employed Leitch to build a ground to replace the Crystal Palace, and the terraces were raised with waste from the Piccadilly line. These were extended on three sides with the North Bank being the main feature.

Humphreys, meanwhile, built the main stand on the east side in Avenell Road, with a multi-span roof and 9,000 seats, although it lacked a central gable. Indeed, the first game took place in September before the work was completed, and the workforce nearly walked off the site.

Henry Norris then took some significant actions and used his influence at the League A.G.M. in 1919, thus Arsenal were promoted to Division One (and have remained ever since). They had finished in fifth place in the lower division before the war, and went up with Derby and Preston, but it was Tottenham that were relegated.

There was an international against Wales in 1920, whilst Norris brought the manager Herbert Chapman to the club from Huddersfield in 1925. All of these actions were soon repaid in full when Arsenal became the strongest team in the country in the 1930s. There was a record attendance of 73,295 against Sunderland in 1935, but the main stand was not cost effective and was replaced by William Binnie's structure the next year.

---

[18] Trevor Francis went from Birmingham to Nottingham Forest for the first £1 million fee in 1979, and helped them to win the European Cup twice.

Meanwhile, Charles Quilter was the manager of the Aston Lower Grounds and Aston Villa played there before moving to Wellington Road in 1876-97. Both staged Cup semi-finals and the latter an international, whilst Frederick W. Rinder a surveyor for the corporation joined McGregor on the Villa committee in 1887. The club won the Cup that year, but were disqualified from the next contest due to severe crowd problems at a home game.

In fact, Wellington Road was always limited and Rinder took them to the Lower Grounds, below Aston Hall, in 1897. The Villa Park venue initially had barrel-roofed stands and curved around an athletics track, while there was raised banking at each end, and the club offices were situated in the old buildings of the pleasure park.

Aston Villa won six championships and five Cups before the First War, and there were internationals at Villa Park in 1899 and 1902. Rinder then contacted Leitch and together they produced 'a master-plan' for the ground in 1914, which might raise the capacity to 104,000. The track was removed and the terraces extended, whilst the main stand in Trinity Road was built with gable in 1922-24. It was more elaborate than Leitch had planned due to the aspirations of Rinder. [19]

Wednesday F.C. played at Olive Grove and were elected to the League in 1892, then won the F.A. Cup in 1896; but were given notice to leave and moved to Owlerton, four miles north of the city, in 1899.

Edwin Clegg kicked-off the first game against Chesterfield in Division Two, and his brother also sat on the board. Indeed, they were promoted soon afterwards and won the League in 1903/04 and also the Cup in 1907, while the ground was developed from 1913-14.

The club raised a large bank or Spion Kop at the Penistone Road end, whilst Leitch built a main stand on the south side with seating for 5,600, a terrace, and a pitched roof/gable. This made the capacity 50,000 although the ground failed to hold a smaller number soon after. There was a change of local boundaries in 1914 and it was renamed as Hillsborough, whilst the club won the League title again in 1929 and 1930. [20]

Leitch's only other work before the war was in Scotland and initially he increased the capacity at Ibrox to 63,000, whilst he built a small main stand for Hamilton Academicals at Douglas Park in 1913, and a larger one for Hearts at Tynecastle in 1914-19.

---

[19] The Holte End was extended by February 1940, and a record crowd of 76,588 attended a Cup-tie against Derby in 1946.

[20] Leitch's stand was renovated in 1992-96, and a second tier was added with 3,200 seats, whilst the roof was replaced and had a replica gable.

His success was clearly apparent and he enjoyed the life of a gentleman, moving to "Etruria House," 49 Lonsdale Road, Barnes in early 1915. The house was situated on the south side and the name was engraved on the gateposts. A driveway went past the front door with a small coach-house to the left, whilst there was a columned porch, two-storeys, and a moulded cornice at roof level with some large chimneys. [21]

Leitch no doubt became familiar with the area when he worked on Craven Cottage, whereas Hammersmith Bridge with its functional design features and criss-cross ironwork may have provided some inspiration.

He had multiple offices around the country and in addition to those in Scotland had temporary offices in Manchester, Northern Ireland, and at 2 Southampton Street, Bloomsbury, in 1915; but such success was tainted when his daughter Jane died at Lonsdale Road in 1918.

GRAND DESIGNS

After the war his first contract was to rebuild Dens Park for Dundee F.C. The club themselves moved there in 1899 which was rather a bold decision, since their main rivals the Wanderers played across the road at Clepington Park. The latter became Dundee Hibernian and United in 1923, whilst the neighbour's venue was renamed as Tannadice.

Meanwhile, Dundee F.C. employed Leitch to develop their ground, and he built terraces on three sides with raised banking to the south due to a slope, and a cinder track around the pitch.

A two-tier main stand was built on the north side, angled at the centre, due to the shape of Sandeman Street (like at Ewood and Molineux). There was decorative ironwork, a red brick exterior, and an entrance with brass door-handles, marble surrounds, wood panelling, and a plaster ceiling.

---

[21] Josiah Wedgwood (1730-95) founded the Etruria Works and daughter Susannah was mother of Charles Darwin. Thomas (1734-88) was a cousin and partner, and his son Ralph had a pottery company but moved to Oxford Street by 1810.

Ralph Wedgwood junior married Hannah English at St. Paul's, Covent Garden in 1818 and was a stationer who invented carbon paper. The family moved to Barnes and his son John Raphael lived at 4 Park Villas and "Etruria House," 49 Lonsdale Road. It was the last property until new developments in 1906.

R. Wedgwood & Son traded in London, and Margaret his widow left a diamond ring given to Ralph by the Emperor of Russia and all her Wedgwood ware in her will of 1908. She died in 1913 and the estate was worth £86,553. The Wedgwoods were all buried at Barnes Old Cemetery.

In fact, the work was not finally completed until 1921 and the ground is little changed today, being "home of the city's oldest club." Indeed, it is an impressive stand of its time, and the blue cladding contrasts with the orange and black of Tannadice just one hundred yards away.

Leitch then secured several more contracts in the capital and took some permanent offices in London, firstly at 3 Queen Street by Southwark Bridge in 1920-22, and then at 18 Victoria Street in 1923-29; the latter being near to the offices and works of his partners Humphreys.

In the first instance he designed two new covers for White Hart Lane, one at the Paxton Road end in 1921 and another at the Park Lane end in 1923. Indeed, with his original main stand the covered capacity was 30,000, and only Goodison had more shelter at this time.

Charlton Athletic moved to the Valley in 1919 but had little money and employed Leitch in 1921. The main stand was built by Humphreys on the west side, but was reminiscent of the Rabbit Hutch at Fulham, and had just four spans and only 2,500 seats. However, there was a large terrace known as the East Bank and the capacity was 50,000, whilst the club joined the Third Division (South) with Aberdare Athletic in 1921.

The club had done well with limited resources, but they were un-settled and Humphreys also laid out a temporary home at the Mount, Catford, in 1923 - although they returned to the Valley after just thirteen games. [22]

Clapton Orient F.C. played at Millfields Road and joined the League with Chelsea, Hull City, and Leeds City in 1905. They were a relatively small club and remained in Division Two, but paid Leitch the considerable sum of £30,000 to develop their ground in 1923.

Their old stand was sold to Wimbledon and erected at Plough Lane, while Humphreys built a large Kop terrace on the north side, and a main stand with five-span roof on the south side. They were forced to sell to Clapton Greyhound Stadium Co. in 1927 and another multi-span roof was inserted above the Kop. Over 35,000 attended games against Millwall and Spurs in 1928-29, but they had to leave the next year and after a period at Lea Bridge Road, went to Brisbane Road (as Leyton Orient) in 1937. [23]

---

[22] The record attendance at the Valley was 75,031 for a Cup-tie against Aston Villa in 1938. The main stand was renovated in 1979 and new stands built at each end, whilst the club vacated to Selhurst and Upton Park from 1985-92.

[23] Leyton F.C. were formed in 1868 and played in the Southern League in 1905-12. They had two periods at Brisbane (Osborne) Road, and fielded Charlie Buchan who played for Sunderland and Arsenal. The greyhound stadium at Millfields Road was closed in 1974, but Leitch's stand remained until the end.

**Sir Frederick J. Wall
(1858-1944)**
F.A. secretary from
1895-1934

**22 Lancaster Gate,
Hyde Park**
Home of the F.A. in
1929-72

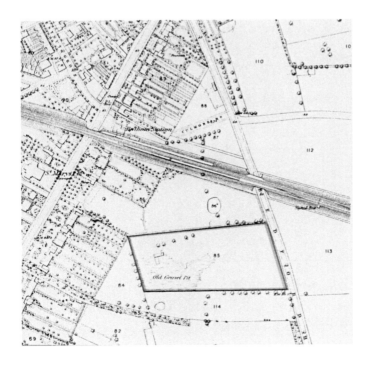

Balham (1872)
Rangers F.C. played
at the cricket ground
in 1875-88

Sir John Charles Clegg (1850-1937)

He played for Sheffield, became F.A. chairman in 1890, and was president from 1923… "Nobody gets lost on a straight road!"

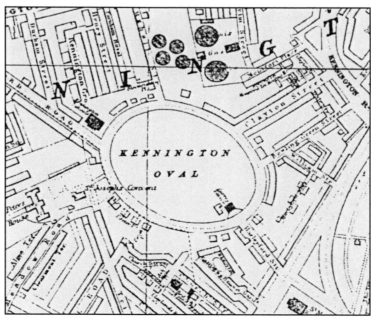

The Oval - Cup Finals 1872, 74-92
Alcock was secretary of Surrey C.C.C. from 1872; Marindin was referee in 1880 and 1884-90, and Clegg in 1882/92

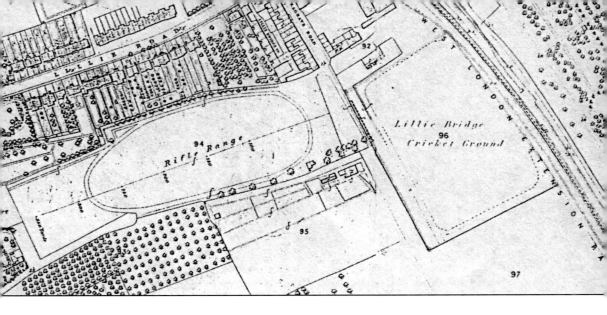

Lillie Bridge Athletic Ground - Scene of the 1873 Final, and a riot in 1887

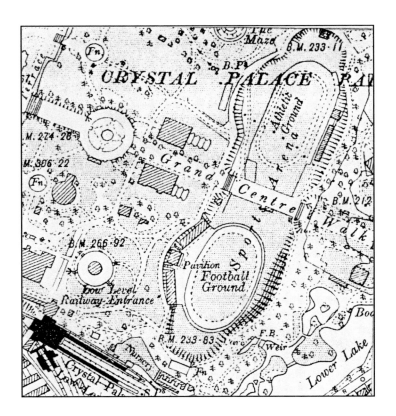

The Crystal Palace (1929) - Staged Cup Finals from 1895-1914

Crystal Palace Panorama - Cup Final (1911), Bradford City v Newcastle (0-0) 69,098

Wembley

All the Cup Finals
and replays from
1923 to 2000
(except a replay
in 1970)

40 St. Enoch's Square, Glasgow

Archibald Leitch had his offices here, from 1897 to 1907

Corner Pavilion and Main Stand, Fulham

Designed by Leitch in 1905

Etruria House, Barnes
A home of the Wedgwoods, and also of Leitch in 1915-22

Dens Park, Dundee
Built by Leitch in 1919-21

South Stand, Ibrox Park
By Leitch, "Ready" in 1928

New Brighton Tower (1899)

League football in 1898-1901

…and again with New Brighton in 1946-51

Blackburn Rovers (1893)

Alexandra Meadows and Leamington Street - home from 1878-90 (note Rover Street)

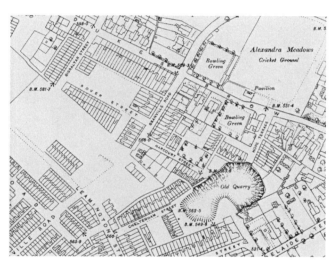

The age of the Kop

St. Andrew's, Birmingham - the terrace alone held 48,000

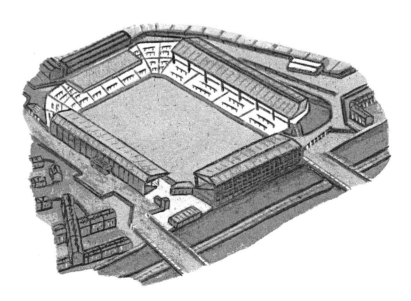

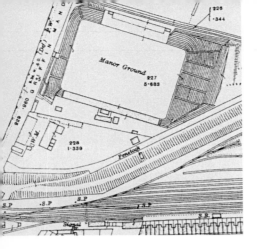
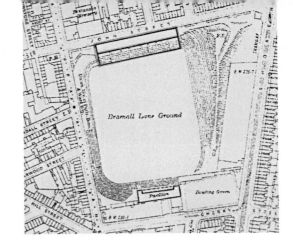

Arsenal (1914) the first Kop of 1904… and **Sheffield (1924)** the John Street Stand

Highbury

Art Deco style care of William Binnie (1936)

Wembley (1966)

It fulfilled the aspirations of the founders

Crystal Palace F.C. moved to Croydon Common Athletic Ground at Selhurst in 1919 and renamed it "The Nest." However, the site was limited with one entrance and they sought a new venue soon after their arrival. The lease expired in 1924 and the ground then became a railway depot, thus they moved a short distance to an old quarry at Selhurst Park. [24]

Leitch and Humphreys laid out a ground with a main stand on the west side without gable, and earth banking on the other three, but it was very basic and much like those built at Chelsea and Fulham twenty years earlier. Some claimed that it was the largest in London, but this was just publicity, although there was an international against Wales in 1926. [25]

In fact, Leitch had reached the apex of his career and moved to a grand residence "Bourneside," The Bourne, Southgate, in 1924-28, which was in a rural location since the underground had not yet arrived.

This was twice the size of his previous home with a large front wall, red brick gateposts, and the name engraved upon them (still survives). Further to this there was a double-front, two or three storeys, a central tower, and a long veranda reminiscent of the colonies. Indeed, it was truly Gothic in style and had stables and half an acre of neatly formed lawns. [26]

Meanwhile, his son Archibald Kent trained as a structural engineer and resided with his father, and may have fought in the First War. They both joined the Incorporated Assoc. of Architects & Surveyors in 1925, citing tube works and football grounds in their application (it became the Assoc. of Building Engineers in 1993).

Leitch then turned his attention to further work around the country and in particular the South Coast, the Midlands, and the North of England. Some businessmen established Portsmouth F.C., and their ground was laid out at Fratton Park in 1898 (used for an international in 1903), whilst the offices were in a mock-Tudor pavilion on Frogmore Road from 1905.

---

[24] Croydon Common played in the Southern League, Division One in 1909-10 and 1914-15. A small stand was laid out on the north side but they folded in 1917.

[25] The Park Road stand at Selhurst Park was built in 1969 and the main stand was refurbished in 1979, followed by a record crowd of 51,482 that year. Indeed, both of these stands are little changed and still survive today.

[26] "Bourneside" was built in the 1860s, and John Miles a resident involved in local affairs lived there for fifty years until his death in 1921. The house was then rented out or sold and was demolished in the 1930s.

John Bradshaw a gentleman and philanthropist lived next door at "The Grange," until 1939. The house passed to Southgate Co. and was demolished in the 1970s, whilst there is a blue plaque to him situated on the boundary wall.

The club were twice champions of the Southern League and joined the Third Division in 1920, thus Leitch was hired in 1925 and Humphreys built a south stand for £12,000 - which was linked to the pavilion. There was an upper tier for 4,000 with criss-cross balcony and a paddock, whilst the rear was plain since it backed onto nearby housing (and remains today).

Molineux was the home of Wolves from 1889; however there was little development of what was basically an athletics venue. Leitch built a new main stand on the west side next to Waterloo Road in 1925, with two tiers of seating for 2,750, and a paddock in front for 4,000 spectators.

The stand which cost £15,000 included a basic pitched roof, but without gable, and was angled at the centre to accommodate the shape of the site. In fact, it included the first proper changing rooms, even though the club had staged early internationals and won the F.A. Cup in 1893 and 1908.

John McKenna the League president opened the new Fratton stand on 29 August and that at Molineux on 12 September 1925, while Leitch returned to Goodison Park which was still one of the country's top venues.

The ground hosted the Cup Final replay in 1910, and enjoyed crowds of 69,000, whilst George V and Queen Mary visited the grand venue in 1913. Leitch then developed the Bullens Road stand in 1926, which was a large construction costing £30,000. This was comprised of two-tiers of seating, a criss-cross balcony, and an extensive terrace to the front.

Meanwhile, Newcastle East End became United and moved to St. James's Park in 1892, then joined the League the next year, whilst a main stand was erected on the west side like that at Middlesbrough in 1905 (but not by Leitch). The ground also staged two internationals but then fell behind and the engineer was consulted during 1926.

He provided plans for a two-tier stand at the Gallowgate end and a low cover on the other two terraces. However, only the one at the Leazes Park end was built and there was a record of 68,386 against Chelsea in 1930. In fact, little was altered, until the innovative east stand arrived in 1973.

Southampton F.C. moved to The Dell in 1898 (used for an international in 1901) and had won the Southern League six times by 1904. They joined the new Division Three in 1920 and were promoted as champions two years later, then stayed in Division Two for the next thirty-one years.

They contacted Leitch in 1927 and he designed a new west stand, whilst Humphreys and the Clyde Structural Co. did the ironwork with an upper tier for 4,500 and a paddock for 8,500. It was of typical design with a criss-cross balcony and took the capacity up to 33,000. Leitch was present for the opening just after Xmas, and a new east stand was added in similar style the next year (both remained until the move to St. Mary's in 2001).

Indeed, his son became a full partner by the Articles of Partnership dated 30 December 1927, and this change brought new impetus to the business, and the firm then did some of its most extravagant work. In addition, his daughter Jessie married Robert William Easton, son of a company secretary from Palmer's Green, at St. Columba's, Pont Street, in 1928.

FOR KING AND COUNTRY

David Mills Duncan worked as a draughtsman for Leitch in Scotland, but established the firm Duncan & Kerr in 1927. He then built a main stand for Partick Thistle at Firhill Park in a similar style, with angled construction, a central gable, and oval terrace around the pitch. Indeed, there was a record crowd of 54,728 for an international against Ireland the next year.

Ibrox Park, meanwhile, remained a huge open arena in the 1920s, with a basic wooden stand on the south side and a double-cover on the north side. However, the club did not approach Duncan but came back to Leitch in 1928. No doubt his son was then heavily involved, and a new south stand was built - but on a completely different scale.

The façade was reminiscent of a stately home with a red brick exterior, numerous doors and arches, a lower tier of windows, round ones above, and a fine roof cornice. The central and end sections were especially grand with the club name and pediments, whilst the entrance had a mosaic floor, marble and wood panelling, and a moulded ceiling.

It was just as impressive within the ground with seating for 10,000 and a paddock for 9,000, plus a criss-cross balcony and central pediment-gable. The stand opened on 1 January 1929 and the venue then witnessed some very large crowds. In fact, Duncan & Kerr also built the new south stand at Parkhead for Celtic that same year. [27]

Meanwhile, the remainder of Leitch's work was at grounds he had already visited, and he returned to Roker Park in 1929. The Fulwell end had been increased in size which raised the capacity to 60,000; however Leitch then built an impressive new main stand on the east side.

This cost the club £25,000, but constraints of space resulted in an upper tier with 5,875 seats and criss-cross balcony, a lower tier of terracing, and a paddock in front. The record attendance of 75,118 was for a game against

---

[27] Ibrox Park had the record League attendance in Britain of 118,567 against Celtic in 1939, but there was a disaster in 1971 and the banks were removed and new stands built in 1978/80. Leitch's structure became central to the plan and it was upgraded as Ibrox Stadium in 1990-94, including a new third tier, the main feature being impressive art deco stairways at either end.

Derby in 1933, whilst they won the League in 1936 and the Cup in 1937. In fact, they spent sixty-eight years in the top flight and were only relegated in 1958. In addition, the lower tier was seated and offices were added ready for the World Cup in 1966 (and the stand remained until 1997).

Leitch and his family left Southgate and lived at 99 Barkston Gardens, Kensington near Earl's Court Station in 1930-34. This was a city mansion (83-101) with a classical porch, wood panels, and brass hand rails, beside a leafy square. In fact, his son took on the day-to-day affairs, and Archibald Leitch (& Partners) traded at 66 Victoria Street from 1930-55.

They had already worked at Molineux, but soon afterwards the north terrace was aligned with the pitch, and the massive South Bank was raised to a depth of 50-yards (and held 30,000 spectators alone). Indeed, Leitch was called back in 1932 to tackle the final side on Molineux Street.

This presented a considerable problem as it tapered to a point at the north end, but he built a multi-span roof of seven gables with seats for 3,450 and a paddock for 4,500. The cost was £20,000 and the partners also added a new façade to the Waterloo Road stand. [28]

In addition to this the company did designs for Dalymount Park, Dublin and Windsor Park, Belfast in the early 1930s. These had replaced Solitude as a venue for Ireland internationals, although Lansdowne Road was also used from 1900-26 (and replaced Dalymount Park in recent years).

Both the father and son lived at 99 Barkston Gardens, whilst there was a shock when the daughter Agnes died of tuberculosis in 1933. By this time Leitch was nearly seventy and his work almost completed, thus he moved to "Braehead," 113 Belmont Avenue, Cockfosters (on the Piccadilly line) in 1934. This was a corner semi-detached property with Tudor-style gable, and his daughter Jessie lived a few doors away in Mount Pleasant.

He then returned to White Hart Lane to develop the east terrace, which was to be a major construction. The club purchased all the houses behind and re-housed the occupants, whilst Leitch built a colossal stand with an austere brick façade looking down onto the road.

There were two tiers including 5,100 seats in the upper tier and 11,000 standing on the "shelf" below, whilst the front paddock had a terrace for 8,000, resulting in a total capacity of 24,100 (the size of a small ground). Indeed, the balcony included the familiar Leitch ironwork but this time with some vertical blue struts.

---

[28] The record attendance at Molineux was 61,315 in 1939, and they played in the U.E.F.A. Cup Final in 1972. The Molineux stand and 71 houses were demolished in 1975, and were replaced by the John Ireland stand costing £2 million in 1979. The Waterloo Road stand and South Bank were re-developed in 1992-93.

The top of the stand was crowned by an elongated gable that doubled as a press box, and the total cost was £60,000. The stand opened in September 1934 and the record attendance of 75,038 was against Sunderland in 1938; whilst the ground remained little changed for the next forty-six years and the east stand was refurbished in 1989 (with roof supports).

Leitch then proposed plans to develop the Riverside Terrace at Fulham in 1935 (but the club declined), and also returned to Roker, and replaced the Clock Stand (of 1898) with a basic pitch-roofed structure in 1936. The rear consisted of wooden steps on steel supports with standing for 15,500, and this was built just after Sunderland won the League title.

In addition, he returned to Glasgow where it all began, and designed a north stand at the rear of the terrace at Hampden Park in 1937. This was a modest structure with 4,500 seats, and prepared the ground for its record attendance of 149,415 against England that year. [29]

His final piece of work was his crowning glory and had a Royal stamp of approval. Indeed, the partners then constructed the Gladwys Street stand at Goodison Park in 1938, with an upper tier of seating over a terrace and criss-cross balcony, all being joined to the Bullens Road stand.

The cost was £50,000 and Leitch & Partners had built the whole ground, a fact which was acknowledged when George VI and Queen Elizabeth visited the venue later that year. The club then won the League in 1938-39 and the record attendance was 78,299 against Liverpool in 1948, whilst the ground hosted five World Cup games in 1966.

The son married Muriel E. Ingram at Ham Church in 1938, however Archibald Leitch died at "Braehead" on 25 April 1939 and his will was proved by his solicitors in Liverpool, the estate being valued at £17,221. The offices at 34 Argyll Arcade were then closed, whilst the son lived in Hammersmith and ran the business until 1955. He provided a new plan to develop the Riverside Terrace at Fulham, which was again declined.

Today, only a few examples of Leitch's important work survive and many have disappeared since the Taylor Report in 1990, but the best examples are surely at Fulham and Glasgow Rangers.

---

[29] The north stand was demolished and the terraces concreted in 1981-86, then it was all seated in 1992-94 and the capacity was just 37,000. However this changed after the south and west stands were rebuilt in 1995.

CHAPTER 17

The Re-Election Lottery

League football had kicked off in 1888-89 with twelve teams, however some of the prospective candidates had missed out therefore a second tier called the Football Alliance was started just a year later.

The initial members were then Birmingham St. George's, Bootle, Crewe Alexandra, Darwen, Grimsby Town, Long Eaton Rangers, Newton Heath, Nottingham Forest, Small Heath, Sunderland Albion, Walsall Town Swifts, and the Wednesday (from Sheffield).

The Alliance lasted for three seasons and the champions were Wednesday, Stoke, and Forest on each occasion, whereas Long Eaton Rangers were demoted at the end of the first season then played in the Midland League, and also took part in the Cup from 1883-98.

Meanwhile, Sunderland first played games at Blue House Fields in 1879, and moved to Newcastle Road in 1886, but the next year they were expelled from the Cup for fielding ineligible Scottish players. As a result Jimmy Allen (one of the founders) and some other members left the club, and formed Sunderland Albion back at the original venue.

The latter made a strong challenge and had two seasons in the Alliance, and in fact finished third and second, but the success of their rivals in the League meant they withdrew in 1891, and folded up the next year.

There were further developments with the introduction of the penalty, and the first was scored by John Heath of Wolves against Accrington on 14 September 1891. In fact, the Corinthians (see later) could not accept such a challenge to the concepts of 'fair play,' and their keeper would stand defiantly by the goalpost as the spot kick was taken.

Another team, Birmingham St. George's, played at Fentham Road near Villa Park from 1875 and entered the Cup in 1881, but finished bottom of the Alliance in its last season and folded up. They fielded John Devey and Dennis Hodgetts who later appeared for Aston Villa.

Indeed, the League was increased in size to 14 members and Darwen and Stoke were elected, whilst Ardwick, Burton Swifts, and Lincoln City were admitted to the Football Alliance. The latter was replaced by Division Two in 1892 and Forest, Newton Heath, and Wednesday went into the top tier, whereas the others formed the backbone of the new division.

As a result the founders of Division Two were: Ardwick, Bootle, Burton Swifts, Crewe Alexandra, Grimsby Town, Lincoln City, Small Heath, and Walsall Town Swifts - plus Darwen (who were relegated) and new members Burslem Port Vale, Northwich Victoria, and Sheffield United.

Initially, there were 16 teams in the First Division and 12 in the Second, however there were important additions the next year with the arrival of Liverpool, Newcastle United, and Woolwich Arsenal, whereas promotion and relegation was settled using test matches until 1898.

The Southern League was established soon after and the first contest was in the 1894-95 season with nine members: Chatham, Clapton, Ilford, Luton Town, Millwall Athletic, Reading, Royal Ordnance, Southampton, and Swindon Town. Millwall were champions during the first two seasons, and Southampton won six times from 1897-1904. [1]

The latter lasted for twenty-five years and other members who joined the top division were: Sheppey U., Tottenham, Wolverton (1896), Bedminster, Brighton U., Royal Artillery (1898), West Ham (1899), Kettering T. (1900), Wellingborough (1901), Leyton (1906), Bradford (1907), Croydon Common (1909), and Stoke (1911).

Meanwhile, the bottom three or four League clubs were put forward for re-election each season, and on the vagaries of the committee their futures were decided. A comprehensive list of those that lost out is shown below, including several whose names have gone down in football history; whereas others survived the process simply by a degree of good fortune.

Accrington (1888-93) - They were formed in 1878 and played at the local cricket ground in the Lancashire Combination by 1882, but were expelled from the Cup for paying their players. After some poor League results they were forced to resign in 1893, then folded up two years later.

Bootle (1892-93) - They played at Hawthorne Road and appeared in the Cup from 1887, then had three seasons in the Alliance. They were briefly the second team in the city after Everton, but their last Cup game was in 1892 and they resigned the next year.

Middlesbrough Ironopolis (1893-94) - The club formed at the Paradise Ground, south of Linthorpe Road, in 1889 but had small crowds of 1,500 or below during their one League season. They withdrew due to losses and disbanded at the same time.

---

[1] The amateur teams Ilford, Leytonstone, and Walthamstow Avenue later merged to create Redbridge (Forest) F.C. in 1979-88.

Northwich Victoria (1892-94) - They began at the Drill Field in 1874 and first played in the Lancashire Combination. During their second season in the League they won just 3 out of 28 games and scored 30 goals but let in 98. They were founder members of the Northern Premier League in 1968 and of the Alliance Premier (Conference) in 1979.

The Drill Field claimed to be the oldest football ground in the world in continuous use by one club, and the game was watched from the Dane Bank terrace for over a century - they left in 2002. However, Maidenhead, who with Marlow played in every F.A. Cup contest, also made the same claim for their York Road ground (used since 1870).

Darwen (1891-99) - Nathaniel Walsh a local mill owner sent his three sons to Harrow, and with Mr. J.C. Ashton they formed the club from two local mill teams in 1870. They moved to Barley Bank by some cotton mills in 1874, and a floodlit game was played after the one at Bramall Lane in 1878. There was considerable Cup success in 1879, with a record attendance of 12,500 against Blackburn Rovers in 1885.

The cricket team left Barley Bank three years later and the club joined the Alliance and were promoted to the League in 1891, whereas the ground had a stand that could seat 1,000 spectators.

Indeed, the club can be thanked for some of the most extraordinary score lines, and they lost 12-0 to West Bromwich (a record for the First Division), and won only four games and conceded 112 goals in 1891-92. [2]

They then played in Division Two setting some staggering records during their last League season. They lost 18 games in a row (10-0 three times, 9-0, 9-2, 8-0, 8-1, and 7-0), lost all their away matches except for a single draw, and in total won only two games and conceded 141 goals!

As a result they then moved to the Anchor Ground and played in various Lancashire leagues, whilst they also lost 11-1 to Arsenal in 1932. The old ground was covered by Hindle Street and a girls' school.

Loughborough Town (1895-1900) - They played at the Athletic Ground which also saw an appearance by W.G. Grace for a cricket match.

Their first Cup game was in 1890 and they were champions of the Midland League by 1895. They replaced Walsall Town Swifts in the League, however finished near the bottom during their five seasons. In the last season, they won only a single game having scored 18 goals whilst conceding 100, and were beaten 12-0 by the Woolwich Arsenal.

---

[2] Nottingham Forest also defeated Leicester Fosse 12-0 in 1909. They were already relegated with 102 goals against, and the previous day went to a wedding.

New Brighton Tower (1898-1901) - James Atherton first laid out New Brighton, The Wirral as a speculative venture in 1830, and there were grand seafront developments in the 1890s. It was a popular resort rivalling others in the area, and a tower larger than Blackpool's was erected in 1897.

The Tower Grounds covered 35 acres with numerous attractions, whilst an athletics stadium was at the south end and had two stands. There was a first-class cycle track (which staged the world championships in 1922).

The owners formed a team and they joined the League with Barnsley, Burslem Port Vale, and Glossop when it increased in size by four members in 1898. Their best finish was fourth in Division Two in 1900-01, but they could not continue and resigned that year. The tower was dismantled in 1919-21 and the theatre and ballroom were demolished in 1969.

Burton United (1894-97, 1892-1901, 1901-07) - The town was a hotbed of soccer and sported three League teams. Burton Wanderers were formed at Derby Turn in 1871, and claimed to be the fourth oldest League club, but were developed by John Parker from 1885 and soon progressed well. They joined Division Two with Bury and Leicester Fosse from 1894-97, and went to a local cricket ground two years later.

Burton Swifts were established from another side in 1883 and went to Peel Croft, Lichfield Street, in 1891. The ground had a pavilion and cover, and was situated amongst the railway lines and breweries. They played in the League in 1892-1901, then merged with Wanderers to form United at Peel Croft - but folded up in 1910 and Burton Albion started in 1950.

Gainsborough Trinity (1896-1912) - A cricket ground was established at Northolme, just north of the town near the River Trent, during the 1850s. The vicar of Holy Trinity Church started a football team in 1873, and they were champions of the Midland Counties League by 1891, thus they were elected to the League with Blackpool and Walsall.

They finished mainly in the lower half of Division Two and in the last season won only five games. Lincoln City then took their place, whilst they continued at Northolme with a record of 9,760 against Scunthorpe in the 1940s, and were founder members of the Northern Premier League.

Glossop North End (1898-1915) - This was an unlikely venue for League football and the town was situated on the edge of the Peak District. A club were formed at North Road in 1886, and they shared the venue with a local cricket club whose ground was just to the west. They initially played in the North Cheshire League in 1890 and became professional in 1894.

After making three applications to join the League they were admitted with New Brighton Tower in 1898, when it increased in size by four members. Indeed, they were runners-up to Manchester City in 1898-99 and both were promoted to Division One. They were the first clubs promoted by right, and Glossop became the smallest town to host top flight football.

They became Glossop F.C. in 1903, whilst the owner Sir Samuel Hill-Wood and a player T.T. Fitchie both moved to Arsenal. They lost 9-2 to Chelsea in 1906-07, and in their final season won only six games and came last. Leicester Fosse who finished just above them returned as City in 1919. They played in the Lancashire Combination or Manchester League after the war, and then in local leagues at Surrey Street from 1955.

Meanwhile, the Third Division started with 21 teams who came from the Southern League, plus Grimsby Town who were relegated, in 1920. The Third Division (North) started the next year with 20 teams, some of them former League clubs and the others from northern regional leagues.

Stalybridge Celtic (1921-23) - Herbert Rhodes established the club at the Bower Fold in 1909, and they played in both the Lancashire Combination and the Central League. Meanwhile, they finished as runners-up to Stoke in the Southern League, Division Two in 1914-15.

As a result they entered the League in 1921 and beat Chesterfield 6-0 in their first game, whereas 27,000 watched a Cup-tie at the Hawthorns in 1922-23. However, they resigned due to a lack of funds and were replaced by New Brighton. More recently they played in the Conference and the ground was raised up to League standard.

Aberdare Athletic (1921-27) - A number of Welsh teams appeared in the Southern League, Division One from 1912 and then joined the League viz. Cardiff City, Merthyr Town, Newport Co., and Swansea Town.

Aberdare and Charlton Athletic replaced Crystal Palace (promoted) and Grimsby (who moved north), when the Third Division (South) started in 1921. They played at the Athletic Ground, Ynis and in their last season conceded 101 goals and were replaced by Torquay United.

Merthyr Town (1920-30) - The club played at Penydarren Park and were in the top flight of the Southern League by 1912. Home and away games were played back-to-back (until 1924) and the record crowd was against Millwall on 26-27 December 1920, with 26,000 at The Den and 21,686 at Merthyr. In the last season they let in 135 goals and were replaced by Thames F.C., but became M. Tydfil in 1945 and were successful in the 1940s-50s.

Durham City (1921-28) - Their early games were played at Kepier Hughes in the North Eastern League, and after joining the League they went to Holiday Park in 1923. They were replaced by Carlisle and returned to play in the former league, but had folded up by 1938. However, they reformed at Ferens Park in 1950 and remained there until 1994.

Ashington (1921-29) - The Colliers formed as early as 1888 and moved to Portland Park in 1909. They played in the Northern Football Alliance and were champions in 1914, whilst Jackie Milburn and his relatives Bobby and Jackie Charlton came from the town.

   Their first home game in Division Three (North) had a crowd of 10,000, and there was a record of 11,837 for a Cup-tie against Villa in 1924, but the team let in 115 goals and finished bottom during their last season. They then played in the North Eastern League at the same ground.

Nelson (1921-31) - They joined the Lancashire League in 1889, entered the Cup in 1893, and played in the Central League after the war. With thirteen other non-reserve teams they joined the Third Division (North) in 1921. The first League game at the Seedhill Ground had a record of 9,000, whilst they were champions ahead of Bradford P.A. in 1923.

   To celebrate the success they went on a Spanish tour and played teams like Real Madrid, but were relegated the next year. They were inconsistent and scored 104 goals in 1927, but conceded 136 in 1928 - indeed they came last again and were replaced by Chester in 1931. The ground was covered by a motorway and they were reformed at Victoria Park.

Thames (1930-32) - The Custom House Sports Ground was located on Bingley Road, near the Royal Victoria Dock and just south of Upton Park. Initially, it was aligned from east to west, and had a small pavilion to the south and some earth banking on the other three sides.

   West Ham Greyhound Stadium replaced it on Nottingham Avenue in the 1920s, and the pitch was aligned north to south. There were covered stands on two sides and terraces, while the new sport of speedway came from the Crystal Palace in 1928. In fact, top riders Roger Frogley and Ron Johnson earned £100 per meeting, when soccer players earned £8 per week.

   The owners then formed a soccer team and they joined the League in place of Merthyr Town, but lacked support with attendances below 1,000. They were the only London club to lose their League status (to date), and were replaced by Newport County; whilst the ground remained until the 1960s then was replaced by housing.

New Brighton (1923-51) - South Liverpool played near to New Brighton in the Lancashire Combination in 1911-21, but left a vacuum when they folded up. A new club New Brighton were then formed, but they declined to use the Tower Ground which was offered by Harrowby F.C. Indeed, the cost of such a move was prohibitive at £50,000.

Instead, they found a vacant site on Rake Lane, Wallasey just to the south which became Sandheys Park. The pitch originally had a large slope but was prepared after the issue of 10-shilling shares, whilst there was a main stand to the north, and "The Lodge" in Osborne Avenue was the club offices.

They took over South Liverpool's fixtures in the Lancashire Combination then replaced Stalybridge in the League. Meanwhile, the Martlew brothers were directors and had links to the Wirral Railway, thus they invited Dixie Dean to come there - he previously played for the railway team. However, he went to Tranmere in 1924 and to Everton the next year.

George Camsell of Middlesbrough set the record of 59 League-goals in 1926-27, but Dixie Dean beat this by one with a hat trick on the last day of the next season. Indeed, he was much sought after and Herbert Chapman offered Everton anything they wanted for him.

New Brighton started off well in the League with a third place finish in 1924-25, and beat Sheffield Wednesday 2-1 at Sandheys Park in front of a record crowd of 12,408. They also reached the 4th round of the F.A. Cup three times. However, Wallasey Corporation requisitioned the ground in 1944 and built pre-fabricated houses on the pitch!

There was no League football in 1945-46 but Derby beat Charlton 4-1 in the Cup Final at Wembley, whilst the club secured the Tower Ground and played in the League until replaced by Workington in 1951. They were then in the Lancashire Combination, but Wallasey Council purchased the Tower Ground in the 1960s and the club then faded.

Gateshead (1919-30-60) - South Shields Adelaide or the Tynesiders were formed in 1899, and entered the F.A. Cup, whilst they were runners-up in the North Eastern League in 1908-09.

They became South Shields the next year and played at Horsley Hill, whilst they won the local league in 1914-15 and were elected to Division Two in 1919. They then played for nine seasons at this level, but were relegated after conceding 111 goals in 1928.

After financial problems they became Gateshead F.C. at Redheugh Park, on Ropery Road, in 1930, just south of the Tyne amongst iron works and paper mills - and then played in Division Three (North). Indeed, they were runners-up on two occasions.

Meanwhile, the record attendance was 17,692 during a Cup quarter-final against Bolton in 1953, and they joined the new Fourth Division in 1958, but finished in 22nd place in the 1959-60 season. However, circumstances went against them and they lost their spot to Peterborough. Such a decision seemed harsh, since they had only applied for re-election on one occasion and Oldham and Hartlepools finished below them.

The club applied to the Scottish League but were rejected and joined the Northern Premier League by 1968, but Bradford Park Avenue took their place in 1970. In fact, they suffered the ignominy of replacing their own reserve team in a local league, and after playing in the Midland League had folded up by 1973. Redheugh Park was then demolished.

A new South Shields team played at Simonside Hall (20,000 capacity) in the North Eastern League from 1936 to the 1970s. They joined Gateshead Town to form United, and played at the International Athletics Stadium, whilst successors Gateshead F.C. played a friendly against Newcastle with 11,750 in 1995. However, the latter had also folded up by 2004.

Accrington Stanley (1921-62) - A team called Stanley Villa was established at Stanley Street, slightly south of Peel Park, in 1891. They became semi-professional when Accrington were disbanded and played in the Lancashire League, then joined the Combination which mainly included the reserve teams of League clubs. In fact, they were champions ahead of Manchester City (reserves) in 1902-03.

They went to the Moorhead Ground (where Accrington had their last season) in 1910, but the League clubs transferred to the Central League the next year and they then had less competition. The club reformed in 1919 and Peel Park was established with a 20,000 capacity.

The ground was off Burnley Road towards Hillock Vale, in the east of Accrington, and had a large stand with pitched roof on the north side, and a further stand to the south near to Peel Park Hotel. A bowling green and pavilion nearby suggests that it was previously used for cricket.

The club played in the Lancashire Combination in 1919-21 and joined the Third Division (North) in 1921. There was some concern that the northern clubs were not financially viable, but Accrington suggested they all paid a deposit to the League committee to quell any such fears.

Initially, the club had limited success, but then fielded a team entirely of Scottish players and scored 96 goals in 1954-55 - only Blackburn and Bristol City scored more. Meanwhile, they featured on television in 1955, and came second to Scunthorpe in 1957-58 then joined the new Third Division; but this was in fact to be the high point.

Some bad financial decisions were made, in particular the purchase of a new stand from the Aldershot Tattoo for £14,000 in 1958. These problems were then transferred to the pitch, and they were relegated in last place in 1959-60, having conceded 123 goals. [3]

This was the beginning of the end and they were unable to complete the 1961-62 season, while their last game was in a snowstorm at Gresty Road. They owed £60,000 and the League forced them to resign after 33 games, although they pleaded for more time. Significantly, they were replaced by Oxford United (who were Headington until 1960) that year.

They had one season in the Lancashire Combination, but then folded up and Peel Park was finally closed in 1966. Accrington Stanley then reformed at the Crown Ground, Livingstone Road, in 1970, with the specific aim of regaining their League status. They eventually played in the Conference and replaced Oxford (yes Oxford) in the League in 2007.

Bradford Park Avenue (1908-70) - They played in the Southern League in 1907 then joined the League with Spurs the next year. County cricket was played at the nearby Horton Park, whilst the club played in Division One for three seasons from 1914-21. They then had two consecutive relegations but came third in Division Two in 1928-29.

Both Len Shackleton and Ron Greenwood played for the club, while Bill Shankly applied to be manager in 1953. However, they went into a decline and with Bradford City were playing in Division Four by 1963.

They came last three times and sought re-election on several occasions, and were finally replaced by Cambridge United in 1970. After one season playing at Valley Parade in 1973-74 they folded up, and Park Avenue was demolished in 1980. They finished one win ahead of City regarding League fixtures and a new team Bradford P.A. was started in 1988.

Barrow (1921-72) - The Bluebirds were formed in 1901 and they played at Holker Street from 1909, winning the Lancashire Combination in 1920-21. A crowd of 16,874 watched at a Cup-tie against Swansea City in 1954, and a similar number saw a game against Wolves in 1959.

They came 22nd in Division Four in 1971-72 eight points ahead of bottom place Crewe, but this was their eleventh re-election and they were replaced by Hereford (who beat Newcastle 2-1 in the Cup that January). They were founder members of the Alliance Premier League in 1979 and beat Leek 3-0 at Wembley to win the F.A. Trophy in 1990.

---

[3] A similar stand from the Aldershot Tattoo was erected on the Shrivenham Road side at the County Ground, Swindon Town the same year.

Workington (1951-77) - The town had its base in coal and iron, and the Bessemer process was developed there. The team were formed in 1884 and played in local leagues, the Lancashire Combination in 1904-10, and had one season in the North Eastern League, but folded up in 1911.

They reformed as A.F.C. Workington in 1921, joining the North Eastern League and their first game was against South Shields reserves. They played Preston at Lonsdale Park in front of 15,000 in the F.A. Cup fourth round in 1933-34, then moved to Borough Park and joined the League in place of New Brighton in 1951.

The club came last at the end of their first season, but Bill Shankly was manager in 1953-56, and they played Manchester United in front of 21,000 in the F.A. Cup in 1958. Their highest position was 5th in Division Three in 1965-66 however they were relegated in last place in 1966-67. In fact, their thirteen directors outnumbered the number of full time players.

They sought re-election five times and with gates of below 1,000 they were replaced by Wimbledon in 1977. The club joined the Northern Premier League and were champions of the North West Counties League in 1998-99, which was in fact their first major championship.

Southport (1921-78) - The club had their origins in a local rugby club and Ralph Rylance a solicitor's manager from Preston was the founder in 1881. They merged as Southport Central and played in the Lancashire League, being the champions in 1903. This took them up to the Combination and they then moved to Ash Lane (Haig Avenue) in 1905.

The Vulcan Motor Co. took them over in 1918, and they were Southport Vulcan for one year, but the League committee did not approve and they reformed as Southport F.C. in 1919. They were the first Division Three club (with Exeter) to reach the sixth round of the Cup in 1931, and there was a record of 20,010 against Newcastle in the fourth round.

They had several re-elections but Billy Bingham became manager in 1965 and they reached the fifth round of the Cup and were promoted. However, he went to Plymouth and N. Ireland in 1968 and they were relegated back to Division Four. The club were champions in 1972-73, but were relegated again and had financial problems with several managerial changes.

There were three successive re-election attempts and Wigan Athletic who had formed in 1932, replaced them in 1978. Haig Avenue, meanwhile, was upgraded and the covered terracing was demolished in 1987, whereas the club later played in the Conference. [4]

---

[4] Wigan Borough played in Division Three (North) at Springfield Park in 1921-31, and the record was 30,611 for a Cup-tie against Wednesday in 1929.

The re-election process was under increasing scrutiny however the most fortunate team certainly came from Hartlepool. A rugby club laid out the Victoria Ground near the docks in 1886, and West Hartlepool F.C. won the Amateur Cup in 1905; whereas the rugby club failed and were replaced by Hartlepools United in 1908 - who hoped to emulate such success.

They entered the League in 1921 and Brian Clough was manager in 1965, but they sought re-election on no less than fourteen occasions. The last clubs to enter the lottery were Exeter, Cambridge United, Preston North End, and Torquay in 1985-86. In fact, it would have been some story if Preston had followed Accrington out of the League.

However, the next season automatic relegation and promotion replaced the rather outdated system, and for many years just one club was demoted. At this point the gulf between League and non-league was considerable and many who went down came straight back up.

Indeed, Lincoln City created a record since they lost their League status in 1908, 1911, 1920, and 1987. Another significant relegation was Doncaster Rovers who had first played League football as early as 1901.

The greatest losses though were Newport County who played at Somerton Park and finished bottom 19 points behind Carlisle in 1988, and Aldershot who played League football at the Recreation Ground from 1932-92. Both of the latter then folded up, but new clubs were formed soon after.

The League structure was greatly altered in recent years with the Premier League and Championship, whereas two teams could join the League from 2002, and since that time there have been more frequent changes.

CHAPTER 18

Speculative Ventures

This last chapter considers some of the founding teams, other aspects of ground development, various idiosyncrasies of the stands, and concludes with a most positive international flourish.

Several professional teams had their origins in the church, in the spirit of muscular Christianity, and some good examples were Barnsley St. Peter's, Christchurch (Bolton), Fulham St. Andrew's, and St. Domingo's (Everton); whereas others were started by cricket and rugby teams.

The Football League kicked off in 1888, but many of the sides played at grounds with less than familiar names. In fact, the only venues to survive with the same clubs playing there are Deepdale and Turf Moor. A list of these grounds is clearly of some historical significance:

Original League Venues

Accrington	Accrington Cricket Gr.	1882-94
Aston Villa	Wellington Road, Perry Barr	1876-97
Blackburn Rovers	Leamington Street	1881-90
Bolton Wanderers	Pikes Lane (Deane Road)	1881-95
Burnley	Turf Moor (Calder Vale)	1883-
Derby County	The Racecourse Ground	1884-95
Everton	Anfield (then Liverpool)	1884-92
Notts County	Trent Bridge Cricket Gr.	1883-1910
Preston North End	Deepdale (with museum)	1881-
Stoke (City)	Victoria Ground	1883-1997
West Bromwich A	Stoney Lane	1885-1900
Wolverhampton W	Dudley Road	1881-89

Regarding the founding clubs there are several additional facts of interest. Blackburn played at Alexandra Meadows from 1878, and an international was staged there against Wales in 1881 (the first away from the Oval), whilst Leamington Street was also used for internationals in 1885 and 1887.

Prince Albert (Edward VII) watched part of a game at Turf Moor in 1886, hence the Royalites, whilst the record crowd of 54,775 was during a game against Huddersfield in 1924. The main feature was the Long Side, which rose to a high point in the northeast corner and was roofed in 1954.

County cricketers started Derby at the Racecourse Ground, which had Cup games and an international, whilst Derby Junction lost a semi-final to West Bromwich in 1887-88. They then moved to the Baseball Ground with its summer baseball tournaments, and staged an international in 1911; whilst the horses left in 1939 and the cricket ground remains.

Everton, meanwhile, have played continually in Division One since 1888 (except for 1930-31 and 1951-54), whereas Notts County were established in 1862 and are therefore the oldest League club.

Like Forest they played at the Meadows Cricket Ground and reached the Cup semi-final in 1883, but lost 2-1 to the Old Etonians. Trent Bridge was laid out in 1838 and the club went there after Forest (1880-82) departed, whilst the main stand was on the Fox Road side. The ground struggled to hold 20,000 and had low attendances, although it staged semi-finals and an international, while the club reached the Cup Final in 1891/94.

William Sudell was a cotton mill manager and his efforts took Preston to the first double, whilst only Aston Villa emulated them in 1897. In fact, the west stand at Deepdale contained many supports and a Belfast roof, lasting from 1906-95, whereas the Fulwood end was built in 1921.

To the south, old boys from Charterhouse established Stoke in 1868, and the main stand at the Victoria Ground was on Boothen Road. The club had to resign from the League in 1908, but reformed and joined Division Two in 1919. They stayed at the ground for over a hundred years and after they went to the Britannia Stadium, only the grass outline remained.

West Bromwich first played at Dartmouth Park, Bunn's Field, and Four Acres - the latter having a crowd of 16,393 for a Cup-tie against Blackburn. Their ground at Stoney Lane had a stand called Noah's Ark, and the first game was against Third Lanark but there were some small crowds. It was later a training ground and was covered by Albion Field Drive.

THE KOP GROUNDS

The English League was introduced in the northern climes in 1888 and the Scottish followed suit with eleven teams two years later, although the first outright winner was actually Dumbarton in 1892. In fact, the League quickly became as important as the Cup competition, and the clubs soon developed some large and permanent grounds.

There were attempts to form a league in the south at this time however only Arsenal, Luton, Millwall, Swindon, and West Herts attended a meeting. As a result the Gunners joined the Football League in 1893, whereas the Southern League was established the next year.

Meanwhile, the golden era of ground development was to follow and sixty clubs opened new venues from 1890-1910. Many of these were to last for over one hundred years, and thus had considerable significance to soccer history and to the game's development.

Quite naturally the history of ground building begins alphabetically with Arsenal (and only Accrington and Aldershot come before them). The side were formed in 1886, and Fred Beardsley one of the founders had played for Forest - hence his old club provided some red shirts.

Initially, they had three venues in Plumstead, and moved to the Manor Ground when they joined the League in 1893. The first large banked terrace or Kop was built there in 1904, and this was the forerunner of many other such terraces around the country.

Indeed, further impressive grounds were built in the capital at Craven Cottage, Stamford Bridge, Highbury, and White Hart Lane, but these were not the only large developments seen in the metropolis.

Thames Ironworks F.C. formed in east London in 1895, and the driving force was Arnold Hills who was the proprietor of a local shipyard. He then laid out the large Memorial Ground on Springfield Road with a west stand and track in 1897, whilst the club joined the Southern League the next year. Indeed, one game against Millwall was abandoned due to thick fog, but it was finished after the return match at East Ferry Road.

However, the club fell out with Hills over professionalism and he invited the (then) amateurs Clapton Orient to come there. As a result they became West Ham United in 1900 and moved to Upton Park in 1904.

Queens Park Rangers were formed from a church side in 1886 and played in that area of London, but had several venues and should have been called "the rovers." Most of their grounds were local, but they moved west and played at the Park Royal Ground, Coronation Road, from 1907-15.

The G.W.R. developed this as a speculative venture and it was built in a similar style to Ayresome Park, with a potential capacity of 60,000. The first game was against Millwall with a crowd of just 20,000, whilst Rangers were champions of the Southern League in 1908 and 1912. However, the army took over the ground and they moved to Loftus Road by 1917 - which was previously occupied by the amateur outfit Shepherd's Bush F.C.

The White City Stadium was built nearby for the Olympic Games in 1908 and had a revival with athletics, greyhound racing, and speedway. Rangers played there in 1931-33 and 1962-63, with a record attendance of 41,097 against Leeds United (1932). However, the latter was demolished for road improvements in 1984. Meanwhile, further north, there was a considerable power base and clubs developed large grounds with huge capacities.

Liverpool joined the League with Ironopolis, Newcastle U., Rotherham Town, and Arsenal in 1893 and became champions of Division Two that year - in fact their team was composed entirely of Scottish players.

The Kop was then developed in 1906 and the first game had a crowd of 32,000, whilst one feature was a 50' flagpole at the south end, which was the topmast of the *S.S. Great Eastern*. The League president John McKenna opened the re-roofed terrace with a capacity of 28,000 in 1928, and the record attendance was 61,905 for a Cup game against Wolves in 1952.

Small Heath F.C. were formed by some cricketers and played at Muntz Street, off Coventry Road, from 1877-1906. At the latter date they became Birmingham F.C. and moved to a new venue on St. Andrew's Street.

The club employed the little known Harry Pumphrey to build a ground in the former brickworks, which had a large Kop reaching around to the Tilton Road end, and a basic main stand on the east side. The terrace was the largest in the country with a capacity of 48,000, and the record crowd was 67,341 against Everton in 1939 (but it was replaced in 1994).

The Rugby League was established at the George Hotel, situated next to the regal Huddersfield Station, in 1895. It was called the Northern Union and the local team played games at Fartown, which was also the venue for two Cup semi-finals. Huddersfield Town, meanwhile, were formed in 1908 and since sharing was discouraged developed the Leeds Road ground.

The club were incredibly successful under Herbert Chapman in the 1920s, whereas the vast east terrace allowed for a record crowd of 67,037 against Arsenal in the Cup in 1932. A new roof was added in 1955, however the ground then declined and the final game was played there in 1994.

Their near neighbours also had connections to the previous history, and Elland Road was first used for rugby in 1878. In fact, Holbeck Rugby Club of the Northern Union purchased the venue in 1897, and local soccer first took place at the ground the next year.

Hunslet F.C. played their games in the south of Leeds but they occupied Elland Road when Holbeck departed, and then formed Leeds City in 1904. They joined the League the next year, whilst the pitch was turned end-on and there was a main stand on the west side. A large bank was erected to the north and east, thus raising the capacity to about 45,000.

The ground was found to be inadequate for large crowds in 1910/12, and the club went bankrupt and sought re-election with Gainsborough Trinity. Herbert Chapman had played there and took over as manager, and for a time matters improved, but the club were then accused of making illegal payments. Indeed, John McKenna announced, "We will have no nonsense, the football stable must be cleansed!"

Chapman denied any knowledge of wrong-doing (on his part), but Leeds City were promptly expelled and the club and its fittings sold off, whilst Port Vale took over their League fixtures during 1919-20.

There was a suggestion that the ailing Huddersfield Town might move to Elland Road, however Leeds United were then formed, and due to a degree of guilt the League committee elected them to Division Two in 1920.

The ground was improved that decade with new roofs on the main and Elland Road stands, and the north Kop was increased to three times its former height. It joined the Lowfields Road terrace and there was a (then) record crowd of 56,796 against Arsenal in 1932.

WEMBLEY OF THE NORTH

Several clubs aspired to build a ground that might claim this accolade, and the most obvious contender was Maine Road, which opened soon after its namesake. A team called Gorton F.C. was established in 1880 and became Ardwick on moving to Hyde Road in 1887. They were founder members of Division Two and were re-formed as Manchester City in 1894.

Facilities at Hyde Road were always basic with a railway line across one corner, and there was talk of moving to the nearby Belle Vue Athletic Ground, but they decided to stay and made basic improvements. Despite this the main stand burnt down in 1920 and the lease expired in 1923, thus they moved to a new site at Maine Road in south Manchester.

Charles Swain designed a stadium in a former clay pit on a grand scale, with a main stand on the west side and a large curving terrace with tunnels at each corner. McAlpine's were the contractors (as at Wembley) and it was the largest English club ground with a 90,000 capacity, whereas the main feature was the huge Kippax terrace.

Indeed, it opened just after Wembley with a game against Sheffield United in front of 60,000, whilst the record attendance for a club game of 84,569 was against Stoke in the Cup in 1934 - likewise, Manchester United set the record for the League of 83,260 against Arsenal there in 1948. [1]

Maine Road arrived after the main period of ground building, but it was clearly the epitome of such aspirations. Meanwhile, the influence of Leitch in the North East remained extensive and he built Ayresome and Roker Parks, while the directors of Newcastle visited Celtic and Hampden before rebuilding their own ground (a copy of Ayresome) in 1905.

---

[1] Manchester United were forced to leave Old Trafford as a result of war damage from 1941-49, and played their matches at Maine Road.

All three grounds attained record attendances in the 1930s-40s; whereas Bramall Lane had a Kop at the Shoreham Street end and despite a cricket pitch achieved a record crowd of 68,287, during a Cup-tie against Leeds, in 1936. Meanwhile, the largest attendance at Hillsborough was 72,841 for a Cup game against Manchester City in 1934.

Several of the founder members also had stadiums of large proportions. Indeed, West Bromwich Albion moved to the Hawthorns in 1900 and built banked terracing on the Handsworth side and at the Smethwick end. The record of 64,815 was for a Cup-tie against Arsenal in 1937.

Their rivals Bolton moved to Burnden Park, which was a wasteland on Manchester Road, in 1895, and initially the ground became a messy bog. In fact, there was a large terrace at the railway end, whilst the Burnden Stand with wooden planking (to the rear) was built in 1928.

The record attendance of 69,912 was for a Cup-tie against Manchester City in 1933. However, there was a disaster due to overcrowding just after the war, and the railway end was sold for a supermarket in 1985. Indeed, from that time there was no railway and no end, whereas Bolton moved to the new Reebok Stadium in 1997.

To the north Blackburn Rovers went to Ewood Park in 1890 (which had an international soon after), and won the championship in 1912/14. As a result they had crowds of 28,000 and won the Cup again in 1928, then had a record attendance of 61,783 during a Cup-tie against Bolton the next year. However, the new Ewood Park was quite unlike the old ground.

In fact, a number of League clubs achieved records of over 50,000 on their sprawling terraces viz. Stoke (1937), Hull City (1949), Portsmouth (1949), Coventry City (1967), and Crystal Palace (1979).

Meanwhile, Nottingham Forest played at the City Ground by the river near to Trent Bridge Cricket Ground from 1898, and had an international in 1909. However, there were few developments until the east terrace and Bridgford end were enlarged in the 1950s, resulting in a record of 49,946 for a Division One game against Manchester United in 1967.

Their rivals Notts County moved just opposite to Meadow Lane in 1910, and actually floated an old stand across the River Trent. Their main stand had a barrel roof (like the one at Preston) and a large Kop was raised at the north end. In fact, they had a golden era with Tommy Lawton, and the record of 47,310 was for a Cup quarter-final against York in 1955 - indeed they reached the semi-final as a Third Division side.

Bradford City also had a large terrace at the Manningham end and this was called Nunn's Kop, after a city dignitary, while the record attendance was 39,146 against Burnley during the Cup-winning season of 1911.

At Bloomfield Road in Blackpool there was a large Kop at the north end of the ground, although the other three sides were restricted. The central railway was close up to the stands, and Blackpool Tower and the seafront illuminations could be seen in the distance. The record crowd was 38,098 for a Division One game against Wolves in 1955.

Both teams were very successful at the time, and Blackpool with Stanley Matthews had just won the Cup, while Wolves with Stan Cullis as manager and Billy Wright as captain had recently won the championship.

All football clubs have their record attendances however some are quite remarkable. Doncaster Rovers played at Belle Vue by the racecourse from 1922, and large banking was erected on three sides. In fact, 37,149 attended a Division Three (North) game against Hull City in 1948, whilst the home side came third and their opponents finished top. However, the banking was redundant in the 1990s and the capacity was reduced to 6,500.

Likewise, Halifax Town were formed after a public meeting in 1911 and the Shay was developed in a natural hollow, once used as a council rubbish tip. The club moved there as founder members of Division Three (North) in 1921, and some large banking was raised on three sides. Speedway came there in 1948 determining the ground's shape, whereas a crowd of 36,885 watched a fifth round Cup-tie against Tottenham in 1953.

Crystal Palace and Millwall set the old Fourth Division record of 37,774 at Selhurst Park on 31 March 1961 (Good Friday), a record unlikely to be beaten. However, little known Thames F.C. had the lowest League crowd (on a Saturday afternoon) of 469 against Luton in 1930.

Meanwhile, Wales had two large grounds, both being in one city. Cardiff Arms Park staged rugby from 1876 and a grandstand was erected in 1885, hence Wales used it for soccer internationals from 1896-1910.

In fact, the Riverside C.C. played nearby and formed Cardiff City in 1899, and after a few trial games turned professional at Ninian Park, Sloper Road in 1910. The ground was sited on a former rubbish tip, and Lord Ninian Crichton Stuart provided the funds then kicked off the first game, a friendly against Villa. The main terrace on the east side was called the "Bob Bank," since it (once) cost just a shilling to stand there. [2]

The club joined Division Two with Leeds United in 1920, and just a year later reached the top division. In fact, they were runners-up to Huddersfield in Division One during the 1923-24 season.

---

[2] Wales played at Ninian Park from 1911, and also used grounds at Swansea and Wrexham. They went to Cardiff Arms Park in 1989, and the Millennium Stadium was built on the site ten years later.

At this time, the championship was decided on goal average; however Cardiff would have won on goal difference (having scored one more goal). Indeed, this was the only time there would have been a different outcome and they were separated by an infinitesimal 0.0241 of a goal.

Meanwhile, the club won the F.A. Cup in 1927 and there was a revival with average crowds of 38,000 in 1952-53. In fact, there was a club record of 57,800 for a First Division game against Arsenal that season. The Bob Bank was then extended and a large roof erected, resulting in a record of 61,566 during an international against England in 1961.

However, in general, the days of the Kop were numbered and only three old-style grounds were opened after the Second War, namely Boothferry Park (1946), Vale Park (1950), and Roots Hall (1955).

Kingston upon Hull was dominated by rugby, although Hull City played at the "Circle," Anlaby Road from 1906, with a main stand backing onto the cricket ground. Meanwhile, they had an uncertain future at the venue, thus they purchased Boothferry Park just west of the city in 1930.

The new ground was not ready for use until 1946, but there was soon a record crowd of 55,019 for a Cup-tie against Manchester United in 1949, and they were promoted that season, leading to average crowds of 37,000. However, in the following years both the club and its ground declined, and the north stand was replaced by a supermarket in 1982.

Port Vale were formed in a district of Burslem in c.1876 and went to the Recreation Ground, Hanley in 1913. Due to some serious debts they sold it to the Corporation in 1943, and purchased Vale Park the next year. There were ambitious schemes to build a "Wembley of the North," but only the paddock and tunnel of the main stand were ever built, and the ground was opened with uncovered terracing on all four sides in 1950.

The first game was against Newport County in Division Three (South) in front of 30,042, whilst the ground was gradually improved with a number of different covers. Meanwhile, the record attendance was an estimated 50,000 for a fifth round Cup-tie against Aston Villa in 1960.

Southend played at Roots Hall from 1906-16 and moved to the "Kursaal" on the seafront in 1919; then to the greyhound stadium in 1934. During this period the original ground was lowered as a result of quarrying, but they returned to the new Roots Hall in 1955, and developed the ground over the next five years (see later).

In fact, this was the last "old-style" League ground to be built and the age of the terrace had come to an end; whereas a new era was ushered in with the opening of Glanford Park at Scunthorpe on 14 August 1988, followed by Bescot Stadium at Walsall just two years later.

IT'S NOT CRICKET

The sport of cricket developed long before soccer and had its origins in London in the 18th century. Its focus was the Noblemen and Gentlemen's Club who were involved in sport mainly for the purposes of gambling.

They were based at Pall Mall and formed the London Cricket Club in 1722 and the Jockey Club in 1750, whilst they also arranged prize-fighting events. The former played their cricket at Kennington or White Conduit Fields, and increasingly at the Artillery Ground in Finsbury, with huge stakes riding on matches against both parish and local county opposition.

This came to a stop during the Seven Years War, fought between England and France over colonial trade in 1756-63, whereas the Artillery Ground became a place of ill-repute. Hambledon was then the centre of cricket for the next twenty years and they beat an all-England side in 1777.

Meanwhile, the gentlemen hoped to re-establish the game in London, and formed the White Conduit Club, Islington, in the early 1780s. The venue was found to be inadequate hence they asked Thomas Lord (1755-1832), one of their players, to find them a new rendezvous.

He initially obtained land at Dorset Square, Marylebone in 1787 and the gentlemen formed the M.C.C. later that year, but they were forced to move to North Bank, Lisson Grove in 1810. The first regular contest between Eton and Harrow was then established; whilst the Regent's Canal was built across the outfield and they had to move yet again.

A new site was found on the Eyre Estate at St. John's Wood in 1814, and this became the famous Lord's Cricket Ground. There were annual games between the Gentlemen and Players from 1819, and a regular North v South contest took place in 1836-38, and each year from 1849. The two regions also played against touring teams and the M.C.C., whilst William Clarke's All England XI traversed the counties from 1846.

Robert A. Fitzgerald was the M.C.C. secretary in 1863-76 and arranged a cricket tour of North America in 1872. In addition, there was an unofficial County Championship from that time, whilst Charles Alcock developed the game at the Oval with the first test against Australia in 1880.

However, there was clearly a close correlation with the development of soccer, and the first official County Championship was started in 1890 with eight county teams taking part at first.

Meanwhile, emerging soccer teams required a venue and many used cricket grounds, which in modern times seems a strange arrangement. In fact, the two sports were often in conflict right from the start.

A number played early games at the County Cricket Ground, and some examples are Brighton, Southampton, and Stoke, whereas Swindon moved to the County Ground in 1896 and remain there today. Such sharing also took place in Derby, Northampton, Nottingham, and Sheffield whereas several clubs played at their local cricket ground.

For instance, Leicester Fosse played some games at the Aylestone Road Cricket Ground and moved to Filbert Street in 1891, whereas Reading went to Caversham Cricket Ground in 1889 but their games were delayed while spectators arrived by ferry. They moved to Elm Park in 1896.

Watford Rovers started in 1881 and were invited to use the West Herts Sports Ground at Cassio Road in 1891, but a condition of the tenancy was that they became West Herts F.C. The ground had a cricket pavilion and some basic banking, whilst a merger saw the name change to Watford F.C. in 1898. The ground was severely tested when 13,000 spectators watched a game against Luton, and they moved to Vicarage Road in 1922.

Bristol South End were established in 1894 and played at St. John's Lane, Bedminster although the venue was overlooked, and they became Bristol City in 1897. Their rivals Bedminster were formed in 1887 and played at Ashton Gate from 1896. Indeed, W.G. Grace played a county cricket match there and it was the venue for two early football internationals.

Both teams played in the Southern League from 1898 but merged in 1900, and were the third southern team to enter the League the next year - only Woolwich Arsenal (1893) and Luton Town (1897) preceded them. At first they used both of the grounds, but only Ashton Gate from 1904.

Greenhalgh C.C. played at Field Mill, Mansfield in 1840 and a soccer team was established there in 1861, making it one of the oldest football venues in the world. There was a complex story of sport locally but Mansfield Town F.C. began in the 1890s, and moved to Field Mill by 1919. The cricket club left three years later, whilst they won the Midland League in 1924, 25, 29, and were thus elected to Division Three (South) in 1931.

Another example was Crewe Alexandra F.C. who started at the Alexandra Recreation Ground, Nantwich Road in 1877. This was the venue for a Cup semi-final between Aston Villa and Rangers in 1887, whereas the club were in the League from 1892-96 and moved to Gresty Road in 1906.

Rotherham Town played at Clifton Lane (cricket ground and racecourse) from 1882, and moved to Clifton Grove where they played League football in 1893-96. A new team Rotherham F.C. was formed at the cricket ground, whilst Rotherham County moved to Millmoor in 1907 and joined Division Two in 1919. However, they finished bottom of Division Three (North) in 1924-25 and the two teams merged to form United.

In fact, several sides had their origins within cricket thus Clapton Orient came from the Glyn C.C., Stockport Co. had links to Heaton Norris C.C., and Darlington were formed at the local grammar school in 1883 but played at Feethams the home of Darlington C.C.

The latter club were a successful amateur side and played in the Cup from 1885, then in the Northern and N.E. League and were founder members of Division Three (North) in 1921. The cricket pitch was next to the football ground for over a century, and was the last surviving example of such an arrangement (they moved to a new stadium in 2003).

Hull City were formed in 1904 and joined the League the next year, then played at the "Circle," Anlaby Road from 1906-46. They missed promotion to Division One by goal difference in 1909-10, thus Hull remains the largest city never to have a top flight team (to date).

A 4,000 seat main stand was built next to the cricket pitch in 1914, and covers were erected over the three terraces in the 1920s. There were a number of sports grounds in the area, but the venue was always restricted with poor access. The record attendance was 32,930 for a Cup-tie in 1930, part of a run that included a semi-final against Arsenal, whilst they returned to the impressive K.C. Stadium (built on the site) in 2003.

Meanwhile, after the demise of Bramall Lane in 1975 the last example of a shared venue was the County Ground at Northampton. The cricket club laid out the site south of Abington Avenue in 1885, and a football club was formed in 1897, but always on terms that were non-preferential. In fact, they were charged more rent than the cricketers, and could not play any games there before September or after April.

However, they became professional and joined both Kettering Town and Wellingborough in the Southern League, whilst Herbert Chapman was one of their players. Initially the team changed in the pavilion and attendances were just 4,000, while a main stand was built in 1907; however Chapman returned as the manager and they won the Southern League in 1909, and were founder members of the Third Division in 1920.

There were several plans to move but without success, and they joined the new Fourth Division in 1958. There was then a remarkable rise up the League, and they went from Division Four in 1961 to Division One in 1965. The average crowds during their one season at the top were 18,000 and the record was 24,253 against Fulham. However, they then experienced one of the fastest slides and were back in Division Four by 1969. [3]

Despite this, the cobblers reached the fifth round of the Cup in 1970 and played Manchester United at home losing 8-2. Indeed, it was the one time

---

[3] Bristol City made an even more rapid descent from 1980 to 1982.

that a stand was allowed on the cricket pitch. Northampton left the County Ground, with its unusual wedge-shaped end terraces, and went to Sixfields in 1994, thus the cricketers took sole charge after 97 years.

In the case of Sheffield the cricket club was expelled, and at Northampton the football club left, but it did not really matter which, since the shared cricket-football venue was truly consigned to history. Owzat!

TIME TO MAKE A STAND

The modern stadiums have heralded in a new era regarding both design and materials, and contrast greatly with those that still remain little changed. Indeed, the difference is often quite striking, and is only rivalled by their progressive appellations and nom-de-plumes.

In the past most grounds were named after a local feature, but football has been infected by a very modern problem. The founders envisioned a game where sport came first and money second, and could not have imagined a time where grounds were named after sponsors.

Clearly a degree of romance has been lost as Feethams, Gay Meadow, the Vetch Field, and many other historic "Parks," have been replaced by the Emirates, Liberty, Reebok, Ricoh, McAlpine &c.

There is no denying that these new stadiums have impressive credentials, but they represent a break with the past, a break that has more to do with modernity rather than just specific to soccer. Some criticise their off-the-shelf uniformity, although the same censure might be levelled at Leitch.

Meanwhile, in the early days clubs used a variety of venues and some were in Victorian pleasure parks, examples being the Lower Grounds, Crystal Palace, and Tower Grounds. All of these had an eclectic mix of sideshows, grand events, dance halls, exotic gardens, and sporting venues.

In fact, Blackpool were formed by old boys in 1887 and first played at Raikes Hall Park or the Royal Palace Gardens. This was a few minutes walk from the seafront, and Raikes Hotel looked out over the cricket-football pitch, near to an ornamental lake and surrounded by a racecourse.

The hotel included an Indian lounge, ballroom, and theatre whilst nearby were a camera obscura, monkey house, and fountains. The club also played at Whitegate or Stanley Park (which was another racecourse) and took part in the League from 1896-99, but lost their status with Darwen.

They then joined rivals South Shore to form a new team at Bloomfield Road in 1899, and re-entered the League the next year. However, their resurgence began poorly, and the first game was a record defeat of 10-1 against Small Heath during the 1900-01 season.

In fact, several teams played their games at racecourses and the one in Derby has already been discussed. Another significant example is Wrexham where the first races were staged in 1807, but the meetings often became rowdy affairs therefore they were banned from 1858.

For several years the site was used just for cricket but the races were then re-instated in 1872, and football was played from that time thus Wrexham (Olympic) were formed in 1884. Indeed, this makes the Racecourse Ground the only League venue as old as Deepdale and Turf Moor.

In the early years the club's activities were centred on the Turf Hotel and a main stand was erected on Mold Road in 1902, the pitch being located across the racetrack. However, the racing ended in 1912 and when the club joined Division Three (North) they developed the ground. One unusual feature was the installation of a deck of seats from the local cinema on the Town End terrace from 1962-78, whereas the Yale Stand was added in 1972 with a view to staging future internationals.

Other clubs such as Hartlepool and Millwall played with a backdrop of sailing ships in the docks. Indeed, there was a Zeppelin raid in Hartlepool in 1916, but it was the main stand at the Victoria Ground that was hit.

Millwall F.C. were established on the Isle of Dogs in 1885 and played at East Ferry Road in 1890-1901, which was an oval arena capable of holding 15,000 - and they won the Southern League there. Indeed, their status was confirmed when they hosted both Preston North End and Sunderland.

They then went to North Greenwich on a former potato field and opened with a friendly against Aston Villa in 1901, the record being 11,000 against Tottenham that year, but they moved to New Cross in 1910.

However, the story might have been different, since the unlikely named Willey Reveley proposed a grand scheme to straighten the Thames across the area in 1796. The plan was dismissed as too expensive, and instead the problem of congestion was solved with some large new docks. [4]

These were clearly days unlike the present and clubs had to be frugal in terms of ground development. In fact, many would re-use existing stands, or borrow those from other grounds. For example: The Wellington Road roof went to Muntz Street in 1897; Noah's Ark was taken to the Hawthorns in 1900; a Hyde Road stand was transferred to the Shay in 1923; and the Swan Passage stand went to Vale Park in 1950.

---

[4] Willey Reveley (1760-99) and his wife Maria both worked with Jeremy Bentham the political reformer, and the former designed the Panopticon a circular prison. The family were friends of the Godwins, whilst Maria remarried and went to Italy. Indeed, the poet Shelley, husband of Mary Godwin, backed a plan by their son Henry W. Reveley to run steamboats from Leghorn to Marseille.

The case of a stand taken from Trent Bridge across the river to Meadow Lane, and the Tattoo Stands at Accrington and Swindon have already been discussed; whereas Mansfield purchased a stand from the recently closed Hurst Park Racecourse in 1959, and raised it in stages behind the old west stand (a similar method was used for Swindon's main stand in 1971).

Indeed, the practice of re-using stands continued into recent times and when Chester left Sealand Road for the Deva Stadium, the roof of the main stand was re-erected at the Hamil Road end of Vale Park.

There were many oddities and Brentford had to clear out an orchard to establish Griffin Park in 1904, while Southampton played at Avenue Road with a footpath across the pitch. Indeed, The Dell was not much better and a swampy stream inundated the ground when they arrived in 1898.

Their neighbours Brighton had a different problem, and a director John Clark lived at Goldstone House near to the home of Hove F.C. The latter established a ground nearby in 1901 and Albion came there the next year, but there was a large druid stone on the site, and this was removed (to a nearby park) when the Goldstone Ground was prepared.

Gay Meadow, Shrewsbury was a historical pleasure site long before the arrival of football in 1910, but was situated next to the River Severn and became flooded on several occasions. Indeed, one supporter Fred Davies retrieved balls from the river in his coracle, charging only a small fee!

There were several stands of a strangely bucolic nature and these included the "Rabbit Hutch" at Fulham, the "Chicken Run" at West Ham, and the "Cowshed" (with the Big Bank attached) in Exeter.

Meanwhile, Singers F.C. were transformed into Coventry City in 1898 and went to Highfield Road the next year. The Kop had the "Crows Nest" at the rear, whereas a roof taken from Twickenham was erected over the west terrace in 1927-67, and the "Sky Blue" period occurred in the 1960s.

Another case was that of Bristol City who had high aspirations and beat Manchester United to the Division Two title in 1905-06, and were runners-up in the League the next year. In fact, they also played United in the Cup Final at the Crystal Palace in front of 71,401 in 1909.

With such success in mind they erected a cover at the Winterstoke End in 1928, which was notable for its great length. It extended way beyond the corner flags and they clearly planned to turn the ground on its axis, but the side were relegated in 1932 and this never took place.

The most astonishing venue, however, was in Norwich and some local teachers started the team in 1902. Initially they played at Newmarket Road and joined the Southern League in 1905, but the site became inadequate, and they moved to a location with even greater deficiencies.

"The Nest" at Rosary Road was laid out in an old chalk pit however there were no other grounds quite like it. The pitch was up against a 30-foot cliff at the east end, and the houses of Rosary Road were close to the goal at the other end. The Newmarket Road stand was placed on the north side, and a cover called the Chicken Run was located just opposite.

In addition the venue was overshadowed by a timber yard, tin works, gas works, and St. Matthew's Church, whilst the ball often bounced off the cliff face back onto the pitch. Indeed, it was a precarious situation and people watched from the top, thus there was a near disaster in 1922.

Despite this there was an amazing record crowd of 25,037 for a Cup-tie against Sheffield Wednesday in 1935, but a corner of the pitch collapsed into the old workings soon after, and they went to Carrow Road later that year. George VI then watched a Division Two game against Millwall at the new ground in 1938.

In fact, clubs would go to any length to prepare new grounds, and in the case of Southend F.C. the terrace was, "One that I made earlier." As stated, the club had two stints at Roots Hall (once an 18th century house), and they joined Division Three in 1920 then returned to the ground in 1955. Indeed, Sid Broomfield the grounds-man built the south terrace "stone by stone," as money allowed, over the next five years.

There was a record attendance of 31,090 for a Cup game against Liverpool in 1979; however the much-laboured-over terrace was sold to a property developer in 1988. Indeed, it was demolished in just a matter of days!

Regarding the closest League grounds the honour goes to Nottingham, since the City Ground and Meadow Lane face one another across the River Trent. However, some other venues are even closer such as the grounds in Dundee, whilst the undoubted winner is The Firs of St. Leonard's which looks down on the extensive Pilot Field of Hastings F.C.

Queens Park Rangers have played at the largest number of grounds with a total of 13 venues and 17 changes. Four of these were in the Kensal Green area including Kilburn Cricket Ground, whilst they played at the substantial Kensal Rise Athletic Ground on two occasions in 1896-1904, then went to Park Royal, Stamford Bridge, Loftus Road, and White City. The athletic ground was closed in the 1920s and Liddell Gardens were built on the site, but were named after a landowner and not the famous runner.

Meanwhile, Leitch was not the only innovative ground designer, and when Arsenal achieved un-paralleled success in the 1930s they looked to develop Highbury. Initially they employed Claude Waterlow Ferrier an architect who studied in Paris, and an exponent of the Art Deco style; however, his first contribution was to extend the end terraces in 1931.

He then turned his attention to the west side, opposite to Leitch's multi-span main stand, and produced a ground-breaking design with a bold white façade, straight linear lines, club motifs, and an upper tier of seating for 4,100 over a large terrace - at a cost of just £50,000.

The Prince of Wales (later King Edward VIII) opened the stand on 10 December 1932, and Arsenal won the title soon afterwards; whilst Ferrier also designed a cover over the North Bank and the record attendance then followed in 1935 (later re-roofed by Binnie).

There were further Cup and League successes however Leitch's stand was found expensive to maintain and was removed in 1936. William Binnie then designed a replacement which mirrored Ferrier's stand, and had 4,000 seats on each of its two tiers and a small paddock-terrace to the front.

However, the most significant feature was a bold façade in Avenell Road with vertical and horizontal lines, and the club name and a gun carriage motif at the centre. There was also a marble entrance hall with the bust of Herbert Chapman, although the cost was a substantial £130,000. No other stands could compare at the time, and they were the apex of ground design in the early years of the Football League.

Meanwhile, there is one other significant development to consider, and this was the introduction of the cantilevered stand. Such stands had been constructed at racecourses and on the Continent in the 1930s, but they were yet to be seen at British football grounds.

It was no surprise that the first innovation came in Scunthorpe which had long been associated with the iron and steel industry. The local team United were formed in 1899, and played at the Old Showground in the Midland League from 1912-50, being champions on two occasions.

There were small stands on each side of the pitch and a cover at the Fox Street end, whilst Grimsby played there in the war as their Blundell Park ground was by the docks. The club then joined Division Three (North) with Shrewsbury Town, when it was increased in size by two, in 1950. [5]

The ground was improved, and a terrace at the Doncaster Road end was covered in 1954, then they were champions in 1957-58. However, the east stand burnt down soon after, and was replaced with the first cantilevered stand at a British football ground.

It was 50-yards long with bench seats for 2,200 and faced the main stand, whilst it was opened on 23 August 1958. The ground was closed thirty years later, and attempts to move it to the new venue proved impractical. In fact, Glanford Park had columns to support the roof on three sides.

---

[5] Colchester United and Gillingham (a League member in 1920-38) were likewise elected to Division Three (South), making a total of 92 teams.

The second cantilevered stand was erected at Hillsborough on the west side, but was on a completely different scale. There were seats for 10,000 spectators and Sir Stanley Rous opened it on 23 August 1961. Indeed, with the demise of the Old Showground, it is now the oldest of its type at a football ground in the country.

THE INTERNATIONAL GAME

Almost every aspect of football was inaugurated in England, and the first international (unofficial) was played at the Oval in 1870. Such games soon attracted large crowds, especially in Scotland, and the Corinthians F.C. were formed in 1882 with the sole aim of competing in these contests. In fact, the home internationals were started two years later.

A number of famous venues were used for these initial games including the Oval (1873-89), the Crystal Palace (1897-1909), the West of Scotland Cricket Ground (1872-76), the first and second Hampden Parks (1878-90), Celtic and Rangers F.C. (1892-1904), the Racecourse Ground, Wrexham (from 1877), and Solitude, Belfast (from 1890).

Meanwhile, the newly emerging clubs had new grounds which provided some further venues: Alexandra Meadows (1881), Bramall Lane (1883/87), Leamington Street (1885/87), Nantwich Road (1888), Anfield (1889), and the Victoria Ground (1889/93). There were also some less familiar choices such as the Aigburth Cricket Ground in south Liverpool in 1883, and Whalley Range in Manchester in 1885.

Games were then played at League (or Southern League) venues, but two that stand out are Richmond Athletic Ground arranged by Alcock in 1893, and the Queen's Club, West Kensington used in 1895. The Corinthians played at the latter and fielded the full England side in 1894/95 (hence the choice), whereas the Oxford v Cambridge varsity match was at the Oval in 1873-87 and at the Queen's Club until at least 1903.

England was the most successful of the home nations in the 1890s, while Upton Park an amateur side (who played in the first F.A. Cup) represented the country in unofficial Olympic tournaments, at Athens in 1896 and at Paris in 1900 - winning both of them. However, Galt F.C. who represented Canada won at St. Louis, Missouri in 1904.

F.I.F.A. the organisation of international football was formed in Paris at the latter date, the initial members Belgium, Denmark, France, Netherlands, Spain, Sweden, and Switzerland. Initially, the F.A. did not join and there was an amateur-professional split in 1906; however they soon became a member and were then prominent in its affairs.

Meanwhile, Mount Vesuvius erupted in this period, thus the Olympics transferred from Rome to London in 1908. By then soccer had become an official sport at the games, and Great Britain beat Denmark 2-0 at the White City to take the gold medal (and in effect were world champions). Indeed, the marathon distance was altered from 24.8 to 26 miles (to reach Windsor), and 385 yards were added to arrive at the Royal box!

The first overseas football tour was to the Austro-Hungarian Empire in June 1908. This included fixtures in Budapest, Prague, and Vienna, whilst there was another tour to that country the next year; however these were the only games on the Continent before the war.

Indeed, there was further success when Great Britain beat Denmark 4-2 in Stockholm to win gold again in 1912, and the Netherlands took the bronze on each occasion. However, there were new "world champions" at the next three Olympics - Belgium won by forfeit over Spain at Antwerp in 1920, while Uruguay won at Paris in 1924 and at Amsterdam in 1928.

A World Cup was discussed by F.I.F.A. from the start, but the F.A. had several disputes with the body in Zurich, and withdrew in 1918-22 and again in 1928. The England team was superior to continental opposition on foreign tours until the 1920s, but due to the rift there was little chance to test if this apparent superiority could hold on the world stage.

In fact, Uruguay agreed to host the inaugural contest in 1930 after their Olympic successes, and won the World Cup that year, whilst the next two competitions were won by Italy before the war.

England then had major setbacks and lost 2-0 to Ireland at Wembley in 1949, and had further problems in their first World Cup in 1950. The side included players such as Tom Finney, Wilf Mannion, Stan Mortensen, and Billy Wright but they lost 1-0 to the U.S.A. (semi-finalists in 1930), and this ended any hopes they had in the competition.

After the Second War there was a 'golden era' for English clubs however the national side was under increasing scrutiny, and this was confirmed with a notorious 6-3 thrashing by Hungary at Wembley in 1953.

In fact, Uruguay won the World Cup again and it was then dominated by Argentina, Brazil, France, Germany, and Italy. However, England continued to be prominent and Sir Stanley Rous, F.A. secretary was F.I.F.A. president in 1961-74. For a time the country were not the undisputed champions of the world, but this was all put right in 1966, and this one moment alone epitomised the aspirations of the founders of soccer.

Appendix I

F.A. Cup Finals   1872-1939

1872	Wanderers	R Engineers	1-0	2,000	(The Oval)
1873	Wanderers	Oxford Univ	2-0	3,000	(Lillie Bridge)
1874	Oxford Univ	R Engineers	2-0	2,000	(The Oval)
5	R Engineers	Old Etonians	1-1, 2-0	3,000r	
6	Wanderers	Old Etonians	1-1, 3-0	1,500r	
7	Wanderers	Oxford Univ	2-1	3,000	
8	Wanderers	R Engineers	3-1	4,500	
9	Old Etonians	Clapham Rov	1-0	5,000	
1880	Clapham Rov	Oxford Univ	1-0	6,000	
1	O Carthusians	Old Etonians	3-0	4,500	
2	Old Etonians	Blackburn R	1-0	6,500	
3	Blackburn O	Old Etonians	2-1	8,000	
4	Blackburn R	Queen's Park	2-1	14,000	
5	Blackburn R	Queen's Park	2-0	12,500	
6	Blackburn R	West Brom	0-0, 2-0	15,000r	
7	Aston Villa	West Brom	2-0	15,500	
8	West Brom	Preston N E	2-1	19,000	
9	Preston N E	Wolves	3-0	22,000	
1890	Blackburn R	Wednesday	6-1	20,000	
1	Blackburn R	Notts County	3-1	23,000	
2	West Brom	Aston Villa	3-0	32,810	
1893	Wolves	Everton	1-0	45,000	(Fallowfield)
1894	Notts County	Bolton Wand	4-1	37,000	(Goodison)
1895	Aston Villa	West Brom	1-0	42,560	(C. Palace)
6	Wednesday	Wolves	2-1	48,836	
7	Aston Villa	Everton	3-2	65,891	
8	Nottingham F	Derby County	3-1	62,017	
9	Sheffield U	Derby County	4-1	73,833	
1900	Bury	Southampton	4-0	68,945	
1	Tottenham H	Sheffield U	2-2, 3-1	114,815	
2	Sheffield U	Southampton	1-1, 2-1	76,914	

1903	Bury	Derby County	6-0	63,102	(C. Palace)
4	Man City	Bolton Wand	1-0	61,374	
5	Aston Villa	Newcastle U	2-0	101,117	
6	Everton	Newcastle U	1-0	75,609	
7	Wednesday	Everton	2-1	84,594	
8	Wolves	Newcastle U	3-1	74,697	
9	Man United	Bristol City	1-0	71,401	
1910	Newcastle U	Barnsley	1-1, 2-0	77,747	
1	Bradford City	Newcastle U	0-0, 1-0	69,098	
2	Barnsley	West Brom	0-0, 1-0	54,556	
3	Aston Villa	Sunderland	1-0	121,919	
4	Burnley	Liverpool	1-0	72,778	
1915	Sheffield U	Chelsea	3-0	49,557	(O. Trafford)
1920	Aston Villa	Huddersfield	1-0	50,018	(Chelsea)
1	Tottenham H	Wolves	1-0	72,805	
2	Huddersfield	Preston N E	1-0	53,000	
1923	Bolton W	West Ham U	2-0	126,047	(Wembley)
4	Newcastle U	Aston Villa	2-0	91,695	
5	Sheffield U	Cardiff City	1-0	91,763	
6	Bolton W	Man City	1-0	91,447	
7	Cardiff City	Arsenal	1-0	91,206	
8	Blackburn R	Huddersfield	3-1	92,041	
9	Bolton W	Portsmouth	2-0	92,576	
1930	Arsenal	Huddersfield	2-0	92,488	
1	West Brom	Birmingham	2-1	92,406	
2	Newcastle U	Arsenal	2-1	92,298	
3	Everton	Man City	3-0	92,950	
4	Man City	Portsmouth	2-1	93,258	
5	Sheffield W	West Brom	4-2	93,204	
6	Arsenal	Sheffield U	1-0	93,384	
7	Sunderland	Preston N E	3-1	93,495	
8	Preston N E	Huddersfield	1-0	93,357	
9	Portsmouth	Wolves	4-1	99,370	

Attendance is for the first game unless marked r for replay.

Appendix II

League Title 1889 - 1939

1889	Preston N E	40	Aston Villa	29
1890	Preston N E	33	Everton	31
1	Everton	29	Preston N E	27
2	Sunderland	42	Preston N E	37
3	Sunderland	48	Preston N E	37
4	Aston Villa	44	Sunderland	38
5	Sunderland	47	Everton	42
6	Aston Villa	45	Derby County	41
7	Aston Villa	47	Sheffield U	36
8	Sheffield U	42	Sunderland	37
9	Aston Villa	45	Liverpool	43
1900	Aston Villa	50	Sheffield U	48
1	Liverpool	45	Sunderland	43
2	Sunderland	44	Everton	41
3	Wednesday	42	Aston Villa	41
4	Wednesday	47	Man City	44
5	Newcastle U	48	Everton	47
6	Liverpool	51	Preston N E	47
7	Newcastle U	51	Bristol City	48
8	Man United	52	Aston Villa	43
9	Newcastle U	53	Everton	46
1910	Aston Villa	53	Liverpool	48
1	Man United	52	Aston Villa	51
2	Blackburn R	49	Everton	46
3	Sunderland	54	Aston Villa	50
4	Blackburn R	51	Aston Villa	44
5	Everton	46	Oldham A	45

There was no League or Cup football from 1915-19.

1920	West Brom	60	Burnley	51
1	Burnley	59	Man City	54
2	Liverpool	57	Tottenham H	51
3	Liverpool	60	Sunderland	54
4	Huddersfield	57	Cardiff City	57
5	Huddersfield	58	West Brom	56
6	Huddersfield	57	Arsenal	52
7	Newcastle U	56	Huddersfield	51
8	Everton	53	Huddersfield	51
9	Wednesday	52	Leicester City	51

1930	Sheffield W	60	Derby County	50
1	Arsenal	66	Aston Villa	59
2	Everton	56	Arsenal	54
3	Arsenal	58	Aston Villa	54
4	Arsenal	59	Huddersfield	56
5	Arsenal	58	Sunderland	54
6	Sunderland	56	Derby County	48
7	Man City	57	Charlton A	54
8	Arsenal	52	Wolves	51
9	Everton	59	Wolves	55

Games played in a season with regard to the number of League members:
1889 (22), 1892 (26), 1893 (30), 1899 (34), 1906 (38), 1920 (42)

Appendix III

Ground Opening Dates

1860	Sandygate	Hallam	oldest ground
1870	York Road	Maidenhead	oldest one club
1874	Drill Field	Northwich Victoria	was 2nd oldest
1881	Deepdale *	Preston North End	sport from 1875
1883	Turf Moor	Burnley	
"	Feethams	Darlington	cricket from 1866
"	Victoria Ground	Stoke City	
1884	Racecourse Ground	Wrexham (Olympic)	football from 1872
1885	Gigg Lane	Bury	
1887	Saltergate	Chesterfield (Town)	1866, also 1880
1888	Oakwell	Barnsley (St. Peters)	
1889	Bramall Lane	Sheffield United	1855, football 1868
"	Molineux	Wolverhampton W	sport from 1860s
1890	Ewood Park	Blackburn Rovers	
"	Aggborough	Kidderminster H	formed in 1886
1891	Filbert Street	Leicester (Fosse)	
1892	Goodison Park	Everton	
"	Anfield	Liverpool	Everton 1884
"	St James's Park	Newcastle United	Rangers 1880
1893	Priestfield Stadium	Gillingham	Brompton to 1913
1894	St James's Park	Exeter City	United to 1904
1895	Burnden Park	Bolton Wanderers	
"	Baseball Ground	Derby County	sport from 1880s
"	Sincil Bank	Lincoln City	
"	Loakes Park	Wycombe Wanderers	
"	Old Showground	Scunthorpe United	Brumby H to 1899
1896	Craven Cottage	Fulham	
"	Elm Park	Reading	
"	County Ground	Swindon	
"	Fellows Park	Walsall	Hillary St to 1930
1897	Villa Park	Aston Villa	sport from 1875
"	Eastville	Bristol Rovers	
"	County Ground	Northampton	cricket from 1885
1898	City Ground	Nottingham Forest	
"	The Dell	Southampton	

1898	Roker Park	Sunderland	
1899	Bloomfield Road	Blackpool	with South Shore
"	Highfield Road	Coventry City	once Singers
"	Blundell Park	Grimsby Town	
"	Fratton Park	Portsmouth	
"	Hillsborough	Wednesday	Owlerton to 1914
"	White Hart Lane	Tottenham Hotspur	
1900	The Hawthorns	West Bromwich A	
1902	Edgeley Park	Stockport County	rugby from 1891
"	Goldstone Ground	Brighton & Hove A	Hove in 1901
1903	Valley Parade	Bradford City	rugby from 1886
"	Ayresome Park	Middlesbrough	
"	Home Park	Plymouth Argyle	rugby/athletics 1894
1904	Griffin Park	Brentford	
"	Ashton Gate	Bristol City	Bedminster 1896
"	Upton Park	West Ham United	Boleyn Ground
"	Moss Rose Stadium	Macclesfield Town	Hallfield 1897
1905	Stamford Bridge	Chelsea	athletics from 1877
"	Kenilworth Road *	Luton Town	
1906	St. Andrew's	Birmingham City	
"	Sealand Road	Chester City	
"	Gresty Road	Crewe Alexandria	
1906	Boundary Park *	Oldham Athletic	football from 1896
1907	Underhill	Barnet	B Alston to 1919
"	Portman Road	Ipswich Town	
"	Spotland	Rochdale	rugby from 1878
"	Millmoor	Rotherham United	County 1907-25
1908	Leeds Road	Huddersfield Town	
1909	Brunton Park	Carlisle United	
"	Layer Road	Colchester United	Town to 1937
1910	Dean Court	Bournemouth	Boscombe to 1923
"	Ninian Park	Cardiff City	
"	Victoria Ground	Hartlepool(s) United	rugby from1886
"	Old Trafford	Manchester United	
"	The Den	Millwall (Athletic)	
"	Meadow Lane	Notts County	
"	Gay Meadow	Shrewsbury Town	
"	Plainmoor	Torquay United	Ellacombe to 1921
1912	Vetch Field	Swansea City (Town)	sport from 1891
"	Prenton Park	Tranmere Rovers	

1912	Plough Lane	Wimbledon	M.K. Dons 2003
1913	Highbury	Arsenal	
1917	Loftus Road *	Queens Park Rangers	Shepherds B 1904
1919	The Valley	Charlton Athletic	
"	Elland Road	Leeds United	rugby 1878, City 1904
"	Field Mill	Mansfield Town	football from 1861
1920	Springfield Park	Wigan Athletic	Borough to 1931
"	Huish Park (old)	Yeovil Town	
1921	The Shay	Halifax Town	
"	Christie Park	Morecambe	Roseberry P to 1927
1922	Vicarage Road	Watford (Rovers)	West Herts 1891-98
"	Belle Vue Stadium	Doncaster Rovers	
1923	Maine Road	Manchester City	
1924	Selhurst Park	Crystal Palace	
1925	Manor Ground #	Oxford United	Headington to 1960
1926	Recreation Ground	Aldershot (Town)	reformed 1992
1932	Abbey Stadium	Cambridge United	Abbey U to 1951
"	Whaddon Road	Cheltenham Town	
"	Bootham Crescent	York City	
1934	London Road	Peterborough United	Fletton U 1905
"	York Street	Boston United	
1935	Carrow Road	Norwich City	
1937	Brisbane Road	Leyton Orient	Clapton, Leyton 1905
1946	Boothferry Park	Hull City	owned from 1930
1950	Vale Park	Port Vale	
1955	Roots Hall	Southend United	also 1906-16
"	Victoria Road	Dagenham Redbridge	football from 1917
1958	Eton Park	Burton Albion	now Pirelli nearby
1970	Crown Ground	Accrington Stanley	formed 1968
1976	Broadhall Way	Stevenage Borough	Town 1961
1994	Nene Park	Rushden Diamonds	formed 1992

* These grounds had artificial pitches in the following years:
Q.P.R. 1981-87, Luton 1985-91, Oldham 1986-91, Preston 1986-94

The first basic floodlights were at Oxford in 1950, followed by Arsenal, Southampton, and Swindon in 1951, but most were in the mid-1950s.

Bibliography

General Bibliography

Burke's Gentry Baronetcy & Peerage; Butterworth's Business Biography;
Crockford's Clerical Directory; Hart's Army Lists; Law Society Records;
National Biography; Navy Lists; Oxbridge Alumni; Who's Who
Registers for Charterhouse, Eton, Harrow, Westminster, Winchester
19th Century Directories; The Times Newspaper and Index
Godfrey O.S. - Barnes 1867; Clapham Park 1872; St. John's Wood 1868

A.A. Illustrated Guide to Britain - Drive Publications Ltd. (1973)
Heritage of Britain - Readers Digest Association Ltd. (1975)
Bailey, Philip, Who's Who of Cricketers, Hamlyn (1993)
Rennison, N., London Blue Plaque Guide, Sutton Stroud (1999)

General Research

The Football Association Archives, 25 Soho Square, London
The Family Record Centre, Myddelton Street, London -
B.M.D., Census 1841-1901, Consular, Nonconformist, Wills to 1858
Public Record Office, Kew - Army, Navy, Royal Engineers' service
The Genealogical Society, Charterhouse Buildings, London
First Avenue House, High Holborn - Wills after 1858
The Metropolitan Archives, Northampton Road, Clerkenwell
Mormon Family Record Centre, Exhibition Road, Kensington
The Guildhall Library & Map Room, Aldermanbury, London
Westminster Archives, St. Ann's Street, Westminster
Scottish General Register Office, New Register House, Edinburgh
I.G.I., Free B.M.D., G.R.O. online (cert.), 1901 census, P.R.O. census-wills,
Scotland's People, peerage.com, American census, Wikipedia (w)
Internet Website = (w)

Chapter 1 - Codes and Rules

A Short History of Soccer: The Early Rules by Tony Brown -
Cambridge, Sheffield, Uppingham, F.A. soccer.mistral.co.uk (w)
Gibson, A. & Pickford, W., Association Football..., Caxton (1905)
Green, G., History of the F.A., Naldrett (1953) - Ch. 2, Appendix
Fabian, A.H. & Green, G.., Association Football, Caxton (1960)

Ereaut, E.J., Richmond F.C. 1861-1925, Howlett & Son (1926)
Blackheath Prop. School, Ideal Homes Suburbia in Focus, Lewisham (w)
Blackheath Rugby Club History - the first ever 'rugby' club (w)

Chapter 2 - Barnes Association

Local Studies - L.B. Richmond, Old Town Hall, Whittaker Avenue

Ebenezer Cobb Morley
U.R.C. History Society, Cambridge, M. Thompson -
Congregational Yearbook 1863/64, Sources for English Nonconformity
Hull Nonconformist Records; Hull Library - Local History Section
Barnes Cemetery - Barnes & Mortlake History Society (1981)

Robert Watson Willis
St. Margaret's Westminster, St. George's Hanover Square
Westminster Archives - rate books and directories

Robert George Graham
Hinxton Parish Records, Church History; Walker, V., Life & Times
Henry Thornton, Clapham Sect, and E.M. Forster (w)
Sheaf, John and Howe, Ken, Hampton and Teddington Past
Hampton Church - A.H. Wood; Winifred Graham (w)

Chapter 3 - American Links

Arthur Pember
D.J. Brown, Bridgnorth, Shropshire - 18th century family history
Timothy Duke - Chester Herald, College of Arms, London
Brixton and Lambeth Parish Records (Metropolitan Archives)
Lists of Stock Exchange Members (Guildhall Library)
Pember, A., The Mysteries & Miseries of the Great Metropolis with some
Adventures in the Country…, D. Appleton & Co. (1874)

The Municipal Archives, Chambers Street - B.M.D., City Directory
The National Archives, Varick Street - Soundex census
New York Public Library - New York Times and Punchinello
The New York Times Archive, Brooklyn Daily Eagle (w)
N.Y. State Library, Albany - A. Rainey (re book), P. Mercer
Mrs. Coreen P. Hallenbeck - further research in Albany

Bureau Des Guides, Musée Alpin, and Bibliotèque (ENSA) - Chamonix
Christchurch Library, N.Z. - Len Dangerfield, further research
Bohan E., Sinclair K., Fry R. - Dictionary of N.Z. Biography (2003) (w)
Poole's Index to Periodical Lit. 1802-1906: Atlantic Monthly, Lippincott's
Arthur Conan Doyle memoirs and adventures, Crowborough (1924)
Coren, Michael, Conan Doyle his life, Bloomsbury (1995)
Fargo Photographic and North Dakota Census 1885 (w)

Chapter 4 - Alcock and the Oval

Durham Record Office - wills; Sunderland Library - shipping records
Chingford Library - reference Sunnyside and O.S. Map 1914
L.B. of Redbridge (archives) - The Merchant Seamen's Orphan Asylum
Ramsey, W., Epping Forest Then and Now (1986)
Victoria History of Essex Vol. VI (Oxford University Press)
Forest Boy's School Archives - G. Wright

Marriott, C. & Alcock, C.W., The Oval Series of Games, Routledge (1894)
Lemmon, D., The History of Surrey C.C.C., Helm Series (1989)
The Lyceum Clubs 1904-2004 (w)

Chapter 5 - The Wanderers

Morton Peto Betts
Institution of Civil Engineers, 1-7 Great George Street, London -
The Frank D. Smith Collection - W. Betts, E.L. Betts, G. Giles, S.M. Peto
White, Leonard, The Story of Gosport (Portsmouth Library)
Isle of Wight Record Office, 26 Hillside, Newport
Local History, Bromley Library - The Betts family, The Holmwood

Charles Henry Reynolds Wollaston
Lancing School Records; Crockford's Clerical Directory
National Biography - Wollaston; Cambridge Alumni - Reynolds

Thomas Charles Hooman
Local History, Kidderminster Library - 1859 map
Kidderminster since 1800 - Tomkinson Hall
Carpets from Kidderminster - Legat; History of - Burton
Charterhouse School; Highgate Street Directories and Map

Robert Walpole Sealy Vidal
Somerset Record Office - Bridgwater Parish Records (Sealy)
North Devon Record Office, Tuly Street, Barnstaple - Archivist
Helen Naomi Richardson Collection - Vidal miscellany
Public Record Office, Kew - Royal Licence

Chapter 6 - Eton and Harrow

Edward Ernest Bowen
Lineham, Peter J. - Dictionary of New Zealand Biography (2003)
Harrow School Archives, 5 High Street, Harrow
Isle of Wight Record Office, 26 Hillside, Newport
Osborne House and Christchurch, Totland

William Parry Crake
William Crake - Middlesex Victoria County History (1989)
Ealing and St. Marylebone Parish Records; Harrow School Register
Paddington, Ealing History; Charles Thomas Lucas (w)

Edgar Lubbock
National Biography - Lubbock, Whitbread; Who's Who
Local History, Bromley Library - High Elms
St. James's Piccadilly, St. Peter's Pimlico - Parish Records
Moore, Dudley - History of Kent C.C.C.

Albert Childers Meysey-Thompson
Burkes Peerage and Baronetcy; Law Society Records
Thomas's Hotel, Berkeley Square - map 1870, picture 1890
The Times - Deed Poll; Harewood House (w)

Reginald Courtenay Welch
Law Society Records; Local History, Twickenham Library
Richmond Local Studies - Lancaster Lodge, Twickenham 1863
Farnham Library - Army College, Heath End - map 1897, sale 1948

Chapter 7 - The Royal Engineers

Royal Engineers Library, Brompton Barracks - team details
Army Campaigns in the 19th century (w)

Henry Waugh Renny-Tailyour
Burke's Peerage and Baronetcy; P.R.O., Kew - Royal Licence
Cheltenham School Register; Cricketer's Who's Who
Angus Archives, Montrose Library, 214 High Street, Montrose
Lobengulu - Matabeleland, Powerscourt, Clontarf (w)
Isle of Wight Record Office, 26 Hillside, Newport
Guinness Archives, St. James's Gate, Dublin

Henry Bayard Rich
Bayard, Carroll, D'Olier, Crooke (w)
Appleton's Cyclopedia of American Biography (1887-89) (w)
Hart's Army List; World Gazetteer - re British Guyana
Dulwich College, D. Young (w)

Herbert Hugh Muirhead
National Biography - Boulton, Watt, and Muirhead
Soho House (and the Lunar Society); Charles Sturt, Esquimalt (w)

Adam Bogle
Francis Perigal - Middlesex Victoria County History (1911)
Benjamin Du Terreau (w); Harrow School Register

Chapter 8 - Gibraltar Connections

East Sussex Record Office, Lewes - parish records etc.
A walk up The Street, Kingston Village near Lewes
Australian Dictionary of Biography - Chataway; Moberly (w)

Gibraltar - Birth, Marriage, and Death, 3 Secretary's Lane
Archives - Chronicle, Census, Blue Lists, Post Office
Kings Chapel of the Convent; Holy Trinity - Albert Langston

Edmund William Creswell
Local Studies Library, Merton Civic Centre - Brackenbury's
Historic Wimbledon / Two Wimbledon Roads - R. Milward
Bruce Castle Museum; School, G.F. Watts, C.H. Rickards (w)

Hugh Mitchell
Hart's Army Lists; Law Society Records; Isle of Wight R.O.
Danny - The Country House Association

Chapter 9 - The Empire Builders

Edmond William Cotter
St. Anselm's Church, Kingsway, Lincoln's Inn Fields
P.R.O., Kew - Army Service, Memorandum, Muster Rolls
Crimean War History; General Encyclopedia - Zhob Valley (w)

Fort St. Elmo, Fort Ricasoli, Barracca Chapel, Malta, Corfu (w)
St. Paul's Shipwreck, St. Paul Street, Valletta - Father Wilson
St. Dominic's, Merchants Street, Valletta - Father Paul Gatt
National Archives, Santo Spirito Hospital, Rabat - Malta

George William Addison
Huddersfield Local History and W. Brook, Meltham (w)
Local Studies, High Street, Paisley - David Rowands re Paisley
Cheltenham School Register; Local Studies, Bath Public Library
Guinness Archives, St. James's Gate, Dublin
St. Paul's Anglican Cathedral, West Street, Valletta - Michael Calleja
Public Registry, 26 Old Treasury Street, Valletta - S. Bugeja

Alfred George Goodwyn
Richmond, L. & Turton, A., The Brewing Industry: A Guide to Historical
Records, Manchester University Press (1990)
Mathias, Peter - The Brewing Industry in England 1700-1830, Cambridge
University Press (1959) reprint Gregg Revivals (1993)
Guildhall Library - parish records; Barnard, Enderby (w)
Local Studies, Barnet Library - R. Calder re Mill Hill
Bath Public Library; Isle of Wight R.O.

William Merriman
Burkes Peerage and Baronetcy - Merriman and Somerset
National Biography; St. Mary Abbots, Kensington - parish records
Thackeray, Pattle, Prinsep &c. (w)

Chapter 10 - F.A. Scandals

John Forster Alcock
2 Albert Villas, Twickenham - Map 1894-96 (Richmond Local Studies)
Divorce Causes - P.R.O., Kew; Bancroft, Lamb (w)
Stian Bjørnø Kjendal, Matrikkel Skaatø 1905, a register (w)

Kragerø Bibliotek, Nordraaksgt 1, 3770 Kragerø -
Midgaard, J., Sannidal and Skåtøy country book vol. II, book from Skåtøy, published by a committee, Naper - Kragerø (1950)
Nils and Hege Sandvik, Skjørsvik Gård, Stabbestad, Norway
Hertfordshire Local History - Berkhamsted by Scott Hastie

Alexander George Bonsor
Polesden Lacey House, Surrey - National Trust
The Westminster Archives - Combe, Delafield & Co. Ltd.
W.S. Kenyon-Slaney, P.R.O. - Royal Licence; Bonomi (w)
Rudy Vanhalewyn, Knokke Heist Archives, Belgium
Brussels and Vilvoorde, Belgium - Pop. Records (Local Govt.)

First Cup Final, The Sportsman - 19th March 1872

Chapter 11 - The Amateur Game

Sir Francis Arthur Marindin
Burke's Landed Gentry - Davenport and Talbot
Inman, E. & Tonkin, N., Beckenham, Phillimore & Co. Ltd. (1993)
Wedderburn-Colvile, Robert Wedderburn, Craigflower Farm (w)
Gen. Society - Lawrence of Jamaica pedigree; Guide to Mauritius
Carnegie Public Library, Abbot Street, Dunfermline

Chapter 12 - The Professional Era

Lord Arthur Fitzgerald Kinnaird
Burke's Peerage and Baronetcy, National Biography
Queen's Scotland (The Heartland) by Nigel Tranter - Rossie Priory (w)
W. Lamb, Lord Melbourne (w); St. James's, Paddington - Parish Records
Correspondence of W.H. Fox Talbot 1847, Glasgow University (w)
Local History, Bromley Library - Plaistow Lodge

Chapter 13 - Balham F.C.

Sir Frederick Joseph Wall
Essex Record Office, Chelmsford - Rainham Parish Records
Chelsea Library - St. Mark's College; Edmonds, R., Chelsea from five fields to the Worlds End (1956); Denny, Barbara, Chelsea Past (1996)
Sutton Library - Local History; Sutton & Cheam Advertiser 1944

Chapter 14 - Sheffield 'Rules'

Sir John Charles Clegg
Sheffield Local Studies & Archives, 52 Shoreham Street, Sheffield
Sheffield Parish Records - The Cathedral; St. Mary's, Bramall Lane
Who's Who - J.C. Clegg and W.E. Clegg

Chapter 15 - Up For The Cup

Pawson, T., 100 Years of the F.A. Cup, Heinemann (1972)
Butler, Bryon, Official History of the F.A., Macdonald (1991)
and Official History of the F.A. Cup, Headline (1996)
Lillie Bridge 1874, Oval 1888, Stamford Bridge 1888 - O.S. maps
Fallowfield - Looking back at Rusholme & Fallowfield (1984)
Bevan, Hibberd, Gilbert, To the Palace for The Cup, Replay (1999)
Inman, E. & Tonkin, N., Beckenham - Crystal Palace in c.1860
Map of The Crystal Palace 1929-30 (Croydon Library)

Chapter 16 - Archibald Leitch

Topographical & Historical Gazetteer of Scotland (1848)
Scottish Vital Records; New Register House, Edinburgh - certificates
Institution of Mechanical & Consulting Engineers, 1 Birdcage Walk -
Proceedings and Memoirs 1939, volume 141
West London Press, 8th September 1905 - Chelsea & Fulham
Barnes 1894 (Richmond); Bourneside 1896 (Palmers Green)
Dumayne, A., Southgate: A glimpse into the past
and The Bourne, Southgate - Enfield in old photographs
Mrs. H. Brew, Southgate - family history

Chapter 17 - The Re-Election Lottery

Blue House Field, Newcastle Rd O.S 1895-96 (Sunderland)
Excelsior Ground, Birmingham O.S 1889 (Birmingham Ref.)
Burton F.C. History and Peel Croft O.S. 1901 (Burton)
Custom House and W. Ham Greyhound (Newham)
New Brighton F.C., O.S. 1899, O.S. 1926 (Birkenhead)
Redheugh Park, Gateshead O.S. 1939 (Gateshead)
Peel Park, Accrington O.S. 1931 (Accrington)
Bradford Park Avenue O.S 1932 (Bradford)

Chapter 18 - Speculative Ventures

History of Accrington F.C. (Accrington)
Wellington Road, A. Villa O.S. 1889 (Birmingham Ref.)
Leamington Street, O.S. 1893 (Blackburn)
Pikes Lane, Bolton O.S. 1889 (Bolton)
The Racecourse Ground, Derby O.S. 1881 (Derby)
Meadows Cricket Ground, Trent Bridge O.S. 1901 (Nottingham)
Stoney Lane, West Bromwich O.S. 1889 (Birmingham Ref.)

Manor Ground O.S. 1897 (Greenwich) O.S. 1914 (Godfrey)
The Memorial Ground, West Ham O.S. 1916 (Newham)
Kensal Rise Athletic and Park Royal 1914-15 (Cricklewood)
Leeds Road, Huddersfield O.S. 1932 (Huddersfield)

A general history of cricket (w)
Ashton Gate O.S. 1902; St. John's Lane O.S. 1943 (Bristol)
Cassio Road, Watford O.S. 1914 (Watford)
Anlaby Road, Hull City O.S. 1928 (Hull)
Raikes Hall O.S. 1893; Athletic Ground O.S 1912 (Blackpool)
The Nest, Norwich City O.S. 1914 (Norwich)

Other Football Sources

Lindsay, R., Millwall 1885-1991 for fixtures, Breedon (1991)
Smailes, G., Breedon Book of Football League Records (1992)
Guinness Record of the F.A. Cup - semi-finals (1993)
Pickering, D., The Cassell Soccer Companion (1994)
Twydell, D., Football Grounds from the Air, Dial House (1995)
Football Grounds from the Air - Then and Now, Dial House (1998)
Rollin, J., Rothman's Book of Football Records, Headline (1998)
Brown, T., F.A. Cup Complete Results, Soccer Data (1999)
International Federation of Football History & Statistics (F.I.F.A.)
Football Programmes, League and Non-League - about 500

Further Reading

Inglis, Simon, Football Grounds of Britain, Harper Collins (1996)

Booth, Keith, The Father of Modern Sport - The Life and Times of Charles W. Alcock, Parrs Wood Press (2002)

Warsop, Keith, The Early F.A. Cup Finals and The Southern Amateurs, published by T. Brown (2004)

Smart, J.B., The Wow Factor, How Soccer Evolved, Blythe Smart (2005)

Inglis, Simon, Engineering Archie - A. Leitch, English Heritage (2005)

Smart, J.B., Arthur Pember's Great Adventures, Blythe Smart (2007)

Photos, Prints

All photographs were taken by J.B. Smart, whilst the portraits of officials are mainly from History of the F.A. (1953) - these pictures once lined the walls of the corridor at Lancaster Gate. The maps are "out of copyright" and are reproduced from the (date) Ordnance Survey.

  Every effort was made to trace ownership of the images and relevant sources have been listed below, whilst any other pictures due to their age or description (as such) fall within the public domain.

Freemasons Tavern; Eton Wall Game; Ebenezer Cobb Morley (Barnes & Mortlake Historical Society); Arthur Pember (Mysteries & Miseries of the Great Metropolis A.P. 1874); Orphan Asylum at Snaresbrook

Charles W. Alcock; Edward Ladd Betts; Harrow School; Edward E. Bowen (Harrow School Archives); Army College Heath End (sale prospectus from Farnham Library)

Royal Engineers (R.E. Library); Brackenbury's School; Sir Francis Arthur Marindin; William McGregor; Lord Arthur F. Kinnaird; Sir Frederick J. Wall; 22 Lancaster Gate; Sir John Charles Clegg; Crystal Palace Panorama; St. Andrew's (painting J.B. Smart)

Index

Blythe Smart Publications